GUNGA DIN

From Kipling's Poem to
Hollywood's Action-Adventure Classic

By William R. Chemerka

Published in the USA by:
BearManor Media
P O Box 71426
Albany, Georgia 31708
www.bearmanormedia.com

ISBN: 978-1-62933-143-0
BearManor Media, Albany, Georgia
Printed in the United States of America
Cover design by Mike Boldt
Book interior design by Robbie Adkins, www.adkinsconsult.com

Dedication
to Danny Mulroy

Acknowledgments

This book would not have been possible without the assistance, guidance, and encouragement provided by a number of thoughtful individuals.

Tony "Skip" Malanowski's invaluable research efforts at UCLA's Charles E. Young Research Library, where the RKO Radio Pictures Studio Records are kept, were crucial in identifying important details and notes about the making of *Gunga Din*. Tony's extensive background in movie production—from editing and producing to directing and writing—helped me prioritize many of the materials used in this book.

Alice Trego, a fellow member of the Western Writers of America, was kind enough to explore the *Gunga Din* files among the Howard Hawks Papers in the L. Tom Perry Special Collections at Brigham Young University's Harold B. Lee Library. Alice, an experienced and talented writer, provided wonderful notes on one of the *Gunga Din* scripts.

Multiple Academy Award recipient Ben Burtt, one of Hollywood's all-time great sound editors and sound designers (the verbalization of *Star Wars'* R2-D2, among others), graciously shared his thoughts about *Gunga Din*. Burtt and Oscar-winning visual effects supervisor Craig Barron (*The Curious Case of Benjamin Button*, 2008), both admirers of *Gunga Din*, have co-hosted screenings of the motion picture at several film festivals over the years.

Mike Boldt, a multi-talented musician, composer, songwriter, video producer, and artist, helped me secure a number of original *Gunga Din* reference and promotional materials, including several obscure items that were produced in Europe and Asia. He frequently forwarded information and images to me "in order to make sure" I had them. Mike, a knowledgeable film memorabilia collector, who has worked with me on a number of projects, also helped create this book's cover.

Craig R. Covner, an historian, researcher, and artist, was kind enough to keep me in mind during his 2016 stay in Lone Pine, California, the primary site of *Gunga Din's* exterior locations. He provided me with photographs of the *Gunga Din* exhibits on display at the Museum of Western Film History in Lone Pine, and supplied me with additional information, including a copy of Dave Holland's splendid book *On Location in Lone Pine*.

Joseph P. Musso, a veteran Hollywood storyboard artist and production illustrator with over 100 motion picture and television credits to his name, shared his original *Gunga Din* campaign pressbook and supplied me with information on edged weapons used in the film. Musso, a film historian, motion picture memorabilia collector, and documentary consultant on all things Hollywood, provided me with additional details about changes made to *Gunga Din* after its initial release in 1939.

Gary Zaboly, a fellow member of the Company of Military Historians and an accomplished professional artist, created images from *Gunga Din* that were noted in earlier screenplays but never filmed. His extensive background in military history and his appreciation of classic motion pictures helped bring the detailed original illustrations to life. Gary also directed me to some important reference materials about the making of *Gunga Din*.

Daniel A. Martinez, Chief Historian at the WWII Valor in the Pacific National Monument, home of the USS *Arizona* Memorial, shared information and photographs about his second cousin, Juan M. Perez, who worked in *Gunga Din* and later served in World War II.

Bob Ackerman and Roxanne Ackerman Spencer shared splendid family stories about Sam Jaffe, who played the title character in *Gunga Din*. Bob wrote Sam Jaffe's eulogy, which is included in Appendix D.

I appreciate the help provided by the staffs of the New York Public Library; the Naples, Florida Public Library; the Ocean County, New Jersey Public Library System; the Harold B. Lee Library at Brigham Young University; The College of New Jersey Library; and the Charles E. Young Research Library at UCLA.

Thanks also to Robert Sigman, Director of the Museum of Western Film History; Dan Allen of the Victorian Military Society; Danny Mulroy; John W. Morgan; Pastor Rodriguez; Sam Juliano; Nancy Boldt; Dottie Hardin Holmes; Violette Cotter; Samantha Lane; Edward and Sandra Teniente; Bill Groneman; Ken Mahoney; Gary Clark; and my wife, Debbie.

As always, I am thankful for the support of Ben Ohmart, Dave Menefee, Robbie Adkins and the rest of the BearManor Media team.

You're a better man than I, Danny Mulroy!

Table of Contents

Author's Introduction. vii

Chapter One: The Historic Background: Rudyard Kipling's *Gunga Din* 1

Chapter Two: The First *Gunga Din* Film. 7

Chapter Three: *Gunga Din*: From Reliance to RKO 14

Chapter Four: Lester Cohen and John Colton 17

Chapter Five: Howard Hawks, Ben Hecht, and Charles MacArthur 22

Chapter Six: The Dudley Nichols Script 32

Chapter Seven: Early Casting 37

Chapter Eight: Completing the Casting: From Sabu to Sam Jaffe 40

Chapter Nine: Creating Nineteenth Century India. 54

Chapter Ten: George Stevens: Behind the Scenes. 72

Chapter Eleven: Location Problems 78

Chapter Twelve: Budget Concerns. 95

Chapter Thirteen: The Final Battle 100

Chapter Fourteen: The Completed Film 107

Chapter Fifteen: Holland's Comments and Suggestions. 131

Chapter Sixteen: The Promotion and Exploitation Campaign 134

Chapter Seventeen: Release, Reviews, and Reactions 139

Chapter Eighteen: Reading, Writing, and *Gunga Din*. 151

Chapter Nineteen: The Plagiarism Accusation 155

Chapter Twenty: The Reaction from India: Protests and Murder 158

Chapter Twenty-One: *Gunga Din*: TV's "First" Film 165

Chapter Twenty-Two: Cast and Crew After *Gunga Din* 168

Chapter Twenty-Three: Re-releases and Offshoots 173

Chapter Twenty-Four: *Gunga Din's* Socio-Political Legacy. .186

Chapter Twenty-Five: The Influential *Gunga Din*: Pop Culture and the Planned Remake. . .189

Gunga Din Postscript 200

Appendix A: Rudyard Kipling's *Gunga Din*. 201

Appendix B: Cast and Crew Credits 203

Appendix C: Negative Cost "Gunga Din" March 23, 1940 208

Appendix D: Eulogy for Sam Jaffe 209

Bibliography. 211

Index 214

Author's Introduction

My interest in *Gunga Din* (1939) began on a rainy April 2, 1957 morning, when some of my fellow sixth-grade classmates gathered in the basement of the Robert Waters School in Union City, New Jersey. Whenever it was raining, students were allowed to enter the elementary school before the first bell rang. Once inside, we were dry, safe, and secure; as a matter of fact, the school's basement was a designated fall-out shelter. In case of a nuclear attack during those Cold War years, we could go to the windowless lower level and remain there for an extended time—a very long time, if we had to—because the hallway was filled with huge metal drums of drinking water and preserved foods. To us, though, the basement's emergency inventory was nothing remarkable nor did it cause us too much concern. After all, we were "duck and cover" drill veterans, who knew what to do in case a large radioactive mushroom cloud appeared over nearby New York City.

That morning, my classmates and I discussed what we had seen on television the night before. I mentioned to my friends that I had enjoyed *The Black Swan* (1942), a lively motion picture about pirates, starring Tyrone Power, Maureen O'Hara, and George Sanders. I sang the film's praises until one of my classmates interrupted me. "You should have watched *Gunga Din*," countered Danny Mulroy, who said he had seen the motion picture the night before on *Million Dollar Movie*, a popular television program, which aired on New York's WOR-TV. "It was great, really great!" stated Danny. "You should have watched it." My other classmates nodded in agreement and added their own comments about the memorable action-packed film. It appeared that everyone had viewed *Gunga Din* except me. So much for *The Black Swan*. I felt as if I had just walked the plank.

Danny followed with an interesting statement. "My father said there was a lot more in the movie that was left out," he said. Since *Million Dollar Movie* was a 90-minute program with commercials, *Gunga Din* had been drastically edited to fit on the small screen. However, it was still ninety minutes I had missed. Fortunately, *Million Dollar Movie* showed a single film twice each evening and multiple times on the weekend for an entire week, so I hadn't really missed it. Based upon my classmates' enthusiastic recommendation, I couldn't wait to see it.

That evening, I viewed *Gunga Din* for the first time. Danny was correct: *Gunga Din* was "great." It was filled with robust action and adventure, essential stuff for elementary school students, who had been captivated by Walt Disney's exciting *Davy Crockett* series a few years earlier. *Gunga Din* featured majestic panoramic cinematography, and its themes of bravery, friendship, loyalty, and sacrifice were inspiring. The motion picture's musical score was captivating, too, and the film's vivid ending was memorable. *Gunga Din* left a lasting impression on me.

Over the years, whenever it was broadcast on television, usually during some post-midnight time slot, I watched it. The film still had the same impact on me, but I came to appreciate the performances, the direction, and the stunning camera work even more.

On January 30, 1974, I attended Radio City Music Hall's Art Deco festival, which screened

Gunga Din, although the film was a grainy, edited 16mm version. I brought my girlfriend, Debbie, along. She married me anyway.

Years later, when I was a high school history and economics teacher at Madison High School in Madison, New Jersey, I had a special *Gunga Din* experience. Under my faculty photograph in the *Alembic,* the school's 1979 yearbook, was a notation that stated that *Gunga Din* was my favorite film. The inconspicuous statement caught the eye of Roxanne Ackerman, a member of the class of 1980. Although she wasn't in any of my classes, Roxanne approached me in the hall one day and told me that her uncle had worked in the film. I was thrilled to hear that, and assumed that he may have been one of the many extras.

"What did he do?" I asked.

"He was Gunga Din," said Roxanne.

I was pleasantly stunned. After catching my breath, I asked her, "Your uncle is Sam Jaffe?"

"Yes," she replied, with a courteous smile, "and he's coming over to our house this weekend."

I froze for a moment, and then blurted out meekly, "Could you get his autograph for me?"

"I'll see what I can do," she replied.

On Monday morning, Roxanne walked up to me in the hallway and handed me a manila envelope. Inside was an 8x10 glossy photo. One half of the photo featured a contemporary image of Jaffe, the other was a picture of the actor as *Gunga Din.* "To William Chemerka, with warmest regards, Sam Jaffe," read the inscription. What a way to start a school week!

In 1990, two good friends, Craig R. Covner and his wife, professor Nina Rosenstand, traveled from their home in San Diego to Lone Pine, California, where they explored the "sacred ground" that was part of the *Gunga Din* set in 1938. Craig found a small piece of the film's temple set and mailed it to me with an accompanying color photo. Thank you, Craig!

In time, like all classic films, *Gunga Din* was eventually made available as a videocassette, laser disc, and DVD. No longer did I have had to wake up at all hours of the night to see my favorite film.

Fast forward to the present day.

This book is more than just a "making of the movie" project. It includes chapters about Rudyard Kipling's poem, the first *Gunga Din* film, behind-the-scenes stories, the filmmaking climate on the eve of World War II, the plagiarism charge against the production, the deadly reaction to the film in India, attempts to remake the film, its role in the early days of television, and the influence of *Gunga Din* on popular culture. Of course, there is much about the making of the film, including information about the various script incarnations and scenes that were written but never filmed. Furthermore, the endnotes provide additional details about the motion picture and other related items.

In my research efforts, the most important information came from the RKO Studio Records and other archived information. The records contain important script details, production data, cast and crew rosters, telegrams, notes, and assorted correspondence. Whenever possible, I examined the original sources that were used or referenced by RKO staffers, including such obscure books as *Confessions of a Thug* (1839), *Twelve Years of a Soldier's Life In India: Being Extracts from the Letters of Major W. S. R. Hodson* (1860), and *History of the 42nd Highlanders—"The Black Watch"* (1893).

Other published efforts, like George Turner's "The Making of Gunga Din" in *American Cinematographer* in 1982 (revised as part of *The Cinema of Adventure, Romance & Terror* in 1989), and Dave Holland's *On Location in Lone Pine*, a superb 1990 photo-laden book (revised in 2005) about the popular California filming area, contained important and useful information. Additional books, newspapers, periodicals, trade publications, and movie magazines provided content that was essential to help tell the story of *Gunga Din*.

The screenplay that eventually became *Gunga Din* in 1939 is an interesting eclectic assemblage that contains creative elements from every previous outline, synopsis, and script, including earlier written works that were based upon a number of historical events and personalities.

Upon its release, *Silver Screen* magazine called *Gunga Din* "a wow of a picture!" In fact, it was much more than that. The full story of the film follows in the pages ahead. I hope you enjoy this book.

William R. Chemerka

CHAPTER ONE

The Historic Background: Rudyard Kipling's *Gunga Din*

It supposedly began with a poem.

"Inspired by Rudyard Kipling's heroic lines," stated posters for *Gunga Din* (1939), RKO's big-budget action-adventure film about British soldiers in late nineteenth century India. However, the words "and by British imperialism" could have been added to the posters, because the actual source of inspiration for *Gunga Din* was Great Britain's involvement in the Asian subcontinent, an international engagement that began over a century before the celebrated British writer penned his memorable poem about a brave native water carrier.

The story began when King George II was on the throne. On June 23, 1757, forces of the British East India Company, led by Robert Clive, won the Battle of Plassey in Bengal against Siraj ud-Daulah, the Nawab of Bengal, and a small force of French artillerists. The military operation was a retaliation against the Nawab of Bengal's mistreatment of British soldiers and civilians who had been captured by native forces at Fort William in Calcutta on June 20. The prisoners had been packed into a small jail cell—the "Black Hole of Calcutta"—and most died of suffocation and shock during the overnight and early morning hours.

The Plassey victory marked the beginning of an expanded British presence in India and other Asian lands. The campaign was part of Great Britain's participation in the Seven Years War (1756-1763), an international con-flict in which the country waged war against the French on several continents.

The East India Company, supported by the Crown, promoted the development of tea in India in an attempt to break China's commercial monopoly on the popular leaf. To achieve its goal, the company exploited the native population in the region, and acquired cotton, copper, and sugar cane, among other natural resources. The East India Company ran much of India until the British Crown assumed control of the territory in 1858, when Queen Victoria was on the throne. It was the time of the British Raj, a period when the British Union Jack flew over much of the Asian subcontinent.

The Crown sent British soldiers, royal officials, and government workers to India in increasing numbers. According to the 1861 *Census of the British Empire*, 40,371 British-born subjects (not counting members of the army or navy) lived in India.[1] Among the thousands of transplanted British subjects were John Lockwood Kipling and his wife, Alice, who arrived in India in early 1865. John became the Head of Department Architectural Sculpture at the government School of Art in Bombay. Before the year was over, they became parents.

Rudyard Kipling was born on December 30, 1865 in Bombay. When he was five years old, he traveled to England for his formal education. After completing his studies, he attended United Services College, a public boarding school for the sons of British military officers and civil servants. Kipling returned to India in 1882, and became an assistant newspaper editor at the *Military and Civilian Gazette*, where he wrote extensively about India, its people, and his fellow transplanted Englishmen.

Kipling's appearance was highlighted by a bushy mustache and thick eyeglasses. "He used to wear double-decked glasses, the top deck for viewing distant objects, and the lower deck for objects nearer in," said Major-General Sir George Younghusband, a veteran of Indian campaigns, who knew Kipling. "Rudyard Kipling and I had met in former years at Simla and Lahore [when he] was sub-editor of the *Civil and Military Gazette*."[2]

Kipling had already established himself as one of England's most promising writers, when *Gunga Din* was first published on June 7, 1890, in *The National Observer*, a British newspaper (it was previously called *The Scots Observer*). The poem was later included in Kipling's *Barrack-Room Ballads and Other Verses* collection in 1892. That same year, he married Caroline Starr Balestier. The couple had an international honeymoon, which included a stop at the Balestier family home in Brattleboro, Vermont. A return trip to the Green Mountain State was celebrated by the Kiplings with the birth of their first child, Josephine, on December 29, 1892. Caroline later gave birth to two more children: Elsie (February 2, 1896) and John (August 17, 1897).

Kipling had already written such popular works as *The Man Who Would be King* (1888), *Wee Willie Winkie and Other Child Stories* (1888), and *Soldiers Three* (1888) before he brought to life the poetic tale of a humble water carrier who served in the British Army in India during the 1880s.

Kipling's writings reflect nineteenth century British imperialism, a policy that was designed to deliver a manipulated benevolence to its conquered subjects. However, imperialism manifested itself in the exploitation of native peoples and their natural resources. Nevertheless, Kipling celebrated Great Britain's growing empire. "[He] was throughout his literary career an outspoken and uncompromising imperialist, inveighing against 'little Englanders,' advocating vigorous national expansion, and claiming for the white race in general and for the English in particular virtues not possessed by the 'lesser breeds without the law.'"[3]

In *A Song of the White Men* (1899), which was originally written to celebrate Queen Victoria's Diamond Jubilee in 1897, Kipling championed his race with lines like "Oh well, for the world when the White Men tread." Kipling's White masculine ideal is as much "an idea, a persona, a style of being [that] seems to have served many Britishers when they were abroad," wrote Edward S. Said in *Orientalism*. "The actual color their skin set them off dramatically and reassuringly from the sea of natives, but for the Britisher who circulated amongst Indians . . . there was also the certain knowledge that he belonged to, and could draw upon the empirical and spiritual reserves of, a long tradition of executive responsibility toward the colored races."[4]

In *Recessional* (1897), which replaced *A Song of the White Men* as a poetic nod to Victoria's tenure on the throne, Kipling firmly acknowledged Great Britain's empire and its Christian foundation: "Dominion over palm and pine—Lord God of hosts be with us yet, Lest we forget—lest we forget."

George Younghusband stated it succinctly: "The sun never sets on the dominions of the King of England, and in righteousness and justice does he reign over half the world."[5] The *Census of the British Empire* boldly proclaimed: "Nations rise and fall, but the great mass of Mankind still continues to increase in numbers, and to overspread the most distant regions of the World. The British Empire, it's 'Colonies,' 'Foreign Possessions,' and 'Dependencies,' contain somewhere about the one-fifth of the Human Race, who dwell under the protection of the British Crown, and who overspread nearly one-sixth part of the earth's surface."[6]

Kipling believed that the British Empire had "to be maintained, defended, and protected—from rival world powers and from the rebellious governed." However, he warned of a nation "drunk with sight of power."[7] The Empire's primary instrument of power was the British Army, and in its ranks were men from every socioeconomic background. Private soldiers primarily came from the lower ranks of society, and some seemed to enjoy their "superior" status over the colonial peoples whom they controlled.

George Younghusband stated that British military leadership was the key ingredient to success on the Asian subcontinent. "The fighting classes in India, and on its borders, are splendid men, brave and fearless in action; nevertheless, to be at their best, they require to be led by British officers," he wrote. "It does not matter how young these officers are, but British they must be." The major-general also noted that "in those days the British soldier stood as a rock and sure support, should anything go wrong with his Indian comrades."[8] In time, something would go very wrong with Britain's Indian comrades.

Kipling's writings avoided detailed tributes to generals and other high ranking officers. Instead, he concentrated on the "Tommy," the conventional nickname for a British enlisted man, an unpretentious soldier, whose language is coarse and whose service to Her Majesty is generally unappreciated, except by his comrades.

Kipling's *Gunga Din* is an apology of sorts, delivered from the perspective of a "Tommy." The enlisted man describes the difficulties of infantry life and the plight of a regimental *bhisti*, a native who carried a *mussick* (goatskin water bag) and brought water to any soldier who called his name.

"Water, get it! Panee lao!
"You squidgy-nosed old idol, Gunga Din!"

According to Ralph Durand's *A Handbook to the Poetry of Rudyard Kipling*, "the *bhisti* or water carrier must not be confounded with the 'pani wallah,' who performs for Hindoos the service that the *bhisti* performs for Mohammedans. The 'pani wallah' must always be a Brahman, so that Hindoos of all castes can accept water from him."

Kipling may have based his heroic character upon an actual water carrier.

"The courage of the Indian *bhitsi* [had] become proverbial: at the siege of Delhi a *bhisti* named Juma, attached to the Queen's Own Corps of Guides, so distinguished himself for heroism during the performance of his duty that he received the star 'For Valour,' till recently the highest distinction an Indian soldier could earn."[9]

Younghusband provided additional details about the brave water carrier (whose name he spelled differently) in *Forty Years a Soldier*. "Jumma was a historic person, immortalized by Rudyard Kipling as Gunga Din, the *bhisti*," he said. "At the siege of Delhi, in 1857, he was with the Guides during the desperate period, at the hottest time of year, in the hottest region on earth, as a camp follower, a *bhisti*. Not a soldier at all, but a humble regimental servant, a carrier of water for the soldiers, engaged in a monthly salary of six shillings."[10]

Following the siege, a collective award was going to be presented to the soldiers who, in turn, would have one of their own accept it for all. "With one accord the soldiers voted that the medal should be given to Jumma," noted Younghusband. "Yet, quite unarmed as he was, and unafraid of the bullets of the enemy, he carried his great *mussack* [sic] of water up to the most forward line, and gave us to drink, when we were nearly dead with the heat, and the exhaustion of fighting. Therefore, this man is the bravest of all."[11]

Unlike Kipling's heroic title character, Jumma (or Juma) survived the fighting and was allowed to join the army as a soldier. "So Jumma was enlisted, and so fine a fellow he was, that in spite of his humble origin, and in spite of caste prejudices, he rose to be an Indian officer."[12] Later, Jumma won another award for bravery at Kabul in 1879. Sadly, Jumma was cashiered out of the service when he lied, in order to protect a senior officer from a charge of negligence (a rifle and two packets of ammunition were missing during a roll call). However, Jumma struggled to regain his good name. He traveled to England, where he was befriended by a Colonel Jenkins, a former officer in the Guides. Jenkins brought Jumma to the India Office, where officials heard his case and provided assistance to him. According to Younghusband: "When he arrived in India he was given a post of trust in the Canal Department, and lived in fair plenty and contentment for the rest of his life."[13]

The Kipling Journal confirmed the Jumma story, but referred to the brave *bhisti* by another similar sounding name. "Younghusband, who knew Kipling and his sister well, claims Suma as the inspiration of the poem."[14]

Another theory about the inspiration of the Gunga Din character originates in the American Civil War. A poem titled *Banty Tim*, written by John Hay, appeared in the April 15, 1871 issue of *Harper's Weekly*, and described the story of a brave Black servant in the Union Army who died at the Siege of Vicksburg in 1863. Hay's poem is delivered in the style of a rough and tumble enlisted man named Tilmon Joy, who suffered from "a rib caved in, and a leg on a strike" as gunshots rang and the "hot sun . . . br'iled and blistered and burned." Tim finds Joy on the battlefield and carries the soldier away until a shot "brought him once to his knees." Despite "a dozen stumbles and falls" and "his black hide riddled with balls," Tim manages to carry Joy to safety. However, Tim dies of his wounds. "And here stays Banty Tim: He trumped Death's ace for me that day, and I'm not goin' back on him!"

Like *Gunga Din*, *Banty Tim* is told from the perspective of a veteran enlisted man, who is wounded in battle, suffers from thirst, and is saved by a mortally wounded man of color. "Kipling was undoubtedly familiar with Hay's poetry for quite some time before writing *Gunga Din*, and shortly before the two finally met in 1892 Kipling wrote to Hay: 'I've been wanting to meet you for a matter of some several years and shall attend with joy.'"[15]

Another inspirational source for Kipling's poem may have been an old barracks song. Lieutenant-General Sir George MacMunn, who served in the British Army for over thirty years, including a tour of service in India, suggested: "When Kipling was a young journalist, and dined in clubs and messes with the young bloods, evening sing-songs usually ended with a most popular song, Gunga Deen."[16]

The song, "Gunga Deen," which was sung to the refrain of "Scotch Lassie Jean," included the following introduction: "Now in India's sultry clime, where you have to spend some time/Without your English servants, you must do." The song's lyrics tell of "a dusky son of sin . . . my bearer, Gunga Deen." The tune includes the line "Oh Deen, Deen, my bearer Gunga Deen."[17]

Kipling's *Gunga Din* contains a passage that is similar to "Gunga Deen." It reads: "Now in Injia's sunny clime, where I used to spend my time." However, the song's lyrics weave an innocuous tale of Deen's daily work routine instead of a story of battlefield heroism.

Like Jumma, Kipling's *Gunga Din* is courageous, brave and caring; however, the poetic character was frequently threatened and chastised by the men in ranks.

> "You 'eathen, where the mischief 'ave you been?
> "Or "I'll *marrow* you this minute
> "If you don't fill up my helmet, Gunga Din!"

During a battle, the soldier is wounded and Gunga Din comes to his aid, providing him with water, and attempting to treat his wound.

> I was chokin' mad with thirst,
> An' the man that spied me first
> Was our good old grinning,' gruntin'
> Gunga Din.
> 'E lifted up my 'ead,
> An' 'e plugged me where I bled

However, the *bhisti* is mortally wounded as he carries the soldier to safety. In the poem's conclusion, the soldier apologizes for his behavior.

> Though I've belted you an' flayed you,
> By the livin' God that made you,
> You're a better man than I am, Gunga Din![18]

Kipling's poem quickly made its way across the Atlantic and was first printed in American newspapers during the spring of 1892. *The New York Tribune* published *Gunga Din* in its May 22, 1892 edition, and other newspapers followed. Chicago's *Daily Inter Ocean* printed it on May 31, 1892, and New Orleans' *Times Picayune* ran the poem on June 12, 1892. Within months, it was published in nearly every major newspaper in the United States.

Gunga Din was not the only poem Kipling wrote about the British soldier's service in India and other Asian countries; in fact, between 1878 and 1890, he wrote nearly twenty military-themed poems, including *Tommy* (1890), *Troopin,'* (1890), and *Danny Deever* (1890), *The Young British Soldier* (1892), and *Sappers* (1896).

Kipling became the most famous British writer of his time. His prolific creations included poems, short stories, speech collections, essays, novels, and histories. Imaginative works, such as *The Brushwood Boy* (1895) and *They* (1904), were particularly inventive. Film historian Rudy Behlmer called him "the grand interpreter of Anglo-Indian themes, the army and British Imperialism." However, as academicians George K. Anderson and William E. Buckler noted: "All in all, it is a great mistake to think of Kipling as the exponent of imperialism alone: he has too much sympathy and too broad a vision."[19]

Among Kipling's most important and memorable works are *The Jungle Book* (1894),

Captains Courageous (1897), and *Kim* (1901). In 1907, he received the Nobel Prize for Literature and, three years later, his famous poem, *If,* was included in *Rewards and Fairies* (1910).[20]

His personal life was filled with misfortune during the next five years. His mother died in 1910, and his father died the following year. Kipling supported Great Britain's role in World War I with patriotic enthusiasm, but became heartbroken when his son, John, an eighteen-year-old infantry lieutenant in the British Army, was killed at the Battle of Loos in Loos-en-Gohelle, France on September 27, 1915. His first-born child, Josephine, had died on March 6, 1899, in New York from pneumonia. Elsie, however, lived until May 23, 1976, and was buried in England.

Kipling held strong opinions on politics and helped form the *Liberty League,* an anti-Communist organization, in 1920. He was featured on the cover of *Time* magazine on September 27, 1926, and continued to write and deliver speeches until the mid-1930s. He warned of Nazi Germany's threat to Europe in a 1935 speech to the Royal Society of St. George, an English patriotic organization. Kipling's last work was *Souvenirs of France,* an essay collection published in 1933.

He died on January 18, 1936, "after an illness which followed an operation for a perforated stomach ulcer."[21] His cremated remains were buried in Westminster Abbey in London. Next to his final resting place are the graves of Charles Dickens and Thomas Hardy. The three celebrated English writers penned some of the most popular novels, short stories, and poems in history, and their memorable works were transformed into some of the most treasured motion pictures of all time.

Chapter One Notes

1. *Census of the British Empire: Compiled From Official Returns of the Year 1861* (London: Harrison, 1864), 177.

2. George Younghusband, *Forty Years a Soldier* (London: Herbert Jenkins, Ltd., 1923), 203.

3. George K. Anderson and William E. Buckler, eds., *The Literature of England: An Anthology and a History From the Dawn of the Romantic Movement to the Present Day* (Glenview, IL: Scott, Foresman and Company, 1966), 1423.

4. Edward S. Said, *Orientalism* (New York: Vintage Books, 1979), 226.

5. Younghusband, *Forty Years a Soldier,* 320.

6. *Census of the British Empire: 1861,* 307.

7. Dr. David Cody, "Kipling's Imperialism," The Victorian Web: http://www.victorianweb.org/index.html.

8. Younghusband, *Forty Years a Soldier,* 65.

9. Ralph Durand, *A Handbook to the Poetry of Rudyard Kipling* (London: Hodder & Stoughton, 1914), 27.

10. Younghusband, *Forty Years a Soldier,* 80.

11. Ibid. A somewhat similar account is provided in Frederick Sleigh Roberts, *Forty-One Years in India* (London: R. Bentley, 1897), 190-191.

12. Ibid., 80-81.

13. Ibid., 83.

14. *The Kipling Journal,* October 1944, 10. Younghusband claimed that Kipling's sister, "a nice pretty girl of eighteen, used to give me a dance now and then, so I got to know him."

15. William P. Cahill and Michael Harrowood, "Banty Tim: A Possible American Source for "Gunga Din," *The Kipling Journal,* December, 2004, 28.

16. Lieutenant-General Sir George MacMunn, "The Original Gunga Deen," *The Kipling Journal,* July 1943, 3-4.

17. Ibid.

18. See Appendix A for the complete poem and an explanation of terms used by Kipling.

19. Anderson and Buckler, *Anthology,* 1424.

20. It took the Nobel committee three months to locate Kipling, who was on a tiger hunt in Indonesia.

21. *Times-Picayune* (New Orleans, Louisiana), January 18, 1936, 7. Kipling's remains were buried on January 23, 1936. His original gravestone was replaced by a new one in 1966.

CHAPTER TWO
The First *Gunga Din* Film

Gunga Din was popularized in the early twentieth century, when public speakers and actors recited the poem at colleges and universities, Y.M.C.A. facilities, clubs, churches, literary organizations, Vaudeville theaters, and other venues.

Clifton Crawford, who successfully combined comedy and dramatics, was praised for his "mien of refinement," when he recited the poem as part of a Vaudeville lineup at Chicago's Auditorium in October 1907. *Variety* reviewer Frank Weisberg stated that Crawford's recitation of *Gunga Din* was one "of extreme merit." Ainsley Scott, a ninety-year-old veteran of international stages, who had established himself as a well-known minstrel performer in the mid-nineteenth century, recited *Gunga Din* to appreciative American audiences in 1910, and the highly regarded Clinton E. Lloyd delivered the poem to crowds across the United States in 1911.

The early presentations of *Gunga Din* were demonstrated in a dignified manner; however, Vaudeville comedians soon integrated Kipling's poem into their acts with humorous twists. Vaudevillian Wellington Cross mixed songs with light comedy and concluded his performance with select lines from the poem; entertainer Doc Wilson delivered *Gunga Din* in Swedish for laughs; comedian Frank Westphal distorted the poem's classic ending with a comedic ode to a Ford automobile: "You're better than a Packard, hunk o' tin." George Jessel delivered a *Gunga Din* parody, and the song and dance team of Ames and Winthrop sang *Gunga Din* to a ragtime arrangement.

The comic performances did not go unnoticed; in fact, some publications were critical of the disrespectful performances. "Once upon a time, *Gunga Din* was a favorite recitation with great actors," noted the June 25, 1912 issue of New York's *Morning Telegraph*.[1] The criticisms were ineffectual and the irreverent Vaudeville performances continued.

Robert Emmett Keane delivered a routine of English stories that included a comedy version of *Gunga Din*. Ed Corelli and Charles Gillette specialized in complex acrobatics, but occasionally added humorous dialogue to their physical routines. During one performance, Gillette recited *Gunga Din* in a serious style, but was quickly interrupted by Corelli, who turned his partner's straight man recitation into a comedic sequence.[2]

Entertainment critics did not accept the efforts of all Vaudevillians who attempted to manipulate Kipling's popular poem for laughs. For example, one performer received a negative review in *Variety* for including the poem in her singing act. "Buhla Pearl made things worse by reciting a parody of *Gunga Din*, entitled 'Hunka Tin.' What Miss Pearl doesn't know about Kipling would make a plot for a three-act tragedy."[3] The interpretive tug of war between comedic Vaudevillians and serious orators over *Gunga Din* continued for decades.

Besides the printed word and public orations, *Gunga Din* was incorporated into another medium, when Clifton Crawford made a 78-rpm recording of the poem on Victor Records (#70028). The poem could now be enjoyed by anyone at any time, as long as they had a record player, such as a Victrola, an early "talking machine" that was marketed for the home.

Following one of Crawford's stage performances, a British Army veteran and Victoria Cross recipient informed the entertainer that "Gunga was the water carrier of his regiment, and was no myth." Intrigued by the veteran's story, Crawford planned to search army records in order to "publish a book telling about the remarkable Kipling character."[4]

Nineteen years after Kipling's poem appeared in *Barrack-Room Ballads and Other Verses*, *Gunga Din* made its debut on the screen in a 1911 black and white silent film, which was produced by Patrick Anthony Powers (aka P. A. Powers), an early filmmaker, who had established Powers Motion Picture Company the year before in New York City. Most of his Powers Picture Plays were twenty-minute two reelers, a common format in the early days of silent motion picture production.

Powers was a productive filmmaker. In 1910, he produced over 100 films with such diverse titles as *A Frozen Ape*, *Legally Dead*, *The Burglar and the Baby*, *A Woman's Power*, *Who Wins the Widow*, and *The Tramp Bicyclist*. He made *Gunga Din* and more than 100 films in 1911. Besides filming at his indoor studio, he also used locations around New York City, including the wooded Palisades area across the Hudson River in New Jersey. During his career, Powers produced over 900 films from 1909 to 1936, including such full-length films as *The Galloping Cowboy* (1926), *The Wedding March* (1928), and *The Love Kiss* (1930). Always looking to improve the quality of his

productions, especially animated cartoons, Powers secured the services of Ub Iwerks, Walt Disney's legendary animator, who helped create Mickey Mouse. In 1930, Powers set up the Iwerks Studio, which produced animated short subjects, but it wasn't successful. Before the decade was over, the two parted ways; Iwerks went to work for Leon Schlesinger Productions, and later Columbia Pictures, before returning to Disney in 1940.

A Powers Pictures Plays ad in the April 15, 1911 issue of *Moving Picture News* noted that the studio "will embrace the most exclusive of classical themes, representing enormous investment. For instance: *Gunga Din* from the war poem by Kipling."[5] A number of other ambitious films were made in 1911, including *The Immortal Alamo*; *Defence of Sevastopol*, an epic Russian production about the Crimean War; *The Battle*, D. W. Griffith's Civil War spectacle; and Robert Louis Stevenson's *The Black Arrow*, which starred Charles Ogle, filmdom's first Frankenstein monster. Powers wanted *Gunga Din* to be as grand as the other literary and historical films.

According to *Moving Picture News* and *Motography*, *Gunga Din* was released on May 20, 1911. Two weeks earlier, the Powers studio proclaimed to theater owners in an ad: "*Gunga Din*—read the poem by Rudyard Kipling; then talk turkey to your exchange man." However, the publication offered little information on the film. The periodical categorized *Gunga Din* as an "educational" film with a moral: "Be a G. Din and Kipling will do the rest." No cast or crew members were mentioned in the article. On another page, *Moving Picture News* identified the film as a "dramatic" production, which generated a "good" review. Yet, other films released at the time were described more favorably with such descriptions as "impressive," "big," "fine," and "enthusiastic." The publication also printed a copy of Kipling's poem, but offered nothing else about the film, which unfortunately has been lost.[6]

World War I contributed to the public's interest in the common British soldier, and *Gunga Din* helped to satisfy the demand. An ad for the author's printed work appeared in March 1915 issue of *Motion Picture Magazine*. "*Gunga Din* recalls the deathless heroism of plain men in battle," stated the promo.

On December 19, 1915, Harry E. Humphrey, a well-known popular speaker, who specialized in recordings of Lincoln's Gettysburg Address, the Declaration of Independence, and passages from The Bible, recited *Gunga Din* on a 78-rpm disc for Columbia records (he was billed as an "elocutionist" on a Pathé version of the recording). Humphrey's histrionic performance is punctuated with exaggerated moments and alveolar trills that set his recording apart from other more conventional recitations. A year later, *Variety* belatedly reported that *Gunga Din* was recorded "on the phonograph records."

Gunga Din continued to be performed by both serious performers and comedians. In 1918, Vaudeville comic Jack Wilson introduced "You're a Better Man Than I am Gunga Din," as one of three new songs that he added to his act, and in 1919, Harry E. Humphrey recited the poem in a solemn manner on an Edison Diamond Disc.[7]

In 1925, Kipling's poem was set to music courtesy of Charles Gilbert Spross, who had created numerous compositions, and provided instrumental accompaniment for the great tenor Enrico Caruso and other famous vocalists of the early twentieth century. Spross' interpretation of *Gunga Din* was published by The John Church Company of New York and London as a 14-page piece of sheet music. According to *Variety*, operatic baritone Reinald Werrenrath, an accomplished recording artist, performed Spross' song during a radio broadcast on October 4, 1925.[8]

A *Gunga Din* movie production was heralded by screenwriter Curtis Benton, who placed a self-promotional ad in the December 29, 1926 issue of *Variety*. In the prominent advertisement, Benton stated that he was "under contract with Universal," and listed a number of his credits for films and studios that had been released, including *Might Lak' a Rose* (1923; Edwin Carewe/First National), *Uninvited Guest* (1924; Submarine/Metro-Goldwyn-Mayer), and *Sporting Life* (1925; Universal). He also named some others scheduled for release, such as *The Sunset Derby* (1927; First National), and *Down The Stretch* (1927; Universal). *Gunga Din* (Famous Players) was also listed on his roster, but nothing additional is mentioned about Kipling's work. Since Benton's screenwriting credits began in 1915, four years after the 1911 *Gunga Din* release, it is difficult to assess the validity of his claim in the advertisement, including his alleged association with the Famous Players Film Company, which was formed by Adolph Zukor in 1912.[9] A few years later, Zukor's enterprise joined forces with the Jesse L. Lasky Feature Play Company, which had created *The Squaw Man*, the first feature ever filmed in Hollywood in 1914. The Zukor-Lasky partnership later purchased its corporate distributor, Paramount.

The trade publications reported that another *Gunga Din* film was in the works. *The Moving Picture World* reported that J. E. D. Meador, President of Meador-Roberston Productions; director John S. Robertson;

Gunga Din by Charles Gilbert Spross. Author's collection.

Joseph P. Bickerton, the company's secretary and general counsel; actress Maude Adams, and others were traveling to Europe from New York on October 10 to confer with Kipling on a production of *Kim*. Reportedly, Kipling "will actively assist in the production." Meador noted that Adams, who owned the screen rights to *Kim*, had conferred with Kipling about the project two years earlier.[10] *The Film Daily* also noted that the company was also interested in filming *Mandalay* and *Gunga Din*, which became a popular Little Blue Book title in 1926.[11] Despite the optimistic reports, Meador-Roberston Productions never made any of the aforementioned titles.

The popularity of all things Kipling was manifested in The Kipling Society, which was created in February 1927. Membership was open to all those who professed an interest in the author and his writings. The following month, the British-based literary organization produced its first official quarterly: *The Kipling Journal*.

Interestingly enough, the character Gunga Din had made appearances in several silent films. In the action-adventure film, *The Red Blood of Courage* (1915), Gunga Din is depicted in a synopsis as a "wild Hindu Prince" who kidnaps a heroine named Lydia Duane. One exciting action scene features Din and his band chasing after Duane and her rescuers over a "swaying bridge," a dangerous walkway that would be reprised in the 1939 epic.[12] In the melodrama, *Thunderclap* (1921), the eighth-billed character, Gunga Din, a "Black friend" of one of the protagonists, was portrayed by Thomas McCann. Several years later in *The White Wing's Bride* (1925), a two-reel Harry Langdon comedy, a character named Gunga Din is the chief antagonist, who battles others in a search for a stolen diamond, which had been removed from an Indian idol.[13]

Kipling's character remained fodder for entertainers. In England, Charles "Nat" Star, performing under the pseudonym Bernie Blake and his Orchestra, recorded "Gunga Din and His Lute" on Sterno Records, a subsidiary label of London's Homophone Company. The 78-rpm recording was identified as a "comedy foxtrot" and included the refrain, "See the little snake wag its tail/ when old Gunga begins to wail/on his funny lute."[14] *Variety* hailed the *Keep Kool* Vaudeville revue in its May 14, 1924 issue. "Hazel Dawn is happily cast all the way. She debuts in a monolog [sic] in a cleverly written parody on *Gunga Din*."[15]

Eddie Foyer, the so-called "man of a thousand poems," countered comedic interpretations of *Gunga Din* with a serious recitation of Kipling's work as part of a "Dance Poems" autumn program at Loew's State Theater in Los Angeles.[16] *Gunga Din* was also part of a special production that included Indian performers at the Empire Theatre in Nottingham, England.[17]

Gunga Din was seemingly everywhere in the 1920s, except on movie screens. However, there was renewed interest in bringing *Gunga Din* to the screen. On January 5, 1929, *Motion Picture News* reported that "*Gunga Din* will be produced as a special for next year's program by MGM. Jack Neville is now writing the adaptation."[18] Later in the year, the *Hollywood Filmgraph* reported: "W. S. Van Dyke, now making *Trader Horn* in Africa, may not return to America when the film is finished. It is said that Metro-Goldwyn-Mayer plans to have him go to India make a "filmation" of Kipling's *Gunga Din*."[19] However, Van Dyke, who had directed over forty films by 1929, never made the film about the famous *bhisti* for MGM or any other studio.

MGM, though, was still interested in *Gunga Din*. Sarah Y. Mason, who won a Best Adapted Screenplay Oscar for *Little Women* (1933); John Howard Lawson, who was nominated for Best Writing Oscar for *Block-ade* (1938); and the prolific C. Gardner Sullivan, who had been associated with over 175 scripts since 1912, created embryonic *Gunga Din* treatments for the studio, but nothing was developed further.[20]

Five years later, *The Film Daily* reported that "Ghunga [sic] Din . . . will be produced by Reliance for United Artists release, it was stated yesterday [October 3, 1934] by Edward Small, Reliance producer."[21] Small and Harry M. Goetz had created Reliance Pictures in 1932, and had scored a big hit with the first sound version of *The Count of Monte Christo* (1934).

"Rubeigh J. Minney, co-author of both the stage and screen versions of 'Clive of India' has been assigned by Reliance Pictures to do the screenplay for *Gunga Din*," noted *The Film Daily* in its October 15, 1934 issue. In November, Minney produced a synopsis, which focused on a love story in which two friends, "Hugh Harding and Kenneth O'Brien, [compete] for the same girl, Eve." After Eve marries O'Brien, Harding departs for India. The married couple visit India, but Eve is kidnapped by tribesmen. The men and "the faithful Gunga Din" rescue Eve, but O'Brien and Din are killed.

Colonel J. C. Hanna, a member of the British Board of Film Censors, thought that the synopsis was harmless, but added: "There is no justification for connecting this story with Kipling's poem. It is obviously written by a man who knows nothing about the service or about India."[22] Colonel Hanna was also criti-cal of a proposed remake of *King of the Khyber Rifles* (1929) and other so-called "Imperial" films because of the "ridiculous caricaturing" and falsely "imagined" description of British soldiers.

Nevertheless, pre-production was under-way. "Edward Small . . . announces that camera work for *Gunga Din* will start in January [1935]. It will be released though United Artists."[23] Small planned to travel to England in late 1935 "to confer with Rudyard Kipling on *Gunga Din*."[24] But the journey was never taken, and Minney's idea was shelved. Small, though, did not give up.

Kipling died on January 18, 1936, which also marked the writer's 44th wedding anniversary. Small purchased the rights to *Gunga Din* from the late poet's wife, Caroline, who managed her husband's estate.[25] Kipling's widow sold the rights to a number of her husband's other works, and within a five-year period, a half dozen of Kipling's literary creations were made into motion pictures: *Elephant Boy* (1937), *Captain's Courageous* (1937), *Wee Willie Winkie* (1937), *Gunga Din* (1939), *The Light That Failed* (1939), and *The Jungle Book* (1942).

An Indian dignitary raised a concern about Kipling's visions of India. Maharaja Mourbhanj, described as one of the "most picturesque potentates of India," visited the United States and commented on Kipling's literary works. "I do not agree with Mr. Kipling at all," he said, in an interview while in New York. "I have read all of his stories which deal with India, especially the frontier life, which I know so well, and I have no hesitancy in saying that he does not show India in the proper light."[26] Many more critical Indian voices would be heard when Kipling's works were finally translated to the screen.

Chapter Two Notes

1. *Morning Telegraph* [New York], June 25, 1912, mentioned in *Variety*, June 28, 1912, 30.

2. *Variety*, March 8, 1918, 28; *Variety*, June 28, 1912, 30; *Variety*, June 15, 1917, 18; *Variety*, June 27, 1919, 21; *Variety*, September 17, 1915, 16; *Variety*, May 10, 1918, 23; *The Billboard*, February 16, 1918, 9.

3. Variety, May 10, 1918, 23.

4. *Plain Dealer* (Cleveland, Ohio), May 15, 1908, 4.

5. *Moving Picture News*, Vol. IV, No. 15, April 15, 1911, 40. *Gunga Din* wasn't the first film to have a Kipling connection. Kevin Brownlow's article, "Rudyard Kipling and Early Hollywood," in the June 2011 issue of *The Kipling Journal*, stated: "The first appearance of the Kipling name on the screen was...*The Vampire* (1910) [which] was, according to the Selig [Films] Release Bulletin, inspired by Sir Ed Burne-Jones' famous painting with suggestions from the world famous poem by Rudyard Kipling." Kipling, who was a nephew of Burne-Jones, wrote *The Vampire* in 1897, the same year that Bram Stoker wrote *Dracula*.

6. Ibid., Vol. IV, No. 20, May 20, 2011, 18, 20, 21, 24. The highest rated film during the week of *Gunga Din's* release was *Gen. Marion, the Swamp Fox*. The film about the famous Revolutionary War leader received an "enthusiastic" rating.

7. *New York Clipper*, March 20, 1918, 12. The song was subsequently published by Harry Von Tilzer; *Variety,* October 13, 1916, 9. Humphrey's Columbia recording of December 9, 1915 was identified as #45808 in the label's series. Humphrey's recording for Thomas A. Edison's West Orange, New Jersey-based company was #50575. It featured a "molded label," which differed from Edison recordings that had pasted labels, a production process which began in 1921. Edison Diamond Disc recordings were produced between 1912 and 1929. Note: Collectors will notice that Edison's products were marked with an Orange, New Jersey identification because West Orange's mail went through adjacent Orange before delivery.

8. *Variety*, September 30, 1925, 4.

9. Ibid., December 29, 1926, 114. Unfortunately, no other information on Benton's association with *Gunga Din* (1911) could be found.

10. *The Moving Picture World*, October 24, 1925, 630.

11. *The Film Daily*, September 29, 1925, 1, 3. *Mandalay* appeared with *Gunga Din* for the first time in *Barrack-Room Ballads and Other Verses.* The Little Blue Book series was published by the Haldeman-Julius Publishing Company of Girard, Kansas. The firm produced nearly 2,000 diverse titles; *Gunga Din* was #795 in its series.

12. *Moving Picture World*, February 20, 1915, 1173.

13. *Exhibitor's Trade Review*, July 11, 1925, 42.

14. For some reason, on "Gunga Din and His Lute," written by Bourne and Wright (no first names were listed on the label), the stringed instrument was substituted for the more appropriate flute. Great Britain's Sterno Records was in production from 1926 to 1935. "Gunga Din and His Lute" featured no production year on the label but identified the song with S702 and #395, which suggest that the recording was issued in the early 1930s. Bernie Blake was one of several pseudonyms used by Star, Homophone's dance music director, during his career.

15. *Variety*, May 14, 1924, 17.

16. Ibid., November 24, 1926, 21.

17. Ibid., 48.

18. *Motion Picture News*, January 5, 1929, 38.

19. *Hollywood Filmgraph*, August 17, 1929, 1612.

20. Rudy Behlmer, *Behind the Scenes* (Hollywood: Samuel French, 1990), 88.

21. *The Film Daily*, October 4, 1934, 2.

22. Jeffrey Richards, *The Age of the Dream Palace: Cinema and Society in Britain 1930-1939* (London: Routledge & Kegan Paul, 1989), 140.

23. *The Film Daily*, October 15, 1934, 19. Subsequent news releases coincided with the debut of "Professor Gunga Din," a fictional lonely hearts advisor who answered questions from readers in Jacksonville's *Florida Tattler* newspaper.

24. *Motion Picture Daily*, August 21, 1835, 10.

25. The alleged amount was either £5,000 or $5,000. Joel Sayre Papers, The New York Public Library, Humanities and Social Sciences Library, Manuscripts and Archives Divisions, C. Articles, Box 6, Folder 21, "You're Better Than I Am," 4.

26. *Trenton Evening Times*, August 12, 1910, 2.

CHAPTER THREE
Gunga Din: From Reliance to RKO

IN APRIL 1936, *Variety* announced that "Edward Small's first picture as associate producer with [RKO] will be *Gunga Din*." RKO—the Radio-Keith-Orpheum holding company—was created in 1928 by David Sarnoff, who was RCA's general manager at the time, and Joseph P. Kennedy (father of future U. S. President John F. Kennedy) of Film Booking Offices of America. Part of the company's name included a reference to the Keith-Albee-Orpheum Vaudeville theater chain, which was also part of the new enterprise.

In another article, *Variety* noted that Small had signed William Faukner to write the screenplay.[1] It was an impressive selection. At the time, Faulkner was a fairly successful writer, having penned numerous short stories, short story collections, and novels. However, he was not as financially secure as his readers may have thought. During the early years of the Great Depression, he sought additional writing work in Hollywood. "Bill, like a lot of people, didn't make any money until paperbacks came in and until France and other countries found him," said director Howard Hawks.[2]

By time he was signed by Small, Faulkner had written several screenplays, including *The Road to Glory* (1936), which was directed by Hawks and co-written by Joel Sayre. Later, of course, Faulkner became one of the nation's most celebrated writers. He was awarded the 1949 Nobel Prize for Literature, and was later presented with two Pulitzer Prizes and a pair of National Book Awards.

Faulkner quickly went to work on the *Gunga Din* project. He researched and produced historical "Notes on India," a chronology of events from 1774 to 1904.[3] He underlined an important note that he would later incorporate into his preliminary script: "January 1, 1877—Queen Victoria was proclaimed Empress of India at a durbar of great magnificence held on the historic 'Ridge' overlooking Delhi." He also wanted to include the famous British Prime Minister Benjamin Disraeli in the story. Faulkner explored the writings of such British historians and biographers as James Anthony Froude, Thomas Edward Kebbel, Harold Edward Gorst, and Sir William Fraser. At the top of his list was *The Public Life of the Right Honourable the Earl of Beaconsfield* by Francis Hitchman, which described the Sepoy Mutiny of 1857. "There was a very uneasy feeling amongst the Sepoys, who had been told that the new [rifle] cartridges which had been served out to them were greased with the fat of pigs and oxen, and that the object of making them bite them was to destroy their caste," wrote Hitchman.[4] The insurrection of the previously loyal native troops in the British ranks provided Faulkner with a dramatic story element.

He wrote six pages of notes in a document tentatively titled *Pukka Sahib*, dated April 10, 1936.[5] The notes, dictated to studio staffer Kathleen Jones, identified a Captain Holmes, a twenty-five-year-old commander of an outpost in the Khyber Hills, who has a son,

Das, with a native woman. The officer later marries an English woman who bears him a son. Das learns of his father's marriage and seeks revenge against him.

Faulkner's notes jump to 1915-1916. Das is rescued from a dangerous situation by a young officer, which happens to be his father's other son. Das is unaware of the situation and exhibits a "dog-like devotion" to the officer. Later, a warring Indian leader tells Das about his brother and uses it to influence him in an effort to attack the English. The young Holmes learns about his half-brother and is thrust into a situation which tests his loyalty. Holmes is forced to decide between "fratricide and the admission of treachery." His superiors give him the option to commit suicide with either his service pistol or poison, but Das provides important information that saves his life and helps thwart the attack.

Faulkner was dissatisfied with his initial notes, especially the ending, and wrote ten new pages three days later. In his new version, the Indian character is called Din, who is described as "a braggart, a petty thief, a gambler, always in hot water and quite incorrigible." Holmes reappears along with Smith, a fellow officer and a rival in romance. Holmes wins the day and marries the girl, who later gives birth to a son. While on patrol, Holmes learns that his wife is in "serious condition" and seeks permission to see her; however, he is denied the opportunity to return to her.

Din steals some papers from headquarters and uses them to allow Holmes to visit his ailing wife. Holmes briefly reunites with her but returns to his men, who are engaged in a battle. Charges are brought against Din, who is found guilty and sentenced to death by a firing squad. Holmes, a soldier for fourteen years, pleads to his colonel not to have Din executed "in front of the troops." The superior officer agrees. Holmes passes a pistol to Din in his cell, and the native commits suicide. In the conclusion, Holmes and Smith drink to Din. "Here's to Din!" toasts Holmes on the final page of Faulkner's notes. "He was a thief and a liar. We kicked and cursed him around, and doubtless he deserved it."

Faulkner revised and expanded his notes to twenty-one pages on April 16, using the alternative spelling of "*Gungha Din* (scenes and sequences)," which included an introduction featuring Queen Victoria and Benjamin Disraeli. In Sequence One, the British monarch elevates Disraeli to Earl of Beaconsfield. Din carries a water pail and informs the British soldiers that his water is so precious that "in battle you will kiss the boots of he who has it," a line taken from Kipling's poem. Faulkner noted that most of the scenes take place in Afghanistan in 1858 and 1875.

In Sequence Two, Faulkner describes two subalterns, Holm (the writer dropped the "e" from Holme) and Smythe (formerly Smith), and introduces a pair of elephants. Most of these scenes are interiors with little action happening outside of military structures. Another scene notes that Din suffers a beating. Faulkner included five additional pages in which he names three other soldiers: Canning, Napier, and Campbell. He also added more notes about the Victoria-Disraeli scene.

After writing three separate note collections within a week, Faulkner reevaluated his work and started writing a fifty-page effort titled *Gungha Din,* which he completed on May 16. In Sequence One (pages 1-7), he sets the scene in Calcutta, and introduces three subalterns: Robert Holm, Whitten-Grey, and McClintock. Holm's brother, Paul, is also written into the story. Din carries a water pail and again quotes Kipling ("you will kiss the boots . . . .").

In Sequence Two (pages 8-22), the three subalterns become dragoons under the watchful eye of Paul Holm. Faulkner notes that Din, who is married and has a child, seeks military service. "I am a fighting man," exclaims Din. "I could be the sahib's orderly in battle."

Sequence Three (pages 23-39) is set primarily within interiors, and features Anne, a "seductive looking" Afghan spy, who seduces Robert Holm and makes him "unfit for Indian service." In Paul Holm's quarters, Faulkner describes "Din lying drunk on the floor."

In Sequence Four (pages 40-48), Robert, bedridden for five weeks due to too much sun, is "thrown into solitary confinement" for being a traitor. The colonel also suspects Paul of being a traitor. Later the Prince, a tribal leader, wants to "get the troop out in the open where it can be annihilated." The Prince states that he will not attack if a British officer is offered to him in exchange. Paul prevents his brother from sacrificing himself when he instructs Din to knock him out; however, Paul is prevented from volunteering when Din knocks him out instead. The water carrier disguises himself as a subaltern and goes to the Prince in order to save the troop. However, the tribal leader recognizes him as a "low-cast[e] native" and impales him until he dies. In the meantime, Paul drives the enemy away.

Sequence Five (pages 49 and 50) describes a headstone for Din ("a water boy—Queen's Own Punjab Light Dragoons"), and concludes with Robert Holm's eulogy. "Kicked him and beat him, but by God, he was a better man than I was," says the soldier. "A better man than I."

Faulkner edited *Gungha Din* down to forty-nine pages on May 19, but shortly thereafter, he was off the project. Nevertheless, the enterprising Edward Small kept the production alive. Leo Spitz, RKO president, told the Universal and RKO convention in New York on June 16, 1936 that his studio was set to release twenty-two "big" productions, including *Gunga Din*, "in the coming season."[6]

On June 23, 1936, it was reported that RKO became the sole owners to the rights of Kipling's immortal poem.[7] On the next day, a quarter-page ad in *Variety* proclaimed: "Rudyard Kipling's greatest work bombarded to the screen! Tune to the stirring beat of marching men. Written in the blood and glory of an empire marching on. Pictured in the drama of human souls too small to count in conquest; too priceless to forget when the fires of battle die. An Edward Small Production." The ad was accompanied by an interesting illustration of a water carrier and a British soldier in a battle scene.[8] Small's next task was to hire a new writer.

Chapter Three Notes

1. *Variety*, April 15, 1936, 29, 31; *Motion Picture Daily*, April 17, 1936, 10.

2. Scott Breivold, ed., *Howard Hawks: Interviews* (Jackson, Mississippi: University Press of Mississippi, 2006), 88.

3. Notes and Screen Treatments by William Faulkner for RKO film *Gunga Din* with screen play by Ben Hecht, Berg Collection, New York Public Library, Humanities and Social Sciences Library, Manuscripts and Archives Division.

4. Francis Hitchman, *The Public Life of the Right Honourable the Earl of Beaconsfield* (London: Samson Low, Marston, Searle & Rivington, 1881), 242. See also Victor Sutcliffe, "The Causes of the India Mutiny," *Soldiers of the Queen*, September 1995, issue #82.

5. Notes and Screen Treatments by William Faulkner. The Mississippi-born writer also referenced Din as a "nigger," an ugly term that survived in one form or another in all the scripts through the September 26, 1938 version.

6. *Variety*, June 17, 1936, 5.

7. *Silver Screen*, January 1939, 60.

8. *Variety*, June 24, 1936, 20.

CHAPTER FOUR
Lester Cohen and John Colton

In May 1936, *The Film Daily* reported that although "work on the screenplay was started some time ago by William Faulkner," Edward Small brought in Lester Cohen to work on the project.[1] Cohen was best-known at the time for writing such films as *One Man's Journey* (1933) and *Of Human Bondage* (1934).

Cohen produced an outline on June 10, 1936 in which Gunga Din is introduced as "an Indian of the Vaisyas caste" who serves as a "guide and a tonga [light carriage] driver." In another undated incomplete script, the writer noted: "He taps Caste Mark on his forehead, which may or may not be a Swastika." Interestingly, the swastika was an ancient Hindu religious symbol, but it was also adopted by the Nazi Party in the 1920s. While Cohen worked on his screenplay in 1936, Nazi Germany sent troops into the previously demilitarized Rhineland, and provided military support to General Francisco Franco's Nationalist forces during the Spanish Civil War. The *Gunga Din* Swastika idea quickly died on Cohen's page.

In the outline, Din saves his sister from Suttee (a Hindu practice whereby a widow throws herself on her deceased husband's funeral pyre) but, as a result, is "made an outcast." Din is befriended by Gloria Mountcastle, an English woman, who later marries and makes the outcast her servant.

Din is later recruited to assist the British in confirming a rumored native revolt. Din falls in love with Zora, who is sympathetic to the natives. When new Enfield rifles and their animal-greased cartridges are distributed to the native soldiers, the unrest commences. [Note: The loading process was nothing new: muzzleloading shoulder arms had previously been loaded with paper cartridges (the lead projectile and the black powder charge were enclosed in the wrapping) after they were opened by a soldier's bite. The Enfield's paper cartridges were supposedly greased with pork and beef fat, which made them easier to load; however, the so-called "consumption" of meat products violated the beliefs of Muslim and Hindu soldiers.]

Cohen also added notes on Indian culture and the Great Mutiny of 1857-1858. On June 30, he updated his outline and changed the name of the female lead to Gloria Rennel—but on the next day, Gloria became Pamela. When Din attempts to protect her from some British officers, whom he believed were going to mistreat her, one of them, a sergeant major, beats him. Later, Din participates in a successful peace keeping mission and is elevated to the position of head water boy of the regiment.[2]

Cohen's treatment of July 2 depicted Din dying of thirst, but he is saved by Gloria Grainger, the daughter of a regimental commander. Later, Din protects her from an advancing British sergeant major, who is actually in love with Gloria. The non-commissioned officer goes out on a mission disguised as a native, but Din does not betray him. However, once the new Enfield cartridges are distributed, the native mutiny begins. Cohen's rewrites were not developing quickly enough into a coherent screenplay, and RKO decided to make a move. While Cohen was editing his work, *The Film Daily* reported that Anthony Veiller, who had written screenplays for *Jalna* (1935) and *Star of Midnight* (1935), had joined the RKO writing roster.[3] The revolving door of writers was just getting started.

On July 14, Cohen updated his synopsis by adding a background story to the sergeant major character. He also added more details about the disguised soldier's mission in an August 1 revision. However, within weeks, Cohen's tenure with the *Gunga Din* project came to an end.

An undated and unsigned synopsis in the RKO Studio files, which may have been written by Veiller, tells the story of a British officer, who is murdered after he is given a valuable emerald from a native chieftain. Years later, the officer's son, Hugh, plans to join his father's regiment and go to India, but he "decides to give up the army" and remain in England in order to win the heart of Eve. However, she has already accepted a proposal from Hugh's cousin, Ken, "who has wealth and a position to offer her."

Gunga Din, a "faithful water boy in the colonel's old regiment," arrives in England and informs Hugh about the location of the stolen emerald. Before the two depart for India, Eve tells Hugh that she really loves him. He promises to return to her. Hugh and Gunga Din manage to retrieve the valuable gem. Later, Eve persuades Ken to accompany her to India in order to find Hugh. Eventually, they all meet, but Eve is kidnapped by "brigands," who demand the emerald as ransom. A fight breaks out and Ken is killed, Hugh is wounded, and Din is mortally wounded. "Eve, rescued, later marries Hugh."[4]

Small also recruited the services of John Colton, who had written screenplays for *The Werewolf of London* (1935) and *The Invisible Ray* (1936).[5] "John Colton is at work on a screenplay for *Gunga Din*," reported *The New York Times* on August 29. Like his predecessors, Colton altered characters, changed scenes, and developed new scenarios.

Colton provided a 47-page treatment titled *Ghunga Din*, (with this new spelling), which was dated September 15, 1936 and marked "incomplete."[6] His story was presented from the perspective of Linda Brandon, a young woman, who "is en route from England to India to marry the young man she has always loved—Captain Geoffrey Kildoyle of the 17th Highlanders."

The treatment begins on Christmas Eve in 1856, as Brandon sails to her destination. At the captain's table, she is lectured by a missionary woman, who criticizes India's caste system. Brigadier General Cahusac, an old officer, opines that the system will never change. After the ladies depart, he tells the other men that "the Crown must take over the powers which the East India Company has abrogated itself."

Later, Brandon introduces herself to the general and tells him that her grandfather once served under his command. She confesses that she has heard stories about "black-magic and blood sacrifices to Kali," which have frightened her. "You need be afraid of nothing," says Cahusac, referring to the powerful Hindu goddess, who is traditionally depicted with four arms.

At his quarters at Naidanpore, Kildoyle sits in a bath, while the "regimental *bhistie*," Gunga Din, "a keen-eyed lad of, perhaps, eighteen," pours water over him. Din pleads with Kildoyle to allow him to accompany the officer to Calcutta. "He promises Geoffrey he will serve him, wait on him 'to end of time' in repayment for taking him." Din is also grateful to the officer for saving him several times "from the heavy belt strap of Top Sergeant Angus McGregor." In another scene, Din uses a pea shooter to annoy the brutal sergeant, his wife, and some others. McGregor catches up with Din and "begins to unlatch his heavy belt."

Kildoyle has had a relationship of sorts with Mrs. Ivy Beirutzoff, a "volcanic, ruthless woman," who reminds the officer that he is "head over heels in debt to the bazaar money lenders." She warns him that his military career could be jeopardized if the colonel learns of his financial situation. Colton added some additional characters, including a Mr. Beirutzoff, Ivy's second husband, a member of a family munitions business hierarchy, which has made "deals with the East India Company."

Due to late orders, Kildoyle is unable to travel to Calcutta, where he was supposed to meet his fiancé. McGregor goes in his place and confronts Gunga Din, "the Lazurisian imp o' hell," yet again. Later, the *bhisti* interrupts a ceremony in which a young widow was about to "burn herself on the funeral pyre of her dead husband," a passage which seems to have been taken from Lester Cohen's writings. Din stampedes a bull into the crowd, which causes a panic. During the chaos, Din quickly removes the woman from the scene. He discovers that she is Zizanla, his former sweetheart, and plans their escape. Din uses his ability to create voices and sounds—a skill he learned from his "foster father, Gab the wizard"—to confuse the train station guards. He and Zizanla sneak aboard a train and hide in one of the first-class compartments, which happens to be Linda Brandon's quarters.

Brandon enters her compartment and discovers them hiding under the seats. "I am a slave of Captain Kildoyle," says Din. "Have pity of the hapless misery you see." Brandon agrees and prevents officials from searching her compartment for the runaway couple.

Upon arriving at Naidanpore, Kildoyle informs Brandon that their formal wedding and honeymoon can't take place until his gambling debts can be repaid. The colonel of the regiment has given him an ultimatum: pay off the debt within two months or be forced out of the regiment. However, Brandon ignores the circumstances and marries Kildoyle that very afternoon. It becomes a double ceremony, when Din and Zizanla "are united 'Christian fashion.'" Din whispers to his bride, "The priests of Kali will never dare touch us now. Who says I am not a clever man?" Ivy Beirutzoff is incensed over the marriage of Kildoyle and Brandon.

Later, rumors of native unrest are dismissed by Colonel Scott, the regimental commander. Brigadier General Cahusac cautiously remarks, "An Englishman has only to turn around and note how the smiles change to scowls as he passes [through a bazaar]." The general also warns that the new Enfield rifles being produced by the Beirtzoff company will feature cartridges wrapped in pig grease, something that would offend native soldiers. Scott dismisses Cahusac's concern and reminds him of the native soldiers' loyalty. Cahusac states that he will not sign the authorization for the new rifles. Scott reminds Kildoyle of the debt deadline. The young officer, who refuses donations from Cahusac and his fellow soldiers, urges Scott not to force his resignation because of the brewing trouble among the native troops.

Mrs. Bierutzoff tells Linda that if she can persuade General Cahusac to sign off on the new rifle, she will have the colonel postpone her husband's debt deadline and forced resignation. Linda refuses the offer and confides in Cahusac. Gunga Din leads the general and the Kildoyles to the bazaar, where they secretly witness "a vile travesty" mocking all things British.

The old Queen of Oudh and Naidan hosts a large party at her palace. Among the entertainers are Gab the wizard and his assistant, Gunga Din. Local British officials, including Sir Ransom, believe that the queen is harmless, but General Cahusac knows otherwise. The queen tells the general that she is pleased that he has refused to approve the new rifles, but Cahusac believes that she wants the rifles introduced so a mutiny will erupt among the native soldiers. Ransom informs Cahusac that if he doesn't sign off on the new rifles, Mr. Bierutzoff will sell them to Russia, "England's greatest potential enemy."

Gunga Din discovers that the general is going to be poisoned at a social function. The dose is designed to make the officer appear drunk and incapable of negotiating the weapons deal. At the gathering, Geoffrey Kildoyle switches his champagne glass with the general's, drinks the tainted beverage, and quickly becomes foolishly drunk. Escorted to his quarters, Gunga Din serves him Gab's antidote. The general is informed about the plot to poison him, and determines that local British officials are part of a conspiracy with the queen and Bierutzoff, but during the night, the general is killed by a "coral-colored snake" that was placed in his bed.

The new rifles are received, and the mutiny erupts. Geoffrey appeal to the native soldiers in his ranks and convinces some of them to remain loyal. McGregor arrives with carts full of the older muskets, which they use. They safely retreat to the fort, but "for eight terrible months Geoffrey with the small detachment of Highlanders remaining and his loyal 'old guard' withstand siege." Eventually, their supplies and ammunition run low. "There would be no water were it not for Gunga Din who has discovered an old well beyond the fort."

Two Sepoy rebels enter the fort through Gunga Din's tunnel and set fire to the gunpowder magazine. The explosion nearly kills Geoffrey but Din rescues the unconscious officer. After Din serves water to him, McGregor responds in amended Kipling prose: "It's crawling and it stinks but, of all the drinks I've drank, I'm grateful for this. I've beaten you and whaled you, but you're a better man than I am, Gunga Din."

The first Sepoy is killed, but the second one runs with a torch to the other powder magazine. Din rushes after him, but it's too late. The magazine explodes and bursts into flames. Din cries out, "Goodbye, Sahib—Goodbye Zizanla!" Din's wife appears on a wall above the magazine and shouts, "Now I make true Suttee for my true husband," before jumping into the flames.

Bagpipes in the distance signal the approach of the British relief column which ends the siege. Linda shows her injured husband their newborn son. "Another man for the regiment," she says, in the treatment's final scene.

Each writer made a contribution to the *Gunga Din* story, but no script was worthy of the studio's final approval. Nevertheless, RKO moved ahead as if it had a finished screenplay. Due to the fact that the film featured historical impressions of nineteenth century British soldiers, technical advice was sought after. The studio signed Major G. O. Bagley, a retired British Army officer, to serve as the production's technical advisor.[7] More changes were about to take place.

Chapter Four Notes

1. *The Film Daily*, May 26, 1936, 7.

2. William Nutt, "Notes, Comparisons and Synopses of All Material on Gunga Din," January 19, 1939, RKO Radio Pictures, Inc., Studio Records, ca. 1928-1958, *Gunga Din*, Subseries 172, 1936-1939, UCLA Library Special Collections, Los Angeles, California. This RKO document does not identify page numbers.

3. *The Film Daily*, June 15, 1936, 2.

4. Nutt, "Notes," January 19, 1939, n.p.

5. *The Film Daily*, September 17, 1936, 6.

6. RKO Studio Records. This script includes mentions of both Gunga Din and Gungha Din.

7. *Motion Picture Daily*, June 16, 1936, 17.

CHAPTER FIVE

Howard Hawks, Ben Hecht, and Charles MacArthur

RKO sought a director for *Gunga Din*. The studio considered King Vidor, who had directed the highly successful silent film, *The Big Parade* (1925), and received Best Director Oscar nominations for four films he made between 1928 and 1938, including *The Citadel* (1938), which he had just completed. RKO settled on Howard Hawks, who had also made the successful transition from silents to talkies. "*Gunga Din* Next For Direction By Hawks," shouted an entertainment page headline in San Diego's *Evening Tribune* on September 3, 1936.

Besides directing, Hawks had worked as a producer, an editor, a production manager, a writer, and an actor. He directed such worthy motion pictures as *The Dawn Patrol* (1930), his first all-sound motion picture; *Scarface* (1932); *Twentieth Century* (1934); and *The Road to Glory* (1936).

Hawks was an independent type, a creative filmmaker, who enjoyed doing things his way, even when instructed not to. Of course, there were consequences for his behavior. In 1936, Hawks was fired by MGM while directing *Come and Get It*, a rough and tumble film based upon Edna Ferber's novel about the environmental damage caused by the logging industry in Wisconsin. Hawks had made unauthorized changes to the story, and studio head Samuel Goldwyn replaced him with William Wyler. Hawks promptly left Hollywood and seemingly disappeared.

"Hawks left town after he and Samuel Goldwyn came to a parting of the ways over the direction of *Come and Get It*, and for at least a month no one had any inkling as to his whereabouts," wrote syndicated Hollywood columnist Louella Parsons.[1] RKO, however, didn't view Hawks as damaged goods.

Hawks took charge and quickly recruited new writers. On September 19, 1936, *The Film Daily* reported that Hawks had arrived in New York, where he was scheduled to "confer with Ben Hecht and Charles MacArthur on *Gunga Din*."[2]

Hecht and MacArthur had teamed up earlier. The pair co-wrote *The Front Page*, a play in three acts, which debuted on Broadway at the Times Square Theatre on August 14, 1928. *The Front Page* provided a plot element that the pair would work into the *Gunga Din* script. The play traces the efforts of newspaper editor Walter Burns, who tries to persuade his best reporter, Hildy Johnson, from getting married and leaving the newspaper business.

In 1931, the play was made into a film, with Adolphe Menjou as Burns, and Pat O'Brien as Johnson. Bartlett Cormack adapted Hecht and MacArthur's story, and Charles Lederer contributed additional screenplay elements. The film features several scenes that became part of *Gunga Din's* final story line. For example, a potent beverage is used to affect a behavioral outcome (Burns attempts to get Johnson drunk); a character commits suicide by jumping (the ill-fated Molly, played by Mae Clarke, makes a fatal jump); and another character delivers an emotional rant as he anticipates his deadly fate (jail breaker Earl

Williams, played by George E. Stone, makes a demonstrative declaration).

The Front Page (1931) also included a few more subtle touches that would appear in one form or another in the *Gunga Din* screenplay: a character's affection for a musical instrument, talk of an "uprising of radicals," and comments about a hanging. "Hecht and MacArthur were paid $60,000 for the story of *Gunga Din* and they stole it from themselves."[3]

Hawks and the two writers had a creative history. Hecht had provided the story for *Scarface* (1932), which was directed by Hawks, and Hecht and MacArthur had written the Broadway play *Twentieth Century*, which Hawks turned into a 1934 film of the same name. He appreciated the writers. "Hecht and MacArthur were just marvelous," said Hawks in a 1974 interview. "When [we] used to work on a script, we'd sit in a room and work for two hours and then we'd play backgammon for an hour. Then we'd start again and one of us would be one character and one would be another character."[4]

Hawks and his writing companions wanted to bring a sense of authenticity to their fictional story. They researched various sources about India in the nineteenth century, and produced dozens of pages of notes on Sir Richard Francis Burton (1821-1890), the British soldier, foreign service officer, explorer, and writer, who mastered several mid-Eastern languages and dialects. After several weeks, they eventually assembled their research facts as *Notes On Sir Richard Burton*, which read more like an enthusiastic treatment for a big-screen bio-pic. "Visualize a man who was more than a man, a giant in mind and physical strength, whose name was Richard Burton . . . a man who might have been King and who might have followed in the footsteps

of Allah!" The *Notes* included a parenthetical reference to Kipling, who had said that one of his fictional characters, named Strickland, was based on Burton.[5]

RKO staffer William Nutt questioned why research on Burton had been added to the studio's files. "It is a little difficult to understand why this is included in the *Gunga Din* material, since it bears no relation to any of the various versions by Faulkner, Hecht-MacArthur, et al. This is merely a sketch of the tempestuous life of Sir Richard Burton."[6] However, Nutt failed to notice something in the Burton files. The document mentioned that during a six-month period, Burton "in all India he had been spied in different disguises." Three pages are devoted to Burton's journey to Mecca, but no mention is made that, in fact, he was disguised as a Dervish during his 1853 pilgrimage. "The metamorphose was so complete that not only natives but even Europeans never suspected it."[7] The disguise element had been utilized by Cohen in his treatment.

Within a short time, Hawks, Hecht, and MacArthur came up with some ideas. On October 27, 1936, they sent an enthusiastic telegram to RKO: "Have finally figured out tale involving two sacrifices, one for love, the other for England, which neither resembles Bengal Lancers nor the Charge of the Light Brigade and contains something like two thousand deaths, thirty elephants and a peck of maharajahs. We have this now in a cocktail shaker and have poured out some thirty-five pages of glittering prose which look good."[8]

Hawks was so encouraged by the writers' efforts that he wanted to accelerate pre-production as quickly as possible. Louella Parsons filed a column from Los Angeles on October 29: "[RKO's head of production] Sam Briskin

. . . expects Hawks back next week to begin preparations for the picture." The timing seemed right, too, since several other films about India were popular at the time. *Lives of a Bengal Lancer* (1935) and *Clive of India* (1935) had already been released, and more India-based films were on the way, including *The Charge of the Light Brigade* (1936); *Wee Willie Winkie* (1937), which co-starred Victor McLaglen as Sergeant MacDuff; and *The Rains Came* (1939).[9]

"*Gunga Din*—An Outline," dated December 2, 1936, features several general story elements that would be retained in the final 1938 script, and the studio acknowledged Hecht and MacArthur as its contributors. "It is pretty clear, in comparing all the foregoing material by Faulkner, Cohen, and Colton to the revised final script, that none of the ideas suggested by these men have been used for the picture, and that the Hecht-MacArthur material alone forms the basis for the story finally used," stated William Nutt.[10] In an RKO Inter-Department Communication memo, dated January 10, 1939, Nutt informed Ross Hastings, one of the studio's legal advisors, that the two writers submitted a similar outline to Sam Briskin's office on December 1, 1936. The following day's outline was sent to Edward Small's office.

The two writers' story revolved around three enlisted men—Sergeant MacChesney ("Soldiering is for him is the flower of all human activity."), Sergeant Ballantine ("Discipline hasn't taken the joy of life out of him."), and Corporal Cutter ("Full of a childishly romantic faith in the tales of that storied land he had heard in his youth.")—and a water carrier named Gunga Din, who is initially described as "scantilly [sic] clothed and monkeyish in his behavior." The studio promptly alerted

newspapers and trade publications about the film's major characters. One gossip columnist, Sidney Skolsky, misread the news release and incorrectly reported that Hawks needed to rewrite the script and "put Gunga Din in it."[11]

In the outline, the relationship between Gunga Din and the soldiers, especially MacChesney, is a rather ugly one; in fact, it stated that MacChesney "has always hated Gunga Din for his slovenliness." In one scene, Din falls, emptying his water bag, as he approaches the sergeant. MacChesney is enraged and "boots the cowering native out of sight."

Followers of Khan Sufi, a "fanatic" native leader, initiate a street fight with the soldiers over the appearance of the Christian cross-like telegraph poles, which seem to be "symbols of an alien faith." The fight escalates into a roof-to-roof battle. The outnumbered soldiers and Gunga Din manage to escape by leaping into a nearby river, but the water carrier nearly drowns. As the group floats along the river on a bullock skin, Ballantine informs his comrades that he will soon leave the service and get married to "Mildred Gubbins [sometimes identified as Cubbins in the outline], the daughter of Jeremy Gubbins, a wealthy exporter in Calcutta." MacChesney is shocked that his comrade is going to turn into a "into a pale, donkey-livered clerk."

Upon their return to headquarters, MacChesney shows his commander, Colonel Stone, a captured rifle. Stone identifies the weapon as Russian-made, and orders the men back into the field to locate Khan Sufi's arsenal of arms and ammunition. MacChesney doesn't want Ballantine to join them because of his impending retirement from military service, but the engaged trooper wants to be a part of this final mission, which he regards as a kind of a "farewell party." Cutter adds the search for a "golden temple" as an incentive for Ballantine to participate in the operation. The group locates Khan Sufi's forces and engages them in battle. Thanks to a daring "rear sortie movement" led by MacChesney, the Khan is captured.

Cutter and Din follow a Hindu priest into the hills in an attempt to secure the "temple with riches." Upon his arrival at the temple, Cutter, who claimed to be the British commander, is captured by the priest's followers. The priest plans to hold Cutter hostage until the captured Khan Sufi is freed. Gunga Din is sent away with orders to bring back the Khan, or Cutter will be killed. Din reports back, but MacChesney is angered at the water carrier and wants to hang him. Ballantine intervenes on Din's behalf.

Ballantine wants to help MacChesney rescue Cutter, but the senior sergeant explains that he can't allow a "non-combatant" to join him due to regulations—unless, of course, Ballantine reenlists. Ballantine agrees, but informs his comrade that as soon as Cutter is rescued, MacChesney must destroy the papers. MacChesney consents to the proposal.

Ballantine and Din disguise themselves as "two revolutionists," who have captured a high-ranking British officer, MacChesney. In order to convince their adversaries, MacChesney is tied on the back of a mule. They hope that their collective appearance will allow them to enter the Khan's fortress and somehow free Cutter. The trio enters the confines and finds Cutter, who is tied to the end of a teeter-totter. A large can of water at the other end is slowly draining water, which lowers him towards "a bed of glowing coals." The teeter-totter torture device had been used in *The Mask of Fu Manchu* (1932),

which starred Boris Karloff in the title role. Directed by Charles Brabin (King Vidor was uncredited for his directorial contributions), the MGM film's teeter-totter included a slow-flowing sand-filled counter weight that rested above an alligator pit. A number of other elements in the film also seemed to have influenced Hecht and MacArthur.[12]

Ballantine suddenly stabs the priest, MacChesney "rolls off the mule," and a gunfight begins. Cutter is rescued and informs his mates that he knows where the Khan's weapons and ammunition are located. The group is cornered in the temple, but manages to hold out until the next day, when MacChesney successfully uses a heliograph to alert the British of their whereabouts. The natives storm the turret and blow it up. Amid the rubble, Din rescues a wounded MacChesney and gives him water until multiple gunshots fell the *bhisti*. "I hope you liked your drink, sir," says Din, using Kipling's words, before he dies.

The three soldiers attend Gunga Din's funeral. Ballantine departs with his fiancé, but MacChesney informs Colonel Stone that Ballantine is a deserter since he technically reenlisted. "Well, fetch him back," says the Colonel, in *Front Page* (1931) fashion.

RKO seemed pleased with the script's development and began a location search for outdoor scenes, especially mountainous areas that could double for India's North West Frontier. Lou Shapiro, the studio's location manager, wrote to the Yuma Chamber of Commerce in Arizona on January 6, 1937, and requested a tourist's brochure. "We would also appreciate any pictures of Yuma and surrounding territory," wrote Shapiro. The brochure was probably one of the few items the former movie cowboy had not accumulated in his files over the years. "It is his boast that before he goes into a town, he can tell you when it rains and how much, the price of a hotel room, whether it's Democratic or Republican, union or non-union, and whether train whistles will interfere with outdoor shooting."[13]

RKO began to cast the film. On January 12, 1937, Washington's *Spokesman-Review* announced that *Gunga Din* was scheduled to begin production in May, and noted that "John Beal will play the title role of the heroic East Indian water carrier and other leads will be taken by Preston Foster and Walter Abel." Beal, who began his screen career in 1933, had co-starred with Katherine Hepburn in *The Little Minister* (1934) and appeared in *Les Miserables* (1935). The rugged Foster had appeared in *I Am a Fugitive from a Chain Gang* (1932) and *The Informer* (1935), among other films since 1929. Abel seemed to be an appropriate choice, since he had played D'Artagnan in *The Three Musketeers* (1935). In time, however, all three actors were dropped from the production.

On January 4, 1937, Hecht and MacArthur wrote a one-page "Draft Continuity" for *Gunga Din,* which was read fifteen days later by Herbert Hirschman, a member of the RKO story department. The writers made a few changes and set the story in 1880. The revision traces the actions of "the three Musketeers of the corps," who are ordered by Colonel Stone to help stop Khan Sufi, a native leader, who is "once again on the warpath." After a false search for "hidden treasure," the three soldiers and a small detachment, which includes Gunga Din, travel to Bohara, where they engage in a "minor insurrection." They return to headquarters, where they are ordered back to Bohara. Ballantine, who is

getting married once his enlistment expires, is excused from the mission.

In order to keep Ballantine in the service, MacChesney and Cutter secretly serve elephant medicine to his replacement who ends up on the "sick list." Ballantine, "against his will," joins his fellow soldiers to Bohara. At the village, Cutter secures another treasure map and plans to search for it, but MacChesney places him in jail. Cutter breaks out of the confines, thanks to Gunga Din and a jail-destroying elephant. Cutter and Din travel to a temple, but are captured by Khan Sufi "and his fanatical army." Din escapes and alerts MacChesney, who organizes a plan to rescue Cutter. Ballantine signs a reenlistment paper, but informs MacChesney that the senior sergeant must tear up the document once Cutter is saved.

Disguised as a native, Ballantine pretends to be MacChesney's captor. They enter the temple, reunite with Cutter, and manage to capture the Khan. However, the Indian leader "kills himself to deliver the English into his men's hands." Din, who is "very ill," disguises himself as the Khan and helps the men escape.

Ballantine gets married, but MacChesney uses the reenlistment papers to keep his comrade in the service. The continuity document concludes with: "No woman can break up the three Musketeers!"

Pre-production continued. The January 14, 1937 shooting schedule indicated a forty-two-day shoot, which designated Yuma, Arizona as the main outdoor location. Other locations included the studio, the RKO Ranch, and Chatsworth, California. The schedule identified and enumerated twenty-five characters with speaking parts. Among the principals, MacChesney was numbered first in the cast, followed by Ballantine, Cutter, Higginbotham, and Gunga Din. Other designated characters in the ranks included Colonel Stone (#6), Emmy Stebbins (#7), Major Hamilton (#8), Corporal Wetkins (#9), and Captain Warwick (#10). Among some of the additional listed characters were Rebel Leader (#12), Mr. Stebbins (#13), Sergeant Evans (#14), Elephant (#18), Khan Sufi (#24), and Fanatic Leader (#25). The second page of the schedule featured a note that instructed all department heads to submit their respective estimated budgets.

Hecht and MacArthur completed a second draft continuity on February 11, 1937, but, with the exception of some dialogue changes, the basic story remained unchanged. The second draft was satisfactory enough for RKO to authorize a budget. J. R. Crone, RKO's production manager, sent Pandro Berman, the studio's vice president in charge of production, a telegram on February 28: "*Gunga Din* budget based upon ninety-five day schedule . . . $1,493,000."

A third draft continuity was completed on March 16. The new version substituted an orchestrated elephant stampede as the method used by the soldiers to make their escape from the town battle, and *Gunga Din* would have a more painful final scene.

The two writers produced a 161-page screenplay titled *Gunga Din* on March 24, 1937. The script establishes the three lead characters—Sergeant Major MacChesney, Colour Sergeant Ballantine, and Corporal Cutter—who are involved in a brawl with some local Hindus over a so-called treasure map. The locals are conveniently tossed out of windows by the three soldiers, who later explain their behavior to Colonel Stone.

Gunga Din is described as having sold MacChesney an expensive watch that ap-

pears to have been stolen. "It was Gunga Din who replaced my sweeper this morning," says Colonel Stone. Later, Din, appearing a bit "tipsy," is seen wearing a wild-pattern red turban and new shoes. MacChesney catches the "ratty little chimp" and beats him with Cutter's belt.

The script also includes a rather lengthy scene with Ballantine and Emmy Stebbins. Over several pages, she instructs him how to serve tea and presents him with a civilian's derby hat, which, when alone, he destroys. Ballantine expresses his love for his fiancé in military terms. "You're as beautiful as a regiment of cavalry." Emmy questions him about his veiled reluctance to remain single ("If you want to get out of this dull, respectable marriage, it's your last chance."), but he makes a convincing pledge to her ("I will be faithful and bear true allegiance to Her Majesty Queen Emmy.").

MacChesney reminds the colonel that Ballantine "is the only man in the outfit with a thorough knowledge of the hill dialects," but the officer rebukes the sergeant's suggestion to retain Ballantine and notes that "[Sergeant] Evans will accompany you as interpreter." After MacChesney exits, the colonel admits to Captain Warwick that Ballantine's departure will "break the best fighting unit in the regiment."

In Bohara, a crowded Indian village, the soldiers install telegraph poles. Gunga Din, still wearing the red turban, shows Cutter a treasure map that identifies a gold temple. MacChesney warns that Daisy the elephant "goes beserk when she sees red," and the pachyderm promptly goes wild when she see Din's colorful headwear. While the soldiers restrain the other elephants, Daisy causes havoc. Ballantine saves the day, when he tosses Din's turban away, which calms the animal. Ballantine later informs MacChesney that "the hills are full of little brown boys," and that "a great many Afghans [are] among them."

A group of armed natives appear, and a "whiskered leader" demands that the telephone poles be removed because they look like Christian crosses. Sensing danger, MacChesney orders his men into a nearby house. He pushes the native leader, which sparks an attack by the natives. Gunga Din manages to get inside the house despite MacChesney's threat, "Keep out of this army, you!" A prolonged street fight develops (detailed from page 33 to 45), which escalates to the rooftops. During the skirmish, Ballantine mocks Din by calling him a "monkey" and a "dumb git." Ballantine's foot crashes through a roof, but Cutter frees him by using a bayonet to cut around him. Ballantine attaches Din's red turban to his rifle and uses it to excite Daisy and the other elephants into stampeding, which allows the soldiers to escape the village. Three men are lost, and Din suffers a leg wound in the fight.

As the three soldiers ride Daisy back to camp, Ballantine explains that he is leaving the army. His statement sparks an argument, which results in a fight between him and MacChesney.

Sergeant Evans, who is designated to replace Ballantine, delivers pre-wedding party invitations to MacChesney and Cutter. The two devise a plot to disrupt the planned wedding by using elephant medicine to poison Evans. They reason that, if Evans is incapacitated, the colonel will have to retain Ballantine, at least for a while. At the party, MacChesney pours the elephant medicine into a punch bowl. "Save some for the elephant," says Cutter, who later prevents other guests from drinking the punch by deliberately spilling a cupful and putting his hands in the beverage. The two soldiers eventually get Evans to drink the spiked punch, and he becomes severely ill.

The next day, Ballantine and Emmy shop for curtains, and the sergeant's mastery of local dialects is made evident through a conversation with a local merchant. The engaged couple is interrupted by MacChesney and Cutter, who inform Ballantine that, due to Evans' sudden illness, he must join his comrades on a mission. Ballantine is suspicious about Evans' condition, but dutifully responds to the order.

Back in Bohara, a drunken Cutter informs MacChesney that when Ballantine sees the gold temple "he'll be forgetting about "marriage and [the] tea business." MacChesney dismisses the absurd "opium dream" and Cutter threatens to go alone. MacChesney promptly knocks him out and has him thrown into a makeshift guard house located in the elephant stables. The senior sergeant threatens Gunga Din, "You sore-eyed sand rat, stay away from those stables." Higginbotham refers to the water carrier as "scum."

In a later scene, MacChesney reminds Ballantine about the many women they encountered over the years: a Russian girl in China, "pretty scamps in Shanghai," a "beautiful Greek countess in Rangoon," and Irene, a "little blonde who sang." Ballantine subsequently kicks MacChesney out of his quarters. The script also included a note to add "the proper British [military] terms when specific commands are used."

Evans recovers and escorts Emmy to Bohara, where she informs Captain Warwick that she has Ballantine's discharge papers.

In the following scene, Gunga Din upsets Daisy's baby in order to get its mother to batter down the guard house, which she does. Cutter and Din depart on Daisy's back, and the baby pachyderm follows. "Off for that pretty gold!" exclaims Cutter.

They arrive at the temple, where Cutter begins his search for gold. He finds a room filled with guns and ammunition cases, but is promptly captured. Din escapes and returns to the camp. MacChesney threatens to execute Din for helping Cutter escape, but Ballantine steps in on the *bhisti's* behalf. Ballantine volunteers to join a rescue party but MacChesney requires that he reenlist. Ballantine agrees and MacChesney promises to destroy the re-up papers once Cutter is saved. Ballantine, disguised as a native; MacChesney, tied over a mule and pretending to be a prisoner; and Din depart to rescue Cutter.

On a journey through "the jungle," they successfully pass four armed natives and arrive at the temple. The native "Leader" seems satisfied that a "very important" captured officer has been brought before him. In order to maintain their identities, Ballantine tells Din to keep whacking MacChesney, who gets angry at the water carrier's actions. The Leader brings them before Khan Sufi, who gives them some gold coins as payment for the captive. MacChesney is taken away to a tower-level dungeon, where Cutter is tied to the high end of a teeter-totter. A water barrel with a small hole in it is positioned at the other end of the device, which slowly lowers Cutter towards a pair of waiting cobras. Cutter says that despite being tortured he has not revealed anything about the "route of the ammunition train." The two soldiers start arguing again.

Ballantine and Din manage to enter the dungeon and capture the Khan. "He's sacred and they won't dare shoot," reasons MacChesney, who attempts to send a heliograph signal, but it's shattered by a native gunman, who is subsequently killed by the Leader. Cutter is freed from the teeter-totter.

The script jumps to a night scene, four days later: "Neither food nor water has passed their lips." The Khan boasts that he can go without food or water for "thirty days." An adjacent courtyard has a cistern filled with water, but it's surrounded by a large ring of "white hot coals." Din begins a "terrible crawl over the coals" and secures some of the precious liquid in a water-skin, despite being shot at by some nearby guards. Din returns and collapses. "I 'ope you liked your drink," he replies in poetic Kipling fashion. MacChesney calls him a "hero."

The group plans to make a run for it but the Khan states: "No! You are not going to go free. You will die—all of you. You will die the way my people like to kill." The Khan removes a hidden knife and stabs himself to death, thereby eliminating the shield that the soldiers and Din had relied on. Din informs MacChesney about a weapons cache he saw while going for the water. MacChesney goes to the room, which is filled with "boxes of ammunition, rifles" and artillery shells. MacChesney opens a few shells and makes a gunpowder trail.

Din, weakened and suffering from severe burns, gets dressed in the Khan's garments as a way to fool the natives. The group leaves the temple area as Cutter holds a gun to Din's back, but the *bhisti* collapses. "Forgive me, Master," says Din. "Forgive you!" replies MacChesney. "What are you talking about. You're a better man than I am, Gunga Din." MacChesney, whistling "Pomp and Circumstance," leads the group away. A firefight breaks out, and then the ammunition room

"Gunga Din's Terrible Crawl Over the Coals." Illustration by Gary Zaboly. Author's collection.

explodes, which gives them a brief opportunity to flee on horseback. The script suggests that Gunga Din died of severe burns.

Safe and back in the regimental hospital, where MacChesney is recuperating from a wound, Ballantine and his bride thank him for his life-saving efforts and bid farewell to him and Cutter. After the newlyweds exit, MacChesney shows Cutter Ballantine's re-enlistment papers. "He left his tunic in the Gold Pagoda," says MacChesney. "I want you to arrest Sergeant Thomas Ballantine for desertion." Once again, it's a concluding scene right out of *The Front Page* (1931).

Three day later, on March 27, Hecht and MacArthur tweaked the 161-page screenplay but titled it *Gungha Din*. The script was nearly identical to their March 24 version. Although the pair's screenplay would subsequently be revised by other writers, several of their story elements would remain and make it to the final print: the close Three Musketeer-like friendship of the three soldiers; Ballantine's problematic engagement; an important role played by an elephant; a non-commissioned officer designated to replace Ballantine; a comical punch bowl sequence; a disagreement between Cutter and MacChesney over treasure hunting; Cutter and Din's discovery of a hidden temple; Cutter's imprisonment; Ballantine's temporary reenlistment; and a climactic battle that includes Gunga Din's sacrifice.

Chapter Five Notes

1. *Milwaukee Journal Sentinel,* October 30, 1936. "I changed the little lame girl who sang so badly that the woodsmen hooted at her to a lusty wench," said Hawks about *Come and Get It* in Scott Breivold's *Howard Hawks: Interviews.* "He saw what I shot, and it was a shock to him. So Willie Wyler was put on and Wyler photographed six hundred feet of film, and Goldwyn gave him credit for being co-director."

2. *The Film Daily*, September 19, 1936, 1.

3. *Arkansas Gazette,* February 11, 1939, 26.

4. Breivold, 66, 91.

5. RKO Studio Records, Scenario Department Files, *Notes On Sir Richard Burton,* January 23, 1937, 1, 3.

6. Nutt, "Notes," January 19, 1939.

7. "An Old Oxnian" (Alfred Bate Richards), *A Short Sketch of the Career of Captain Richard F. Burton* (London: William Mulland and Son, 1880), 4, 7. Burton, who survived a lance that "transfix[ed] his jaws and palate" while in Africa, was also a prolific author who wrote dozen books, and dozens have been written about him including *The Life of Sir Richard F. Burton* (1893), *Burton: A Biography of Sir Richard Francis Burton* (1963), and *The Tangled Web: A Life of Sir Richard Burton* (2008). *Burton and Speke*, a 1982 novel by William Harrison about the undaunted adventurer's and John Hanning Speke's search for the source of the Nile River in 1857, served as the basis of the motion picture *Mountains of the Moon* (1990). In the film, Burton, is played by Patrick Bergin.

8. Behlmer, *Behind The Scenes*, 90.

9. *The Charge of the Light Brigade's* conclusion was set within the Crimean Peninsula but its introduction and early scenes were set in India.

10. Nutt, "Notes," n.p.

11. *Augusta Chronicle,* January 9, 1937, Section A, 4.

12. *The Mask of Fu Manchu,* written by Irene Kuhn, Edgar Allan Woolf, and John Willard – and based on Sax Rohmer's story – also featured a spacious temple hall that included a large gong and a "divine image of Genghis Khan." In the hall, Karloff delivers a rant-filled speech ("Kill the white man and take his women!") to his excitable torch-carrying followers. One of the principals (Charles Starrett's Terrence "Terry" Granville) is whipped, snakes are seen in an underground cave and an upscale torture chamber, and a gong-striking sequence is part of the film's closing scene.

13. *Arkansas Gazette,* October 30, 1938, 10.

CHAPTER SIX

The Dudley Nichols Script

The revolving door of writers continued. *Motion Picture Daily* announced in March 1937 that Vincent Lawrence was brought in to work on the screenplay.[1] A month later, Dudley Nichols, who wrote the screenplay for *The Informer* (1935), joined the writing roster. *The Informer* received four Academy Awards, including those presented to John Ford for Best Director, Victor McLaglen for Best Actor, and Dudley Nichols for Best Screenplay. Nichols refused to accept the statuette at the 1936 awards ceremony, due to a dispute between the Screen Writers Guild, of which he was a founder, and the Academy of Motion Picture Arts and Sciences. His refusal was a Hollywood first (and one that was not repeated until George C. Scott rejected the 1970 Best Actor Oscar for *Patton*.[2] Nichols later collected his award at the 1938 ceremony.

By June 17, 1937, Hecht and MacArthur's script had been revised by Nichols and Hawks into a mammoth 284-page screenplay.[3] Nichols and Hawks kept the major story elements but slightly altered several scenes.

The script begins with an urgent telegraph message sent from British Army headquarters in Calcutta to the Muri post. The communication warns of Sufi Khan's (formerly Khan Sufi) attempt to acquire weapons and ammunition. In order to prevent the Khan from achieving his goal, telegraph lines need to be extended, a task entrusted to the "Three Napoleons," as Colonel Stone calls them: Sergeant "Mac" MacChesney, Sergeant Tom Ballantine, and Corporal Archibald Cutter. Two fellow soldiers, Warwick and Higginbotham, are sent to bring the three men back to headquarters because the trio went on common leave together, in order to search for emeralds in the sacred Lake Singali. While on leave, they get into a fight with some of the locals in town. When Warwick and Higginbotham find them, MacChesney is holding Yussif Ali, a moneylender, precariously out of a window. When Warwick orders MacChesney to take his hands of Ali, MacChesney drops him onto a trellis.

Back at headquarters, Stone admonishes the soldiers for their foolishness (they admitted that they dove seventeen hours in a lake for the precious stones), but recognizes their value as enlisted men who can get the job done. Since Ballantine can speak the local language, he sets out first to Bohara, where he attempts to gain information about the Khan's whereabouts and activities. However, Ballantine's military efforts will be short lived: he has four weeks left of active duty before he retires from the service and marries Emmy Stebbins.

Later, the patrol arrives in Bohara, where Gunga Din, carrying a goatskin filled with water, provides drinks to all. He is verbally abused by the men, but carries on stoically. MacChesney and Cutter discover Ballatine, who is disguised as a Hindu snake charmer. Ballatine shares some limited information with them, which he has acquired about Sufi Khan and his followers.

A group of native priests, led by the "Bearded One," object to the telephone poles, which appear to them as Christian crosses. The soldiers detain the natives and discover one of them is the Khan. Chaos erupts when Din waves the native leader's red silk scarf, which upsets Daisy the elephant. During the pandemonium, MacChesney calls Din various names including "black numbskull," "brown-skinned beggar," and "scabby misfit."

The Khan escapes and orders an attack, but the soldiers and Din manage to escape by using an elephant stampede to disperse the natives. Din is particularly grateful that MacChesney helped rescue him and gives the sergeant a gold watch. Although suspicious of where Din got the watch, MacChesney is appreciative and gives Din a British Pound note for it. On the way back to headquarters aboard Daisy, a discussion about Ballantine's forthcoming marriage escalates into a fistfight between the two sergeants.

Back at headquarters, Ballantine is reunited with his fiancé. Ballantine is declared exempt from all duties until his enlistment expires; Higginbotham is designated to replace him. Colonel Stone informs the soldiers that the Khan and his supply of weapons must be captured. The commanding officer also discovers that the watch MacChesney displays is his. Later, MacChesney whips Din with Cutter's belt as punishment for stealing the colonel's watch.

At the elephant stalls, the soldiers discover that Daisy is pregnant. They also receive invitations to a betrothal dinner honoring Ballantine and Emmy Stebbins. At the event, MacChesney and Cutter extend their best wishes to the couple, but Ballantine knows better and tells Emmy not to trust them. While the refreshment room is empty, MacChesney empties a bottle of elephant medicine into the punch bowl. The two manage to prevent the guests from drinking from it until they serve Higginbotham a glass. Ballantine's replacement takes a drink and collapses.

The next day, Ballantine and Emmy are shopping at a bazaar, where MacChesney informs his fellow soldier that he must go to Bohara with the rest of the company. Emmy protests, but MacChesney informs her that since Higginbotham is ill her fiancé must join the mission.

At Bohara, Cutter and MacChesney share ideas on how to keep Ballantine in the army. Cutter suggests that a search for a treasure-filled temple might entice Ballantine to remain in the service, but MacChesney counters with another idea. "We're going to start a war."

Later that night, the two start a fire outside of town and toss rifle cartridges in the flames. They quickly return to their quarters and wait for the cartridges to ignite. Once the shots ring out, MacChesney and Cutter react as if Bohara is actually being attacked. The foolish plan becomes nonsensical, when MacChesney makes believe he is dying of a gunshot wound, which was created with a shirt burn from Cutter's cigarette. "I'm dying," MacChesney tells Cutter. "That'll get Ballantine. He'll put his name on the dotted line if he knows I'm dying. Don't you see?" MacChesney get the blood he needs for his wound by punching Cutter in his nose. Din brings Ballantine to MacChesney, who requests that Ballantine reenlist as a death wish. Ballantine plays along for a while until he dumps the contents of large water drum on MacChesney and Cutter. "Your real funeral will be held tomorrow morning," warns Ballantine.

Cutter brings up the search-for-treasure idea, but MacChesney rejects it and locks him up. With help from Daisy and her baby, Din helps Cutter escape. They eventually find the temple, which happens to be the Khan's headquarters. Emmy and Higginbotham arrive at Bohara with Ballantine's discharge papers.

Cutter is captured at the gold temple, and Din returns to Bohara to explain what happened. At first, Ballantine thinks it's another ploy to keep him in the service, but quickly realizes that Din is telling the truth. Ballantine agrees to sign a temporary reenlistment document. "This is an entirely private transaction—between you and me—and only for the duration of our little expedition," promises MacChesney. "When it's over, you can tear 'em up." Emmy learns that her fiancé is going out on a mission, even though he has been discharged from active duty. "Why didn't you come right out and say you don't want to get married!" she tells Ballantine. "And never did! Why did you fool me?" MacChesney, Ballantine, and Din rush to the rescue of Cutter.

Ballantine, disguised as a native, and Din pretend to bring a captured soldier, MacChesney, to the Khan as a way of getting to Cutter and freeing him. Upon arrival, MacChesney is placed in a dungeon, where Cutter is tied to the end of an ornate bronze teeter-totter. At the other end of the balancing device is a water barrel with a hole in it, which is slowly lowering Cutter into a pit filled with cobras.

Ballantine and Din manage to kill a guard and gain entry to the dungeon. They free Cutter and MacChesney. Ballantine manages to take the native leader into custody, but they are surrounded by the Khan's followers. A stalemate ensues inside the temple's tower. MacChesney signals Bohara with a heliograph, but the mirror is shattered by a native's rifle shot. Cutter realizes that a nearby wall featuring the Hindu god Siva is made of gold. MacChesney receives a gunshot wound in his arm.

The standoff continues for four days; the natives will not attack as long as the Khan lives. Din bravely crosses to a nearby cistern, which is surrounded by a twenty-foot ring of hot coals. Din suffers terrible burns and is wounded as he brings water back to his comrades. Despite their predicament, Cutter promises to "buy me all the pubs in Calcutta" with his gold. Cutter digs through the wall and exposes a secret staircase that leads to the Khan's stored weapons and ammunition. The native leader kills himself by jumping into the snake pit. His death eliminates the shield which had protected the soldiers and Din.

Din is disguised as the Khan in an attempt to escape the temple. "And they march out as Din stretches out his hand in a gesture of peace." However, Din collapses, and the Khan's followers attack. Cutter and Ballantine retreat, firing as they go; MacChesney carries Din in his arms. The Bearded One is shot and falls. MacChesney reaches the gate, but an explosion shrouds the area in smoke and debris. MacChesney carries Din through the smoke; Ballantine emerges from the choking clouds. Cutter manages to take a golden leg from the idol. Din dies of his wounds.

At headquarters, all participate in Din's funeral ceremony. Ballantine marries, but MacChesney locates his comrade's reenlistment papers in a small tin tobacco box that Din possessed. MacChesney orders Cutter to "to arrest Sergeant Thomas Ballantine for desertion." Cutter questions the legality of such an order. "At the time I gave him my word he was a civilian!" replies MacChesney. "I never kept my word to a civilian—and I don't intend to start now!

"Cutter and the Snake Pit." Illustration by Gary Zaboly. Author's collection.

RKO president Leo Spitz was pleased with the script and told syndicated Hollywood columnist Louella O. Parsons that "*Gunga Din* will have the flavor of *What Price Glory* [1926], a he-man roistering drama." Spitz added that he hoped "getting it into production early next year."[4]

Location scouting continued. Lou Shapiro sent a memo to Hawks about Yuma, Arizona's weather for the first four months of the year. He noted the high temperatures for each month: January (67°), February (72°), March (78°), and April (85°). "Average temperature from then on would be around 100 up to June," said Shapiro.[5]

The script required a baby elephant, and RKO gave Shapiro the task to locate one, since there were none in any of California's zoos at the time. On April 18, 1938, he sent an inquiry to three well-known animal collectors: Ellis S. Joseph, John T. Benson, and Frank Buck. The telegram read: "Please advise immediately purchase and rental prices your youngest baby elephant on hand for motion picture purposes, preferably a suckling baby elephant if one available."

The next day, John T. Benson, the owner of Benson's Wild Animal Farm in Nashua, New Hampshire, replied to Shapiro by telegram and informed him that he had a baby elephant that stood "fifty-five inches high." Benson stated that the animal was "accustomed to large elephants, being handled by an eleven-year-old girl, acclimated, perfect physically and disposition." Benson offered the animal for $2,500 plus "caretaker's expenses."

That same day, Shapiro received a telegram from Frank "Bring 'Em Back Alive" Buck, the famous animal collector, who had a jungle retreat in Amityville, New York. Buck told Shapiro that there were no baby elephants in the country at the time, but he could deliver one to RKO from Singapore in forty-five days. However, if the studio wasn't too concerned about size, Buck said that the "smallest elephants now available here at my jungle camp stand trifle over five feet." The price tag was $2,000 each.

On April 20, Shapiro received a telegram from Ellis Joseph, who ran an international wild animal business out of New York and Sydney, Australia. Ellis informed Shapiro that he had no baby elephants but anticipated receiving "an elephant measuring about 3 ft. 9 in." in a forthcoming shipment of animals.

The production shifted its focus on casting two-legged performers, but it would prove more difficult than securing baby elephants.

Chapter Six Notes

1. *Motion Picture Daily* March 22, 1937, 5.

2. Ibid., April 26, 1937, 15.

3. *Gunga Din* Script, Revision of Estimating Script, Screenplay by Ben Hecht and Charles MacArthur, Revised by Dudley Nichols and Howard Hawks, June 17, 1937. Register of the Howard Hawks Collection, L. Tom Perry Special Collections, Brigham Young University. Nichols' typewriter had a flawed letter "e" which usually resulted in the letter appearing more like an "o."

4. *Daily Illinois State Journal* (Springfield, Illinois), November 13, 1937, 13.

5. Shapiro to Hawks, December 1, 1937.

CHAPTER SEVEN
Early Casting

While the screenplay was being rewritten, Hawks directed *Bringing Up Baby* (1938), a zany comedy that starred Cary Grant and Katherine Hepburn. The film, which was co-written by Dudley Nichols, went over budget and caused a concern at RKO. In the meantime, casting began on *Gunga Din*.

"We made several tests for the officers' parts among the English actors then on Broadway," explained Marian Roberston, an RKO talent scout. "We also rounded up an assortment of young Hindus for the title role. The first day the call went out, we fine-combed the East Indian shops and boards of trade [in the New York area.] There was a Hindu colony over in [New] Jersey, but the boys were not the pure Oriental type."[1]

Although the initial search for Kipling's brave *bhisti* proved unsuccessful, RKO was more concerned about casting the principal soldiers.

According to *The New York Times*, Philip Merivale, age fifty, was an early choice "for the lead role in *Gunga Din*."[2] The designated leading role was Cutter, and Merivale seemed to fit the role despite his age. The English actor, who stood six-feet-one and was born in India, had appeared as George Washington in the 1934 Broadway play, *Valley Forge,* and was one of the leads in the film musical *Give Us This Night* (1936). However, he was soon dismissed from consideration, when another actor seemed to be a better choice.

In the autumn, RKO secured its Cutter. "Cary Grant is definitely set for lead role, under a commitment settled this week,"

reported *Motion Picture Daily* on November 15, 1937.[3]

Born Archibald Alexander Leach in Bristol, England, on January 18, 1904, Grant left school as a teenager and joined an acting-acrobat troupe. He performed in traditional stage productions in England, and later came to the United States, where he appeared in a number of Broadway productions—as Archie Leach—including *Better Times* (1922-23), *Golden Dawn* (1927-28), and *Nikki* (1931), among others. Broadway led to Hollywood, a name change, and Grant's first feature film, *This is the Night* (1932).

Grant's career rose, when he co-starred with Mae West in *She Done Him Wrong* (1933). Later in his career, Grant said that he learned a lot about comedy from West, who began her career in Vaudeville in 1907, when she was a young teenager. Grant's role as Jerry Warriner in *The Awful Truth* (1937), one of four 1937 films he starred in, generated box office successes, critical acclaim, and fan enthusiasm.

Two films that Grant co-starred in with Katharine Hepburn, *Bringing Up Baby* (1938) and *Holiday* (1938), were financial disappointments, although he managed to receive some good reviews. *The New York Times* stated that "Mr. Grant's Mr. Case is really the best role" in *Holiday*.[4] RKO didn't consider the signing of Grant for *Gunga Din* as a huge risk, but the thirty-three-year-old actor was concerned about the motion picture's fate. "[Grant] realized that his next film needed to be a big box-office hit."[5]

Although there were some light moments in the evolving *Gunga Din* script, the screenplay was primarily a military-themed melodrama—and Grant liked that. "He loved the script, which gave him a chance to break out of the usual comedy role, and he also realized what the association with such a prestigious production could do for his career."[6] Coincidentally, Kipling's *Gunga Din* had been a favorite of Grant's since his childhood. Furthermore, Grant enjoyed being given the opportunity to portray another Cockney character in film. He had played Jimmy Monkley in RKO's *Sylvia Scarlett* (1935), the first time he worked with Katherine Hepburn. The motion picture wasn't successful, but Grant's performance was impressive, although his accent sounded a bit stereotypical.

Grant contacted Douglas Fairbanks, Jr., the son of the legendary silent era swashbuckler, and asked him if he was interested in playing one of the other lead characters. "He explained that such scripted plot as existed so far had been inspired by Rudyard Kipling's *Soldiers Three*," said Fairbanks, Jr. "So I stalled politely and said that since no script existed yet, I'd first read whatever treatment there was before I could give an answer."[7] After examining a newly written rough draft, Fairbanks agreed to join the cast, but he wasn't sure what part he would end up with.

Fairbanks' sophisticated style, handsome looks, and charm matched well with Grant's similar assets. He had worked under Hawks' direction in *The Dawn Patrol* (1930) and had also starred as Grand Duke Peter in *The Rise of Catherine the Great* (1934). Coincidentally, Sam Jaffe played the same role in *The Scarlett Empress* (1934), which was released seven months later. Fairbanks' career was elevated following his appearance as Rupert of Henzau in *The Prisoner of Zenda* (1937), which featured a captivating Academy Award-nominated musical score by Alfred Newman.

On January 12, 1938, *The New York Times* announced that *Gunga Din*, which had been "on and off RKO's schedule for two years, was set for definite production in the late spring." The newspaper noted that Cary Grant and Douglas Fairbanks, Jr. had been named "for the leading roles . . . .with a strong possibility that Joan Bennett will be assigned the female lead." The article concluded with a cautionary note of sorts: "Tentatively selected to direct is Howard Hawks."[8] The carefully worded passage may have reflected RKO's concern with Hawks and his over-budget *Bringing Up Baby* (1938) production.

The Hawks-RKO relationship quickly soured once the box office receipts trickled in.[9] The studio cited "numerous breaches in his contract" and "offered him a termination fee of $40,000 to walk."[10] The media soon broadcast the situation. "RKO has settled its contract with Howard Hawks and the director and the director has left the lot," reported *The New York Times* on April 6, 1938. "He recently completed *Bringing Up Baby* . . . and was scheduled to direct *Gunga Din*, which has now been switched to Gregory La Cava."[11]

RKO was in an awkward position. It had replaced its director and it lacked a completed script, despite the efforts of over a half dozen writers. Furthermore, the studio hadn't completed its casting. In addition, Samuel Briskin, the studio's head of production, was departing for Columbia Pictures, where he had previously worked. RKO wanted to begin shooting *Gunga Din* by late spring; as a matter of fact, *The New York Times* reported that filming was scheduled to begin on May 1, 1938. The problems seemed to increase with every passing week—and to think that only a month earlier, RKO's biggest challenge was finding a baby elephant.

Chapter Seven Notes

1. Marian Robertson, "The Problem of Casting a Motion Picture," *National Board of Review Magazine*, March 1939, 18.

2. *The New York Times*, February 12, 1937, 2.

3. *Motion Picture Daily*, November 15, 1937, 10.

4. Charles Higham and Roy Moseley, *Cary Grant: The Lonely Heart* (New York: Harcourt Brace Jovanovich, 1989), 96.

5. Geoffrey Wansell, *Haunted Idol: The Story of the Real Cary Grant* (New York: William Morrow and Company, 1984), 126.

6. Warren G. Harris, *Cary Grant: A Touch of Elegance* (New York: Doubleday, 1987), 90.

7. Douglas Fairbanks, Jr., *The Salad Days* (London: William Collins Sons and Company, Ltd., 1988), 283-284.

8. *The New York Times*, January 12, 1938, 17.

9. *Variety* reported that *Bringing Up Baby* lost $350,000 during its initial release. For more on the film, see Marc Eliot's *Cary Grant: A Biography*, (New York: Random House, 2004), 260-263, 270.

10. Marc Eliot, *Cary Grant: A Biography*, 270. In Scott Breivold's *Howard Hawks: Interviews*, Hawks told fellow director Peter Bogdanovich that *Bringing Up Baby* was "a mistake" since every character was a "screwball."

11. *The New York Times*, April 6, 1938, 29. Only a few months earlier, Warner Brothers replaced William Keighley as director of *The Adventures of Robin Hood* during filming because he was behind schedule. Michael Curtiz finished directing the film.

CHAPTER EIGHT

Completing the Casting: From Sabu to Sam Jaffe

As the casting process continued, RKO found its new director in house: George Stevens. The thirty-four-year-old had worked as a director of photography on a number of Laurel and Hardy short subjects and Westerns featuring Rex, the King of the Wild Horses, for the Hal Roach Studios. He also directed numerous comedic shorts, including the "Boy Friends" series, which were produced by Roach and released through MGM. However, creative differences with Roach led to Stevens' suspension and an eventual split from the studio.

Stevens went to RKO, where he directed his first comedy feature, the *Nitwits* (1935), with Robert Woolsey and Bert Wheeler. "[Stevens had] a natural flair for gags in general and comedy in particular," said writer Joel Sayre.[1] Stevens developed a creative philosophy that would guide his successful career: "A director's most critical task—giving structure to the story and establishing believable characters."[2] Stevens admitted that he didn't particularly care what film he was given to direct; however, he said that the film's story has to have "something to say" to the audience. "If in the situations the emotions are honest and the reactions natural, it doesn't make any difference to me whether the story is drama or comedy, slapstick or tragedy, musical or Western, cops and robbers or Indians and cowboys," he said.[3]

Stevens followed with *Alice Adams* (1935), a wonderful romantic production starring Katharine Hepburn and Fred MacMurray;

Annie Oakley (1935) with Barbara Stanwyck; and *Swing Time* (1936), a Fred Astaire and Ginger Rogers musical that featured a story line about a group of fellow performers who conspire to have Astaire's character remain single—something akin to a familiar story element in Hecht and MacArthur's *The Front Page* (1931). Next came *Quality Street* (1937), a romantic production set in nineteenth century England, featuring Katharine Hepburn and Franchot Tone; *A Damsel in Distress* (1937), a musical comedy starring Fred Astaire and Joan Fontaine; and *Vivacious Lady* (1938), a comedy starring Ginger Rogers and Jimmy Stewart.

RKO paid Stevens $73,507 to direct *Gunga Din*.[4] "I was doing one thing right after another at RKO with no particular time between pictures," said Stevens. "The studio had a script, but it was all dialogue. They didn't know what to do with it because it was far from any kind of motion picture."[5]

Before Stevens was assigned the directorship of the motion picture, talks had taken place between RKO and MGM about the possibility of using Clark Gable, Spencer Tracy, and Robert Montgomery as the three leads. Although MGM may have been willing to loan out two of its stars, it was not going to part with Gable, the top box office male in Hollywood.[6] On the commentary track of the 2004 Warner Bros. Entertainment *Gunga Din* DVD, film historian Rudy Behlmer noted that RKO asked MGM's Louis B. Mayer to borrow Clark Gable, Spencer Tracy,

Pandro S. Berman.

George Stevens.

and Franchot Tone in exchange for the rights to *Rio Rita* (1929), a successful RKO musical comedy that MGM wanted to remake with the popular Nelson Eddy and Jeanette Mac-Donald. Mayer refused to loan out Gable, but was willing to allow Tracy and Tone to work in an RKO film. Later, MGM was interested in buying the *Gunga Din* rights from RKO in order to produce another Kipling work: *Soldiers Three*. All of the deals fell flat, although MGM's *Soldiers Three* finally reached the screen in 1951.

Stevens was also named as *Gunga Din's* producer, a position that allowed him to coordinate assorted facets of the production. However, Pandro S. Berman, RKO's vice-president, was "in charge of production." The RKO official supposedly had the final say regarding major decisions—especially budget issues—with the film.

Some of RKO's earlier scripts and notes collections penned by the various writers featured two main soldiers, the recent ones featured three. Stevens was set on one lineup. "I wanted a third character so there would be three men, the reason being a simple matter of arithmetic," explained Stevens. "The third character could alternate with the other two, who would be playing against each other, which meant I could be developing the story at the same time."[7]

The use of three soldiers would have another Kipling connection, since three non-commissioned officers were the main characters in the aforementioned *Soldiers Three*. Kipling's martial trio initially appeared in *The Three Musketeers*, first published in the *Civil and Military Gazette* in 1887, a year before it appeared in *Plain Tales from the Hills*.

In 1899, the characters were introduced to a larger audience in *Soldiers Three and other stories*, or simply known as *Soldiers Three*. The fictitious British soldiers—Learoyd, Mulvaney and Ortheris—behave in the "one for all, all for one" manner established in the first *Three Musketeers*, which Alexander Dumas wrote in 1844.

Stories about the casting of *Gunga Din* ranged from speculations to facts. The only actors who seemed to be officially part of the production were Cary Grant and Douglas Fairbanks, Jr., who both happened to share the same management firm: H. E. Edington-F. W. Vincent, Inc. Still, nothing else seemed definite about *Gunga Din* at the time.

Fairbanks explained that the casting was done by chance. "It was Cary's idea for me to be in the picture," he explained. "He wanted to make it a three-star vehicle. He didn't even have a script at the time—only a draft of the synopsis. He told me he'd play whichever part I didn't want. Cary chose the material first and then worried about the part. That was the secret of his success. Ultimately, we tossed a coin."[8]

Pandro Berman remembered it differently. "We had written the script for Doug Fairbanks to play the role that Cary eventually played, and Cary to play the role that Doug played," explained Berman years later. "Well, when Cary read the script, he came in and he said, 'I'd like to do the picture, but I'm not going to do it because I wouldn't dream of playing that flat role. I love the part that you're giving to Doug—the comedy role.'" As a result of Grant's request, Berman said he switched the roles. "Since he was paying Grant $125,000 for his part compared to $117,000 for Fairbanks and $62,000 for McLaglen, Berman had no compunction about giving the actor what he wanted and making the switch, which was a wise one," explained Grant biographer Geoffrey Wansell.[9]

Coincidentally, Fairbanks' mother's family tree included a branch of Ballantines.

"This is a good part in *Gunga Din*—and no love interest, thank God!" said Grant. "Doug Fairbanks gets the girl this time. I had a choice of several parts and settled on this one . . . while I was still doing the screwball comedies."[10] The *Gunga Din* script would eventually include comedic touches and fanciful elements that would showcase Grant's playful talents.

An RKO Budget Detail sheet indicates that the principals were contracted for an initial time period that began on June 1, 1938, and continued until September 3. Despite the figure stated by biographer Geoffrey Wansell, Grant was paid a "flat rate" of $75,000 for ten weeks of work, and an additional $34,375 for three weeks and four days of work. In total, Grant received $109,375 for appearing in *Gunga Din*. According to Hollywood columnist Hedda Hopper, taxes consumed eighty-two percent of Grant's income in 1938.[11]

Another RKO Budget Detail sheet noted that Fairbanks was paid $101,562.50 for ten weeks and five days of filming at $9,375 a week. In his autobiography, *The Salad Days*, Fairbanks guessed that he "made something more than $75,000" for his role in the film.[12]

Casting continued—and so did the rumors.

"RKO is seeking the loan of James Cagney for *Gunga Din*," reported *The New York Times* in March, 1938. The newspaper once again stated that the film would start shooting on May 1. However, Cagney, a major Warner Bros. star, went on to work in *Angels With Dirty Faces* (1938), which started production in June. Cagney was out and the search continued.

Other actors' names emerged, such as Ronald Colman, Robert Donat, and Roger

Livesey.[13] "With only the feminine role remaining unfilled, RKO today [April 22, 1938] completed the cast of principals for *Gunga Din* with the acquisition of Victor McLaglen as the hard-boiled sergeant," noted an article in *The New York Times*. However, according to an RKO radio transcription document, Grant was cast first, McLaglen second, and Fairbanks third.[14]

McLaglen had an adventurous life that read like a movie script. Born in England in 1886, McLaglen joined the British Army during the Boer War (1899-1902), but was dismissed from service when it was discovered he was underage. He later moved to Canada and became a professional wrestler and a heavy-weight boxer. McLaglen crossed the border and participated in five bouts in Washington State in 1908. On March 10, 1909, he went six rounds in an exhibition match against champion Jack Johnson, who had won the crown on December 26, 1908. Two years later in Missouri, McLaglen fought an exhibition bout against Jess Willard, who took the title from Johnson on April 5, 1915. McLaglen eventually became the heavyweight champion of the British Army after serving a stint as an assistant provost marshal in Baghdad.

He became an actor in England and starred in his first film, *The Call of the Road* (1920), in which he played a boxer. One of his brothers, Cyril, also appeared in the movie. McLaglen appeared in nearly twenty films in England before traveling to Hollywood. He starred in his first American motion picture, *The Beloved Brute* (1924), in which he played a Western grappler. McLaglen's popularity grew as a result of his roles in *What Price Glory* (1926) and *A Girl in Every Port* (1928), which was directed by Howard Hawks. In *The Black Watch* (1929), which was directed by John Ford, he played a British officer who gets involved in a daring secret mission in India during World War I.

McLaglen became an accomplished actor, who made a successful transition from the silents. He played an unnamed, rugged British sergeant in *The Lost Patrol* (1934), a splendid drama, co-written by Dudley Nichols. Interestingly enough, McLaglen's character has a brief conversation with a private Pearson (played by Douglas Walton), who proclaims his fondness for Kipling.

McLaglen's autobiography, *Express to Hollywood*, was published in 1934, and his performance as Gypo Nolan in *The Informer* (1935) earned him a Best Actor Oscar. He portrayed Sergeant MacDuff in *Wee Willie Winkie* (1937), which was based on Kipling's short story set in India.

McLaglen, who was fifty-two years old, seemed a solid choice to play the senior sergeant in *Gunga Din*. For his efforts, RKO paid him $56,144.45 for thirteen weeks and five days of work.[15] An interesting RKO note stated: "McLaglen and Grant do not get paid for working Sundays. All other actors are paid."

An undated, uncredited, and incomplete 26-page *Gunga Din* synopsis acknowledged a sergeant major role "to be played by Victor McLaglen," but did not identify any other actors in its pages.[16] The synopsis describes "India of 1850," occupied by "three hundred millions of insecure humans" who have "in their dark and battered souls . . . the spark of fanaticism."

The story is based in the British outpost of Lucknow, where seven years later the city was under siege during the Indian Rebellion of 1857, and contains the familiar historical tale about the questionable rifle cartridges. The outbreak of hostilities began when Indian troops were ordered to use the new Enfield Rifle cartridges. On May 1, a regiment of Indian soldiers under the authority of Sir Henry Lawrence refused to open the cartridges as instructed. This act of defiance escalated into a widespread rebellion that lasted until November. British casualties—primarily British regulars and loyal Sepoys—numbered approximately 2,500. Rebel casualty estimates were much higher.

In the synopsis, a colonel Lawrence confronts the Nana, a regional native leader, who receives an annual allowance of £80,000 from the British government. Lawrence orders to double the guard at the fort's powder magazine prior to the Nana's arrival. The officer also sends his sergeant major to meet and escort Mr. Stebbins, a middle-aged British East India Company official, and his "young and beautiful" bride. Mr. Stebbins insists to Lawrence that India "belongs to England," but the colonel counters that India "has not been conquered, there being no India to conquer."

The Nana arrives with an impressive entourage of elephants, soldiers, and servants, "a helter-skelter picture of Hindu opulence." One of the Nana's horseman is "a white man dressed like a British officer but with a jeweled turban on his head." The synopsis identifies the character as Donat, later described as a disgraced British officer who had allegedly disobeyed orders during a campaign which resulted in the loss of "a score of British soldiers." Donat was subsequently accused of "insubordination and cowardice," but did not offer a defense for his actions. He was "cashiered out of the army" and became the Nana's chief aide. The Donat character exists in the synopsis at about the same time that actor Robert Donat was considered for a part in the film. Besides McLaglen's designated role as the sergeant major and the role of Donat, there are no references to the other non-commissioned officers that would be similar to the characters eventually played by Cary Grant and Douglas Fairbanks, Jr.

The synopsis continues with the Nana demanding £150,000 instead of the former £80,000 payment. Lawrence diplomatically offers the original sum but the Nana refuses, since Russia is also courting the Indian leader. This aspect of the synopsis is similar to a story element from *The Charge of the Light Brigade* (1936) in which the Indian leader, Surat Khan, turns to Russia after Great Britain withdraws its annual payment to him.

McLaglen's character attempts to visit Donat, but native soldiers accost him and drag the sergeant major to the former British soldier's tent. Donat explains to the non-commissioned officer that "it was only natural for natives to mistake him for a thief," since the English had "stolen their country from them." The two discuss the sergeant major's actions years ago which resulted in Donat's court martial. The sergeant major argues that Donat should abandon his service to the Nana, but the former soldier responds by stating that the "whole conquest of India is an example of British greed."

Donat changes the subject by offering the soldier a cold bath—complete with hand-picked "lovely maidens." The two enter an inner tent, where they discover Gunga Din, a "beggarly-looking Hindu in a greasy turban and an even greasier loin cloth," in the bathing tub. Gunga Din confesses that he fell in the tub while trying to steal some scented bath oils. Donat promptly beats him and McLaglen's character rolls "on the ground howling with mirth." Donat attempts to beat Din again but the sergeant major intercedes, which results in a fight between the veteran soldier and his former commander. McLaglen's character wins the fight and gains a new friend: the "dog-like Gunga Din, trotting at his elbow and crying his thanks to the sahib." One week later, Gunga Din presents a stolen watch to the sergeant major.

Colonel Lawrence reminds the sergeant major that "Donat serving under the Nana in such a time as now, is a danger to English prestige." The officer orders that Donat be brought back to the fort. Meanwhile, at a meeting between the Nana and some Russian representatives, the native leader asks a drunken Donat if "he has evolved a plan for attacking Lucknow." Donat replies that he "knows no way of conquering the British." Later, the sergeant major and six English soldiers kidnap Donat and bring him to Lucknow, where a party is being hosted by Mrs. Stebbins. Although Donat is deliberately ignored by the other officers he plays "the part of a social pariah with grace and amusement." He interprets a secret message sent by one of the native servants as a forthcoming attack on Lucknow. The post goes on an immediate alert.

The incomplete synopsis ends with the sergeant major pulling out his watch and Mr. Stebbins recognizing it as his own, "and we have the business of the sergeant's anger at Gunga." Since the synopsis did not reflect Stevens' intent to use three non-commissioned officers as the primary characters, it was never developed further.

The writing continued. Anthony Veiller was associated with a 206-page *2nd Revised Estimating Script* dated February 5, 1938. The script included minor revisions that were made between January 17 and 31, 1938. "Apparently, Mr. Veiller merely did some cutting on the revision dated June 17, 1937 by Nichols and Hawks."[17] However, another piece of written material would alter the story of *Gunga Din*.

An undated and unattributed script notes document in the RKO Studio files introduced a revised story with some new story elements: Khan Sufi is a Thug leader who worships the goddess Kali, and the three principal soldiers are Royal Engineers, members of the British Army, who were celebrated in Kipling's *Sappers*, one of the works in the writer's *Seven Seas* (1896) collection. The script identifies Gunga Din as a young native, who wishes to be a soldier. Din later blows an alarm call on a bugle which disrupts the camp. The notes also include a Thug massacre of a caravan.

Grant was pleased that the screenplay had three leads besides the title character, but he was more concerned about film's outcome at the box office. He was aware of the Hawks debacle with RKO, and had concerns about working with a new director. If *Gunga Din* failed commercially, reasoned Grant, "there would be plenty of 'glory' for everyone to go down in."[18] The ultimate responsibility for the success or failure of the film rested on George Stevens, and he sought experienced crew members who would help make *Gunga Din* a winner.

Stevens' directorial staff included Ed Killy, who had directed a dozen films and worked as an assistant director on nearly twenty others, including *Alice Adams* (1935), which Stevens had directed. As assistant director on *Gunga Din*, Killy was contracted for nineteen weeks of work at $125 a week. Killy would soon learn that his services behind the camera were just part of his job.

Despite the talk about a firm deal with the Grant-Fairbanks-McLaglen triumvirate, another actor's name surfaced. On April 21,

1938, *The New York Times* noted that the film's "comedy element will be expounded by Jack Oakie." Perhaps, Fairbanks' status with the production had not been finalized because the newspaper later stated: "Shooting will start early in the month with Sabu, the lad in *Elephant Boy*, Cary Grant and Jack Oakie."

Oakie was a veteran comedic actor who had been in motion pictures since the early 1920s. He had co-starred with Grant in *The Toast of New York* (1937) and had a reputation of getting along with everyone in Hollywood. In May, the *Independent Exhibitors Film Bulletin* confirmed that *Gunga Din* would feature "Jack Oakie in support ... of Cary Grant in the title role." However, less than four weeks later, *The New York Times* noted that "Jack Oakie withdrew from his role in *Gunga Din* at RKO today [June 4, 1938] on the ground that he was not suited for the part." It appeared that Fairbanks was still part of the cast.

The casting focus shifted to Sabu Dastigir, known simply in Hollywood by his first name. Sabu appeared to be the perfect actor to portray the title role. The fourteen-year-old, who was born in India, had starred in *Elephant Boy* (1937), a popular film based on Kipling's short story *Toomai of the Elephants*. Sabu's next film, *The Drum* (1938), which was released in the United States as *Drums*, was also set in India. The film featured the young star as a pro-British prince, who is threatened by a treacherous uncle. At the time, Sabu was under contract with Alexander Korda's London Films Productions, which had produced *Elephant Boy*. RKO initiated negotiations with Korda for Sabu's services. The basic agreement included a provision that would allow a RKO-contracted player to work on a forthcoming Korda film. The news seemed encouraging.

On April 21, 1938, *The New York Times* reported that "Sabu . . . has been engaged by RKO for one of the principal roles in *Gunga Din*." However, the news report was premature. The performer Korda wanted from RKO's talent roster was none other than one of the studio's most popular stars: Ginger Rogers. The multi-talented Rogers had teamed up with Fred Astaire in some of the most successful musicals in Hollywood history, and the actress was also establishing herself as a first-rate comedic and dramatic performer in other productions. RKO couldn't afford to lose Rogers. The studio was seemingly willing to offer any other performer, but Korda wanted her. The negotiations recalled RKO's attempt to secure Clark Gable from MGM.

The deal fell apart. "Negotiations between RKO and Alexander Korda for Sabu . . . were canceled today [May 27, 1938] when RKO refused Korda the services of Ginger Rogers for that of the boy," noted the *New York Times*. "RKO had agreed for an exchange of players but had not anticipated that a request would be made for Miss Rogers." A month later, the newspaper confirmed that "Ginger Rogers was too high a price to pay for the services of Sabu for the lead of *Gunga Din*." Sabu remained with Korda and went on to star in *The Thief of Bagdad* (1940).

RKO continued the search for an actor to handle the title role. Newspaper articles reported that Pandro Berman "launched an extensive search," since he was "unable to find [anyone] on the West Coast." One newspaper headline proclaimed: "Scouts Searching World For Gunga Din Figure."[19] It was an exaggeration, to be sure, but RKO was getting desperate.

Berman wanted a Hindu or a "Hindu type" to portray Gunga Din, and assistant

(L to R): Cary Grant, Victor McLaglen, Douglas Fairbanks, Jr., Robert Coote. © RKO. Author's collection.

director Ed Killy was given the assignment to find someone to play the important role. Killy left Hollywood and traveled south to El Centro in Imperial County, California where he believed a Hindu colony was located. "No coloney [sic] here," wrote a disappointed Killy in a telegram to J. R. Crone on May 21. "200 Hindu ranchers scattered through valley ... gathering Monday for Hindu funeral. Arranged to attend." Killy also added that he was planning to contact schools in the area for possible talent, but he was unsuccessful in finding someone satisfactory enough to play Kipling's *bhistsi*.

Killy traveled north. "Checked Oregon [and] Washington ... Nothing," wrote Killy in a telegram on May 29. He went to Vancouver, British Columbia, where a community of Indians, primarily composed of Punjabi Sikhs, had been established at the end of the nineteenth century. "Given their exclusion from many professions, Indo-Canadian men gravitated to one of the few economic sectors that offered them employment: wood processing, especially in the sawmills."[20] Killy expected that some members of the community would be eager to leave the sawmills for Hollywood.

On May 31, from Vancouver's Georgia Hotel, Killy told Crone that he had "interviewed thirty boys." That same day, he sent another telegram: "Have covered Vancouver and vicinity [and found] only four possible prospects. Very enthused about one. Although [he] might be too small. He's very good looking, likeable, and intelligent. Height 57 inches. Weight 79 pounds."

Killy was encouraged. He believed that he finally found his Gunga Din: Sucha Singh, a twelve-year-old (born on February 2, 1926), who had arrived in Canada from India in February 1935. Despite having no acting background, Killy believed that Singh was capable of handling the role under Stevens' careful direction. At first, Singh's father, Nama, was reluctant. "Father does not want him to go to Hollywood," said Killy in a telegram dated June 2, 1938. "Apparently someone talked to him against Hollywood." Killy, though, pressed on. He told the studio that he had concluded a three-hour conversation with the father and would "see him again in the morning." The next day, Killy informed RKO that he was "unable to convince boy's father," but would try again "in [a] few days."

On June 4, Killy wired an optimistic message to the studio: "Boy's father will consent in a few days." According to a Western Union telegram, stamped June 6, 1938, Killy arranged for Singh and his father to cross the border at Vancouver, enter Washington, and travel to Stockton, California, where they would be transported to Hollywood. At the studio, a contract would be drawn up for the young man. It appeared that RKO had finally found its Gunga Din. However, at the last minute, Singh's father reconsidered and declined the film offer.

The search for Gunga Din continued, but the proverbial clock was ticking—principal photography was scheduled to begin in less than three weeks. RKO staffers acknowledged that an actual Indian actor was probably not going to be found in time. They looked elsewhere.

Nearly 3,000 miles away, Shakespeare's *The Merchant of Venice* was being staged at Union College in Schenectady, New York. In the cast was Sam Jaffe, who had delivered a memorable performance as the High Lama in *Lost Horizon* (1937), and had concluded a successful Broadway run as Nils Krogstad in Henrik Ibsen's *A Doll's House*, which ran from late December 1937 until May 1938. In between scenes, Jaffe had received a telegram. "RKO Radio wanted him to plane West instanter and go into the water-carrier part without the preliminaries of screen testing. He wanted a new piano, so the idea seemed good and he obeyed."[21]

According to Jaffe biographer Arleen Lorrance, Garson Kanin, who had acted on Broadway and directed RKO's *A Man to Remember* (1938), one of *The New York Times'* ten best films of the year, was instrumental in securing the *Gunga Din* role for Jaffe. Kanin was familiar with Jaffe, having seen him in *The Bride of Torosko* (1934) at Henry Miller's Theatre. Although the Broadway play lasted only a dozen performances, Kanin was so impressed with Jaffe that he urged him to try out for the role of Kipling's tragic hero.[22] Jaffe secured the part, but he was amused that he had recited the poem years earlier in order to gain entrance to the City College of New York's drama club. "I did the *Gunga Din* speech and they wouldn't take me," recalled Jaffe. "I thought I was good. They didn't think I was good enough."[23] RKO paid Jaffe only $11,000 for the title role, which was based on seven weeks and two days of work at $1,500 a week. The studio also paid Jaffe an additional $500 so he and his wife could complete a round trip to New York.

RKO had first sought Sabu, a fourteen-year-old born in India, and later Sucha Singh, a twelve-year-old also born in India, but ended up with New York City-born, forty-seven-year-old Sam Jaffe, the son of Russian Jewish immigrants. It didn't matter to the studio, and when the film was released, Jaffe's age didn't seem to matter to most reviewers, although Rockford Illinois' *Morning Star* described the title character as "an elderly native water carrier"[24]

Meanwhile, media reports stated that the established cast had undergone yet another shakeup. On June 6, 1938, a surprising article in *The New York Times* noted that "RKO has borrowed George Sanders from 20th Century Fox to replace Douglas Fairbanks, Jr. in a lead role in *Gunga Din*."[25] Once again, it appeared that another actor was replacing Fairbanks. However, the speculation was false: Sanders never joined the cast and Fairbanks remained.

Despite earlier reports that suggested Joan Bennett or Madeleine Carroll as the possible "female lead," Joan Fontaine, an RKO contract player, got the part. Fontaine, a British-born actress with nearly a dozen screen credits, was the younger sister of Olivia De Havilland. "Joan Fontaine . . . is slated for stardom at RKO within the year," stated *Hollywood* magazine in 1937.[26] Despite the encouraging press about the future of her film career, Fontaine preferred the stage.

Fontaine had been the understudy for the part of Marguerite in *Faust* at the Pilgrimage Play Theatre in Los Angeles. One night, the lead actress, the singularly-named Margo, became ill and Fontaine took over. She saw this as an opportunity to showcase her talent. Fontaine recalled that the director, Max Reinhardt, was so impressed with her fill-in performance that he was preparing to give her a contract. Fontaine loved the stage and expected that her career in the theater was about to take off.

"Returning home triumphant after this exciting, almost fictional evening, I heard the telephone ringing persistently," said Fontaine. "RKO's assistant director was sending a car for me early the next morning. I was wanted for my small part in *Gunga Din*."[27] Fontaine was cast as Emmy Stebbins, the fiancé of Fairbanks' sergeant Ballantine. She wasn't particularly pleased since it interfered with her stage work, but she was under contract with RKO and in no position to challenge the studio. Fontaine placed her stage career on hold. Little did Fontaine know that teaming up with a fellow *Gunga Din* cast member a few years later would help her win an Academy Award.

Fontaine was twenty years old and single when she began working on *Gunga Din*, and she was treated respectfully by her fellow cast members; in fact, the other actors made it a point to be always polite around her. "[We] always tried to be careful with our language and manners when Joan Fontaine was near," said Fairbanks. "After all, we agreed, this was her first important role, and she was a newcomer to both America and films."[28]

The rest of the cast included veteran performers and relative newcomers.

Eduardo Ciannelli was cast as the Guru, the rabid Thuggee cult leader. The Italian-born actor had a successful European opera career and later appeared on Broadway. He was cast in over a dozen films and specialized in mobster characters in such motion pictures as *Winterset* (1936) and *Law of the Underworld* (1938).

Montagu Love took the part of Colonel Weed, the British commander. The British-born actor (born Harry Montague Love), with a rich authoritarian voice, had the most extensive career of anyone in the cast, having made nearly 150 appearances in films dating back to 1914. Throughout the 1930s, Love created a diverse set of celluloid characters, from Governor Pigot in *Clive of India* (1935) and Detchard in *The Prisoner of Zenda* (1937) to Henry VIII in *The Prince and the Pauper* (1937) and the Bishop of the Black Canons in *The Adventures of Robin Hood* (1938). He

also played Joan Fontaine's father in *Damsel in Distress* (1937).

Robert Coote became Bertie Higginbotham, the supercilious by-the-book sergeant. Coote, another British-born performer, was a stage actor, who had accumulated only a handful of film credits by the time he was cast in *Gunga Din*. However, the twenty-nine-year-old actor proved to be competent enough to hold his own against the top-billed cast members.

Abner Biberman was cast as Chota, the Guru's obedient blood-thirsty son. The twenty-nine-year-old, who was born in Philadelphia (most accounts state incorrectly that he was born in Milwaukee), had appeared only in one film prior to *Gunga Din*, but he had acted in a number of Broadway productions including *Winterset* (1935), which also featured Eduardo Ciannelli. Biberman's solo film credit at the time was *Soak The Rich* (1936), which was written and directed by Ben Hecht and Charles MacArthur.

Lumsden Hare was assigned the role of Major Mitchell, Colonel Weed's second-in-command. The Irish-born actor had scores of motion picture credits, including many from the silent film era. He was particularly effective in military roles, such as the Colonel of the Black Watch in *The Black Watch* (1929), which starred Victor McLaglen; Sergeant Clark in *Clive of India* (1935); and Major General Sir Thomas Woodley in *The Lives of a Bengal Lancer* (1935). He had also appeared with Montagu Love in *The Crusades* (1935).

Cecil Kellaway portrayed Mr. Stebbins, Emmy's father. The Native-born South African had spent years in the Australian motion picture business before traveling to Hollywood in the 1930s. Kellaway, a busy actor, who appeared in ten films in 1938, had a

Joan Fontaine and Douglas Fairbanks, Jr. with Cary Grant and Victor McLaglen. © RKO. Author's collection.

gracious and playful on-screen demeanor that served him well. He had also appeared with Joan Fontaine and Robert Coote in *Blond Cheat* (1938).

London-born Reginald Sheffield was given the role of Rudyard Kipling, and the thirty-seven-year-old performer was made up and costumed to look like the famous author, complete with signature mustache and glasses. Sheffield's film career, which began before World War I, included short subjects, silent features, and an uncredited role as a clerk in *The Lives of a Bengal Lancer* (1935). One of his children, John, became the adopted son of Johnny Weissmuller's Tarzan character in seven films, beginning with *Tarzan Finds a Son!* (1939). The RKO film *Tarzan and the Amazons* (1945), which also featured Johnny Sheffield, had a few *Gunga Din*-like elements: an interior that recalled the temple of Kali; a gold-topped structure; a charismatic mysterious leader, who is guarded by a band of deadly Amazons (instead of Thugs) with spears (instead of strangling cloths); and a mortally wounded Amazon, whose last act is striking a large gong that warns her fellow sisters. Young Sheffield, though, survives the mayhem.

Anne Evers, an extra, was elevated to featured background status, when Pandro Berman made her Cary Grant's dance partner in the betrothal party sequence. Although Evers had no lines in *Gunga Din*, Berman "took an option on her services and gave her an important role in *The Mad Miss Manton* [1938]," which starred Barbara Stanwyck and Henry Fonda. As soon as she completed her scene in *Gunga Din*, Evers portrayed Lee Wilson in *The Mad Miss Manton*, which was released in October 1938, three months before *Gunga Din* debuted.[29]

Finally, there was Anna May, better known as Annie, who happened to be the largest member of the cast. "Anna May is something of a moralist," noted *Photoplay* magazine. "If her manager stays out late, she'll scold loudly until her return. Also, like many women, she harbors a strong affection for Cary Grant. And she eats a bale of hay a day."[30] According to *The Gunga Din Bugle*, Vol. I No. 1, the production's location weekly: "Four bales of hay [are] consumed daily by Anna May and her three elephant friends, who also raise the devil with unpeeled bananas in large groups, carrots by the bunch and other delicacies left around within trunk's reach."

Annie the Indian elephant, who hailed from Mysore (now Mysuru) in Karnataka, was a veteran of many films, beginning with *The Adventures of Kathlyn* (1913), an early silent film serial (Thomas Edison's twelve-chapter *What Happened to Mary* in 1912 was the first American serial), and continuing for the next twenty-five years. Following her work in *Gunga Din*, she was slated to appear in W. C. Fields' *You Can't Cheat an Honest Man* (1939). Her role in *Gunga Din* was so important that RKO took out an insurance policy on the thirty-year-old pachyderm.

RKO rented Anna May, who was also known as Anna Mae, from the Selig Zoo at $250 a week, although her single day rate ranged between $75 and $150.[31] As a principal performer, she had her own stand-in: Martha. The zoo, located in the Lincoln Heights area of Los Angeles, also provided another elephant, Marianne, to *Gunga Din* at a slightly lower rental costs of $225 a week.

Additional unnamed elephants were rented from Goebel's Lion Farm in Thousand Oaks. The farm had acquired its elephants from P. K. B. Acooli and Sons, a Calcutta,

India-based importers and exporters of "foreign and Indian birds and animals." According to the company's price list on November 9, 1936, a female baby elephant was priced at $2,500. On the set, Barlow Simpson was the primary elephant handler. He also did double duty as a stuntman.

Queenie was another Indian elephant in *Gunga Din* who had accumulated screen credits, including *Boy Meets Girl* (1938) and *I'd Give a Million* (1938). Owned by Frank Whitbeck, the twenty-six-year-old former circus performer had a stand-in named Sally. The pair generated $450 a week for Whitbeck.[32]

Film work was demanding for the elephants. "Movies are harder on animals than a circus, because they must be used to sirens, whistles, wind machines, and actors they never saw before," explained George Emerson, a trainer at Goebels Lion Farm, who trained water buffalo for *Gunga Din*.[33] The water buffalo can be seen on the street where Ballantine and Emmy shop for curtains in the bazaar. RKO also added sheep, chickens, mules, and camels to its menagerie.

Interestingly enough, there was another large four-legged animal in the Hollywood area who had a movie resume: Gunga Din, a "temperamental star" bull, who was represented by Wray Bergstrom and had appeared in *Rhythm on the Range* (1936), a Western musical that starred Bing Crosby.[34] Gunga Din missed out on *Gunga Din*.

Chapter Eight Notes

1. Sayre Papers, "You're Better Than I Am," 3.
2. *George Stevens: A Filmmaker's Journey*, Creative Film Center, Inc. 1984. The documentary, written and directed by George Stevens, Jr., was released on a Warner Bros. Entertainment DVD in 2004.
3. *Arkansas Gazette*, February 18, 1939, 25.
4. RKO Budget of Production Cost, sheet #1, July 18, 1938.
5. George Stevens, Jr., "George Stevens," *Conversations With the Great Moviemakers of Hollywood's Golden Age Age at the American Film Institute* (New York: Vintage, 2006), 222.
6. *This Fabulous Century: 1930-1940*, Time-Life Books, 1969, 181. *Motion Picture Herald's* top box office stars of the year for 1938 listed Gable as #2; Shirley Temple was #1.
7. George Stevens, Jr., *Conversations*, 222.
8. Nancy Nelson, *Evenings With Cary Grant: Recollections in His Own Words and by Those Who Knew Him Best* (New York: William Morrow and Company, 1991), 103.
9. Wansell, *Haunted Idol*, 127.
10. *Daily Nonpareil* (Council Bluffs, Iowa), December 11, 1938, 10.
11. *Evansville Courier and Press* (Evansville, Indiana), January 9, 1939, 4.
12. Fairbanks, *The Salad Days*, 287.
13. George E. Turner, "The Making of Gunga Din," *American Cinematographer*, September 1982, 896.
14. Ernest S. Pagano, *Radio Transcription*, RKO Studio Records, January 11, 1939, 4.
15. RKO Studio Notes.
16. "Synopsis of Gunga Din," L. Tom Perry Special Collections, Harold B. Lee Library, Brigham Young University, Provo, Utah.
17. Nutt, "Notes," 1939.
18. Eliot, *Cary Grant*, 283.
19. *Dallas Morning News*, May 30, 1938, 8; *Springfield Republican* (Springfield, Massachusetts), June 12, 1938, 35.
20. Margaret Walton Roberts and Daniel Hiebert, "Immigration, Entrepreneurship, and the Family: Indo-Canadian Enterprise in the Construction Industry of Greater Vancouver," *Canadian Journal of Regional Science*, Spring-Summer, 1997, 124.
21. *The New York Times*, February 5, 1939, Screen, 5.
22. Arleen Lorrance, *Sam Jaffe: An Actor of Character* (Scottsdale, AZ: LP Publications, 2012), 180. Lorrance stated that after signing, RKO allowed Jaffe "two weeks to keep a previous commitment" as Shylock in a production of *The Merchant of Venice* at Penn State University; however, her remarks conflict with a *New York Times* report that identified the play as being staged at Union College.
23. Ibid.
24. *Morning Star* (Rockford, Illinois), March 8, 1939, 14.
25. *The New York Times*, June 6, 1938, 13.
26. *Hollywood*, June 1937, 54.
27. Joan Fontaine, *No Bed of Roses* (New York: William Morrow and Company, 1978), 89.
28. Fairbanks, *The Salad Days*, 286.
29. *The Film Daily*, July 19, 1939, 10.
30. *Photoplay*, February 1939, 68.
31. *Boston Herald*, November 26, 1939, 26.
32. *San Diego Union*, December 15, 1938, 9.
33. *Plain Dealer* (Cleveland, Ohio), September 17, 1939, 90.
34. *San Diego Union*, May 3, 1936, 30.

CHAPTER NINE
Creating Nineteenth Century India

RKO announced that it was producing fifty-four feature films for 1938 and 1939, and the studio designated *Gunga Din* as its most ambitious and expensive production. "It is our duty to furnish the studio with authentic photographs, illustrations and data from which all the sets, costumes, furniture and props that you see in the picture are made," explained Harold Hendee, Director of Research for RKO.[1]

The studio contracted technical advisor Hilda Grenier to research various aspects of East Indian culture, especially the Hindustani language. She worked from April 26 to June 25, 1938, and was paid $150 a week. On May 16, May 18, June 2, and June 13, 1938, she produced pages of English equivalents to numerous native terms and expressions—from *hathi* (elephant) and *chaprassi* (messenger) to *solah topee* (pith helmet) and *cheela* (disciple)—that might be appropriately used in the screenplay. One term on her list, *chota sahib* (small master), found its way into the script when Abner Biberman's character, the son of the Guru, was named Chota.[2]

She also provided an interesting list of every-day terms and expressions that soldiers would use, including "Blighty" (home), "Bully Beef" (tinned meat rations), "Gravel Crushers" (infantry soldiers), and "Vamping" (eating heartily), among others.

Grenier made careful notes and comments about East Asian architecture, trees, plants, flowers, and food. For example, she noted such esoteric information as: "The Wild Date Palm grows in the Basin of the River Indus but is not seen near the Khyber." She even wrote about a detailed description of a bungalow at Peshawar, Pakistan in 1900, which she secured from Jane A. Tracy's book *See India With Me* (1928).[3] Grenier also conducted research into British Army uniforms and provided specific suggestions. "In khaki—a soldier is not allowed to wear medals, only the ribbons," she noted. "When wearing his medals in full dress, no matter how many he has, a soldier must not make two rows of them—they can overlap." All of her information was turned over to the writers and the art department.

Grenier distributed pages of correct translations and pronunciations to all cast members, who had to deliver Hindustani dialogue. George Stevens made sure the language was properly pronounced when he provided lines and dubbed dialogue in post-production to such uncredited background performers as Adbul Hasson, Paul Singh, Jasin Ali, and Dalip Singh, among others. They were initially paid $25 a week, but were later upgraded to $41.25 a week.

Progress was being made on the script, but Stevens still wasn't satisfied. He was concerned that the existing dialogue-driven screenplay was primarily set inside the soldiers' barracks. "I took one look at it and saw there were no outside scenes," said Stevens. "The only thing you saw outside was through the windows of the officers' barracks where some people would ride by occasionally. I was afraid it would be very dreary and just wouldn't have worked as written, so I told the studio that I would take it on but would make a location picture out of it."[4]

Stevens wasn't satisfied with images of the Yuma landscapes, which were supplied to the studio by Lou Shapiro, RKO's location manager, so he became personally involved in the search for land that looked like India. "I wanted three locations: the flatland, the midland in the rocks and the higher ground," said Stevens, who conducted his searches in an airplane. "But the logistics and finances demanded that we do it all in one area."[5]

A number of California locations were also considered, including Convict Lake in Mono County, Sabrina Lake in Inyo County, Lake Arrowhead in San Bernardino County, and Alturas. Typical of the inquiries sent by Shapiro was a telegram he sent to a friend in Alturas: "Send me pictures of your country covering an area of fifty miles surrounding it; information on how many horses we can get."[6]

Nevada was also considered as a possible shooting location; in fact, the Union Pacific Railroad offered RKO a special train that would transport cast and crew on a ten-hour journey from Los Angeles to Moapa, Nevada. The railroad required that the studio purchase at least a hundred first-class tickets, which would cost $2,800.[7] RKO passed on the offer.

The place Stevens eventually selected was the Alabama Hills, an Inyo County, California location, which he described as a "strange rugged rock formation that related to places like Persia, Afghanistan, and the Khyber Pass in India." The majestic Sierra Mountains and Mount Whitney, the tallest elevation (14,505 feet) in the contiguous forty-eight states, served as magnificent backdrop. On one exploratory location journey, Stevens was joined by Harold Barry, the production's construction superintendent, who confirmed the director's choice.

Near the Alabama Hills was the tiny community of Lone Pine in Owens Valley, which had served as the temporary home of numerous film production companies since 1920. *Lives of a Bengal Lancer* (1935), *The Charge of the Light Brigade* (1936), *Hopalong Rides Again* (1937), and *Lost Horizon* (1937) were just a few of the films that utilized parts of the Alabama Hills for their location and background. Lone Pine was situated about 210 miles north-northeast of Los Angeles.

Stevens' vision of *Gunga Din* grew grander, but he realized that the cost of shooting on location, building elaborate sets, and hiring a large supporting cast and crew would be a considerable investment for the studio. Nevertheless, RKO supported him and established a budget of $1,332,025 for "Picture #146, *Gunga Din*," which was verified by the studio's accounting department.[8]

Stevens had a cast, detailed research notes, and a location, but he still lacked a finished script, at least one to his liking. Pandro Berman had given him a start date, Friday, June 24, 1938, and a finish date, September 3, 1938. Although those were "estimated" start and finish dates, according to an RKO Budget of Production Cost sheet, Berman expected Stevens to start on time. However, Stevens wasn't worried about the shooting schedule; in fact, he seemed to welcome the challenge. "It's so interesting to see a film like this play itself out," said Stevens. "It gives a real sense, for better or for worse, of the adventure of filmmaking—the opportunity of having resources and the disadvantages of having no dramatic concept of a story line that is going to hold it together."[9] Still, the director needed help and he sought assistance from two veteran writers with whom he had worked with before: Fred Guiol and Joel Sayre.

Stevens knew Guiol as a director and writer from the Hal Roach Studios, where both had served on a number of films together, including the early Laurel and Hardy comedy short *Slipping Wives* (1927), which was directed by Guiol and filmed by Stevens. Stevens later directed a number of Guiol-penned screenplays, including *Boys Will Be Boys* (1932), *Room Mates* (1933), and *The Nitwits* (1935). Guiol had directed everything from crime dramas to Wheeler and Woolsey comedies, and would provide plenty of frolicsome touches to the *Gunga Din* screenplay.

After producing short stories for *The New Yorker* magazine and writing two successful novels, Joel Sayre went to Hollywood, where he penned several screenplays, including *Annie Oakley* (1935), which was directed by Stevens, and *The Toast of New York* (1937), which featured a writing contribution from former *Gunga Din* writer Dudley Nichols.

Sayre believed that the *Gunga Din* project began as a joke of sorts. "According to studio gossip, the notion of making a feature picture out of Rudyard Kipling's dialect poem about a water boy started as a gag," noted Sayre. "Two wags were supposed to have conned a certain associate producer into capling Kipling's widow an offer for the movie rights. Gag or not, he obtained them—allegedly for $1,200—and assigned writers and a director to preparing the project. Wild rumors flew around the RKO lot. One was that they had made Gunga Din into a girl."[10]

Stevens had his writers but time was running out.

"We had a start date in three weeks' time, and got some books and went to Arrowhead Springs [California]," said Stevens. "Joel read the books; Freddie and I talked about things." One of the books that Sayre probably examined was *Twelve Years of a Soldier's Life In India: Being Extracts from the Letters of Major W. S. R. Hodson, B. A.,* which was edited by the Rev. George A. Hodson in 1860. The book carefully detailed various battles, the activities of native troops, and the exploits of rebel forces. "We needed something to get this whole thing together and Joel came upon it: the cult of Thuggee assassins that existed in India," said Stevens. "We worked it into the theme of the story."[11]

"For a couple of writers to be working on location was most unusual," remarked Sayre, who described Guiol as "huge, dark, mustachioed, glossy-haired [who] had once answered to the name of Chile."[12] The writers respected Stevens and were loyal to him. Sayre even criticized RKO's earlier choices to direct the film. "The British film *Elephant Boy* had been a recent smash, so the RKO director (George's predecessor) undertook to convert *Gunga Din* into an elephant picture that would end all elephant pictures forever," wrote Sayre. "His ultimate aim was to have every elephant in the U.S. that could walk appear in his great wow at the finish; and to this end he had his agents out beating the circuses, carnivals, and zoos for recruits. The girl he was training to play Gunga Din would play the bewitching mahout, only her name would be changed to Girlga Diana."[13]

While at Arrowhead Springs, a mountainous locality in San Bernadino, California, Stevens, Sayre, and Guiol produced four outline sequences by the end of May. They didn't make any drastic changes to the last Hecht-MacArthur script; in fact, they resurrected two earlier script ideas: the soldiers escape from the town skirmish by jumping into the river instead of using the forced elephant stampede, and Gunga Din is wounded from a gunshot instead of being injured from hot coal burns.

However, on June 4, 1938, Sayre provided a new beginning to the story. Chota and a band of Thugs massacre a patrol of Royal Engineers. Colonel Weeks, concerned about a possible Thug revival, orders a small detachment led by three sergeants (corporal Cutter received a promotion) to investigate the missing patrol. (Sayre depicted the Thugs as more menacing than the rebellious natives from previous scripts.) Weeks also orders regiments of Highlanders and Lancers into the field to curb any potential Thug activity in the region.

Ten days later, Sayre revised some of the continuity pages. A new scene featured Chota and his Thugs observing the three sergeants and their men as they repair the telegraph lines. Another scene described a Thug worship ceremony inside the temple.

A "Story Outline," dated June 21, reads more like Hecht and MacArthur than Sayre and Guiol. It did not reflect the changes that Sayre had provided in his June 4 synopsis.

The developing script still wasn't a finished product, but the screenplay was becoming more of what Stevens thought the story should be about—"The concept of a kind of 'Rover Boys in India,'" a reference to the juvenile book series published between 1899 and 1926, about three adventurous brothers, who attend a military school.[14]

Sayre suggested the use of many extras, and Stevens approved. The director estimated that he would need to hire over one thousand background performers to portray Scottish Highlanders, Indian cavalry, Thuggee forces, and civilians. Furthermore, each individual would have to be properly uniformed and equipped. "I went to the studio and ordered costumes for five hundred Highlander foot soldiers who had to have kilts," noted Stevens. "And of course we couldn't do it without five hundred Lancers, too. We found a British unit called the Queen's Own Sappers and Miners, dug up the details on their uniforms and got costumes for twenty-eight soldiers, and three for the sergeants."[15]

The studio budgeted $29,155 for wardrobe costs, of which $26,555 was designated for the men's costuming, which included military uniforms, Thuggee garments, and native civilian clothing.

The British soldiers' costuming, which was provided by Hollywood's Western Costume Company, was fairly accurate. The British soldiers wore relatively correct foreign service helmets, five-button khaki tunics (one type featured a rounded front skirt and the other an inverted "V" cutout below the bottom button) with two breast pockets, khaki trousers, and acceptable footwear. Some of the tunics were previously used in *Wee Willie Winkie* (1937).

The Black Watch—actually the 42nd Royal Highlanders—were satisfactorily outfitted with appropriate helmets, tartan kilts, and white gaiters ("spats").[16] Like other Highlander units, the soldiers' "stockings . . . went up to below the knees."[17] However, Western Costume couldn't provide enough uniforms. The company rented 100 Lancer outfits to RKO, but the studio had "88 made to order." RKO had "130 Dress Scotch Dress Uniforms" in its wardrobe department, but had to make seventy more.

Custom uniforms were made for the principals. On June 15, the wardrobe department requested permission from production to make various uniforms for McLaglen, Grant, and Fairbanks. Initially, each actor was provided with four main uniforms: red dress, evening fatigue, khaki service (field), and khaki service (barracks). At the time, it was estimated that it would cost $420 to outfit each of them. In addition, duplicates of the red dress uniform and the khaki service (field) uniform were made for each actor at an additional combined production cost of $185.

A production document detailed all of the three sergeants' uniforms and costs:

Red Dress Uniform $115.
Red Dress Uniform (duplicate) $100.
White Uniform $75.
White Uniform (duplicate) $75.
Khaki Service Uniform $100.
Khaki Service Uniform (duplicate) $85.
Khaki Service Uniform (Barracks) $85.
2 Khaki Service Uniforms for Doubles $100.
3 Outfits for Stand-ins $60.

The three sergeants' uniforms were also adorned with service and campaign decorations.

On June 22, the wardrobe department requested permission to start the manufacture of Montagu Love and Lumsden Hare's uniforms. Love, whose character was still called Colonel Weeks on the costumers' memo, was initially provided with three uniforms: fatigue, evening dress, and dress. The first two uniforms cost $100 each; the third $115. Lumsden Hare, who was identified as Major Pearson at the time, was at first provided with one $115 uniform, which included Tartan-pattern trousers. Like Love, he would later be costumed in an evening dress uniform.

The wardrobe department estimated that it would cost $460 to properly outfit Robert Coote as Sergeant Higginbotham.

Costuming for Joan Fontaine was relatively easy since no strict historical fashion guidelines were followed. On June 27, 1938, the costume department requested permission to start creating her clothing. Initially, two costumes were made: a "street outfit for shopping" and a "traveling outfit." Each outfit cost $175. Her ball gown was designed by Edward Stevenson, the studio's accomplished costumer, who had worked on scores of films prior to *Gunga Din*, including nineteen films that were released in 1937. Stevenson's work was so highly regarded that he was given an opening credit in *Gunga Din*.

Among the principals, the title character's wardrobe budget cost the least amount of money. Sam Jaffe had six duplicate outfits (a waist covering and a turban), which cost a total of $50. He was also supplied with leather sandals. Ciannelli's costuming (one main outfit and one duplicate) also cost only $50. Biberman's clothing cost $25.

RKO sought technical advice from experienced military veterans, who were familiar with India. "Hundreds of applications were received by the studio from technical advisors, all enclosing credentials to substantiate their claims at having been stationed at various British Army posts in India."[18] On April 25, 1938, Murray Ellman, who ran his own Hollywood-based artists representative company, wrote to Pandro Berman and recommended one of his clients, Bill Deming, for one of the technical advisor positions. "Mr. Deming possesses what is considered the most complete library concerning India, and his actual experiences in that country make him the most recognized authority," wrote Ellman, who noted that Deming was planning to return to India "within the next few months."

Harry H. Lichtig of Lichtig and Englander, another Hollywood talent firm, suggested Dr. Thomas MacLaughlin, who had served in the British Army in India and was particularly knowledgeable about the Indian Army Medical Corps.[19] MacLaughlin also earned a Bachelor of Law degree and served as an uncredited technical director and writer on over a dozen films, including *Arrowsmith* (1931), *A Farewell to Arms* (1932), and *British Agent* (1934).

One potential advisor was upset after being rejected. Captain E. Rochfort-John, who was credited as a technical advisor on *The Lives of a Bengal Lancer* (1935) and *The Charge of the Light Brigade* (1936), wrote to RKO president Ralph Blomberg and told him that he had been recruited by George Stevens. "The next day, I was telephoned by the Director of your Research Department that a certain salary would be paid to me, and if satisfactory to me I was to report for work two days later," stated Rochfort-John, in an undated RKO Studio Records letter. "One hour later, I received a second call saying the arrangement had been canceled. I found that another officer with little or no experience as [an] advisor, had been engaged at a lower figure." The former Royal Engineers officer, who had served twelve years on the frontier of India, reminded Blomberg why the film needed skilled advisors. "You know better than I do just how important absolute accuracy and sympathetic advice must be on a picture whose greatest appeal is undoubtedly to the British Empire market," said Rochfort-John. "If I am wrong in my conclusions, please pardon me." RKO ignored his plea.

RKO assembled a list of the best candidates, and "seven advisors were contracted by the studio," said Ernest Pagano, an RKO writer.[20]

The film's main credited technical military advisors were British. Sir Robert Erskine Holland, Captain Clive Morgan, and Sergeant Major William Briers were responsible for drills, military formations and maneuvers, weapons instructions, and assorted martial responsibilities. Holland, who had been awarded the Order of the British Empire in 1922 for his service in India, worked for the production from June 4 to September 3, and was paid $150 a week. He received an additional $150 a week for "living expenses while in Hollywood."

American newspaper coverage of Holland was favorable, and members of the cast agreed that he was a good choice. He was depicted as experienced, knowledgeable, and diplomatic. "A quiet unassuming gentleman, he was knighted for nearly forty years service for the British government in India, during which time he acted as judge, mediator and advisor to various maharajahs," said Fairbanks.[21] One of Holland's first recommendations to RKO was "to minimize *Gunga Din* because glorification of a native might tend to rekindle the Indian problem."[22] However, that suggestion was rejected by Stevens and his writers.

Morgan, who had served ten years on India's North West Frontier, began working in films in 1929, and had portrayed Captain Norton, an uncredited role, in *The Lives of a Bengal Lancer* (1935). Australia-born Major Sam Harris, who had served as a technical advisor on *The Charge of The Light Brigade*, worked on *Gunga Din* from June 25 to September 3, and was paid $125 a week. Thomas MacLaughlin was also hired as an advisor.

Indian journalists expressed concerns about British Army officers serving as technical advisors. "But why do they seek ex-service men from the British Army as technical advisors when making films about India," remarked Baburao Patel, editor of *Filmindia* magazine and president of the Film Journalists' Association of India. "The producers would not have to go outside of Hollywood to discover a number of Indians, professors and other cultured people who could give them all the advice they wanted, but still it was Sir Robert Erksine Holland whom RKO engaged as technical advisor on *Gunga Din*."[23]

Another *Filmindia* writer was even more critical of Holland. "I discovered that the Technical adviser for this picture is a seventy-year-old retired British officer, Sir Robert Erskine Holland, whose chief qualifications for being an expert on Indian culture and customs is that he was for a long time a member of the high-born services in India, one of our rulers, who, after a whole life spent in India, cannot speak two words of Hindustani correctly," wrote Khwaja Ahmad Abbas.[24] The comment was only a preview of the criticism that was to come from the Bombay-based publication.

A number of the military extras in *Gunga Din* had worked as a member of Carl Voss' movie "army." Voss, nicknamed "Hollywood's Military Generalissimo," had served as a sergeant in the United States Army's 14th Infantry Regiment before he took his skills to Hollywood's celluloid battlefields as a military coordinator. Since *The Big Parade* (1925), Voss and a small group of regulars worked like a precision drill team upon their arrival on the set, while other background actors had to be trained. The basic daily pay rate for background soldiers was $8.25 a day, although some earned as little as $5.50, while others received $11 a day. Voss and his men would later make contributions to such films as *Beau Geste* (1939), *The Fighting 69th* (1940), and

Northwest Passage (1940), among others. Voss and fellow soldier Bernard Breakstone were paid extra for operating the Gatling guns in *Gunga Din's* final battle.

Stevens needed hundreds of Indian extras, but there weren't that many available of military age who could handle the physical demands of an extensive location shoot during extreme summer heat. RKO's casting department went to work again.

"All the Hindus, Hawaiians, and other brown-skinned extras in Hollywood" were cast as background for the film "and more than 250 live in the camp."[25]

RKO also recruited such Lone Pine locals as Juan Perez, a twenty-year-old, who worked at Lone Pine Lumber and Supply. Rusty, the Perez family dog, frequently accompanied Perez to the set.

Whenever possible, the Hindus were strategically placed before the camera. Jaffe was impressed with the background performers. "You heard their explanations in their native tongue," said Jaffe, who also appreciated the set embellishments. "There were elephants, mounted Sikhs and Ghurkas, temple bells, and oxen, and so far as I am concerned it was perfect India."[26]

Once they reported to the set, they were issued a simple cotton waist wrap-around garment and a head covering. At the RKO wardrobe department, the fabric photographed satisfactorily, but "photographed badly at Lone Pine, which is nearly 4,000 feet higher than Los Angeles," noted *American Cinematographer*. "The wardrobe men bought all the available flat white goods—more than 300 yards of it—from the three stores in Lone Pine and confiscated seventy-two bed sheets from the location camp in order to make new costumes

Juan Perez and and the Perez family dog, Rusty, behind a set and its "Dip Hands" station.
Courtesy of Juan Perez Collection, National Park Service, USS Arizona *Memorial.*

in a hurry for the 400-man Thuggee army." Fortunately, the camp linens were quickly replaced to everyone's delight.[27]

Hundreds of Caucasian extras were also hired, but each day many of them had to be transformed into loyal Hindus and Thugs, a process that would consume a large portion of the film's $6,999 make-up budget. The make-up tent was filled with approximately 100 tables and mirrors—and a unique device. "Five men at a time are seated on a turntable. The table turns slowly while spray guns spray on a brown make-up. Each day less and less make-up is necessary, for the sun in [Lone Pine, California] is intense, and has given most of the company a natural tan."[28] A final make-up touch included a hand-dip bowl that was filled with the brown liquid. Bowls were strategically placed behind the sets in case background performers' hands lost their artificial color.

Some members of the cast and crew got sunburned. Annie the elephant received a "severe sunburn" during filming that required medical care; as a matter of fact, a $21.08 disability payment from her insurance company was issued to her handler.[29]

Sam Jaffe's makeup took longer to apply than the quick spray-gun process that was used on the background artists. A special dye was carefully applied to his entire body; only his waist area and head were spared from the makeup. It took nearly two hours to remove the makeup, which took longer than the time required to apply it. Jaffe's appearance fooled some film fans. An *Augusta* [Georgia] *Chronicle* reader wanted to know the race of the movie's title character. "Sam Jaffe, who played the role, is white," answered the newspaper.[30]

Ciannelli had an even more difficult time in the makeup chair, since he had to wear a tight-fitting skull cap to cover his hair. Like Jaffe, Ciannelli looked convincing; as a matter of fact, another audience member later inquired about the actor's race and identity to his local newspaper. "I am sure that I have seen him before but cannot recognize him from the make-up," asked *Milwaukee Journal Sentinel* reader Gordon Franke. "The chief of the Thuggees was portrayed by a white man, a well-known actor named Eduardo Ciannelli," answered the newspaper.[31] The make-up department also provided beards and wigs for the natives, and mustaches for some the British soldiers.

When made up and dressed in his simple costume, some observers thought that Ciannelli's appearance resembled Mahatma Gandhi, the prominent leader of the Indian nationalist movement, who was named *Time* magazine's "Man of the Year" in 1930. Despite his stature on the international stage, Gandhi was occasionally ridiculed in Hollywood. One trade periodical included a description of Gandhi as "the little brown man of India," and actress Marion Davies named her pet dachshund "Mahatma Gandhi." Dixie Dunbar, a performer in George White's Scandals, said that, when she was discovered by White in a nightclub production, she wore "a bib and a huge diaper that would have put Gandhi to shame." Furthermore, Gandhi was depicted as the "skindy man from India" in the 1932 Looney Tunes cartoon, *I Love a Parade*. The animated character sits on rug, playing a flute, while a goat dances in front of him. The Indian leader was depicted in a comedic scene in *42nd Street* (1933), and in *Everybody Likes Music* (1934), a two-reel comedy that starred Shemp Howard of Ted Healy and His Stooges fame, an uncredited inebriated character that resembled Gandhi was played for low-brow laughs. The Indian leader's garments were even insulted in an American fashion publication. *The New Movie Magazine* described men's bathing trunks worn on Malibu Beach as "Gandhi loin cloths."[32]

The most interesting member of the make-up department was Charles Gemora, an actor, who specialized in portraying gorillas in films. The native-born Filipino, who was called the "King of the Gorilla Men," first donned an ape costume in *Goose Flesh* (1927), a short subject. Prior to *Gunga Din*, Gemora had amassed over thirty credits as a gorilla, including appearances in *Murders in the Rue Morgue* (1932), *Island of Lost Souls* (1932), and *Charlie Chan at the Circus* (1936).

The weaponry seen in *Gunga Din*, which was primarily provided by the J. S. Stembridge Company (now Stembridge Gun Rentals), was not correct; as a matter of fact, most of the firearms used in the movie were anachronistic pieces that either hadn't been made yet or were not available for service at the time the screenplay's story took place (1880s). For example, Grant, Fairbanks, and McLaglen carried model 1909 Colt Army Revolvers instead of the Crown-issued Adams Mk II, Adams Mk III, Enfield Mk I, or Enfield Mk II revolvers.

Indians in the British ranks were equipped with Krag-Jorgensen models 1892 and 1896 bolt action rifles; and the Thugs fired Krag-Jorgensens and Springfield model 1873 "Trapdoor" rifles, which were not used in India. Nevertheless, the "Trapdoor" rifle and its carbine version served Hollywood for nearly a century. Some of the popular "Trapdoor" shoulder arms had even been modified as flintlock rifles and were used in such productions as *Last of the Mohicans* (1920), John Wayne's *The Alamo* (1960),

and CBS-TV's *George Washington* miniseries (1984), among others.

One correct firearm seen in the film was the Jezail musket, which was carried by some of the Thugs. The single-shot muzzleloading weapon, with its accentuated wooden stock, was also used in *Beau Geste* (1939), *Lawrence of Arabia* (1962), and *The Man Who Would Be King* (1975), among other films and television productions.

"RKO used 500 rifles in *Gunga Din*," reported *Variety*.[33] According to Paul Harrison's syndicated "Harrison in Hollywood" column, "every last British Lee-Metford [rifle] in the Stembridge warehouse—460 of them—were trucked over to RKO for *Gunga Din*."[34] The Lee-Metford bolt action rifle, which was carried by the native troops who fought alongside the principals in the Tantrapur battle, replaced the Martini-Henry rifle in 1888.

The Martini-Henry, a breech-loading, single-shot lever-actuated rifle produced by the Royal Small Arms Factory in Enfield, England was the proper British infantry shoulder arm of the era depicted in *Gunga Din*. The weapon, which had an effective range of 400 yards, and could be fired a dozen times a minute, was introduced to the troops in 1871. Kipling acknowledged the rifle and the way it should be treated in *The Young British Soldier*, a poem which appeared in *Barrack-Room Ballads and Other Verses* in 1892:

Don't call your Martini a cross-eyed old bitch;
She's human as you are—you treat her as sich
An' she'll fight for the young British soldier
Fight, fight, fight for the soldier

The background players who portrayed enlisted men in the film carried acceptable looking leather accoutrements, which reflected the 1870 Pattern Valise Equipment: a waistbelt, a pair of ammunition pouches, an ammunition bag, and a pair of braces. A complete equipment package would have also included a pair of straps for a great coat, a strap for a mess-tin, a valise, and a pair of valise supporting straps. The waistbelt could also adopt a bayonet frog.[35] However, the accoutrements also seemed similar to the 1888 Slade Wallace equipment, which included buff leather (whitened with pipe clay, except for rifle regiments which had black leather), a pair of bullet pouches, a white canvas haversack, an oval water bottle covered in grey or blue felt, a spare rifle magazine, a mess tin, a valise carried by means of two buff straps, an entrenching tool carrier, and a bayonet scabbard.[36]

The extras, who portrayed the Sepoy infantry and lancers, were costumed and equipped relatively accurately, and since many were Hindu, their on-screen appearance added a sense of ethnic authenticity to the film.

During the film's final battle, the British are depicted firing a Colt Model 1883 Gatling gun, which was not available for use by Her Majesty's troops in India at the time. Instead, the British used a Gardner-Gatling gun, which had a decidedly different appearance.

The field guns used by the Thugs in the film were satisfactory-looking nineteenth century muzzleloading artillery pieces, although the weapons did not recoil as they should have after being fired. The British guns were French 75mm 1897 models, which were designed not to recoil because of the weapon's unique hydro-pneumatic recoil system. To some, the Royal Artillery pieces also looked like RML 9 pounder cwt weapons, which were modified with an iron protection shield. However, for audience members, these detailed martial anachronisms didn't matter. Inside a dark-ened theater, all that was necessary was that the guns went boom and the rifles and pistols cracked loudly.

Despite the anachronistic shoulder arms, hand guns, and artillery pieces, they still had to be fired, cleaned, maintained, and repaired, and the workers from the J. S. Stembridge Company did a commendable job, especially when they had to work overtime after the large battle sequences. *Variety* reported that during one two-week period, 175,000 rounds of blank ammunition were used in *Gunga Din, Stagecoach, Dodge City*, and other films. *Gunga Din* used up most the ammunition: 85,000 rounds.[37] RKO provided a significant amount of pyrotechnics for the film, including 1,000 dynamite caps, 1,000 squibs, and five pounds of flash powder.

The Western Costume Company, which was located near RKO's studio in Hollywood, also provided some weapons to the *Gunga Din* production. "Besides producing everything from evening gowns to uniforms, Western Costume began buying and making all kinds of weaponry and props," explained Joseph P. Musso, an accomplished Hollywood storyboard artist and production illustrator. "By the 1920s, it acquired an extensive collection of nineteenth century military sabers, following the dissolution of the Austro-Hungarian Empire in 1918. Since these sabers, particularly the officers' models, bore a close resemblance to the British versions of the same period, and they became perfect stand-ins for Hollywood's films on the British Empire."[38]

In addition, RKO's miniature shop produced a number of prop weapons, including 250 wooden swords and sabers, 5 breakaway guns, 75 rubber and balsa wood pickaxes, 50 pine pickaxes, and 16 trumpets. An additional $180.24 was budgeted for painting the props.

Stevens also needed to build his three primary sets: the seven-acre British fort at Muri, the village of Tantrapur, and a temple dedicated to Kali, which would be topped with a golden dome. "We designed the set before the script was written," said Stevens, who originally wanted the sets to be constructed at three different elevations, including one situated at about 9,000 feet up in the mountains. Stevens knew that RKO would not grant him the money to film in multiple outdoor locations that were too far from each other, so he modified his plan. "It cost too much to move a camp, so we put it all in one place and those various locations all came within a few minutes' ride of one another with our star, Mt. Whitney."[39]

Besides the three major sets, over twenty other sets were constructed. Some were interiors built on RKO soundstages; others were erected at the studio's ranch, Culver City, Lake Sherwood, and various Lone Pine locations. For example, Set 22 at Lone Pine was designated for the "Bridge, Rocks, and Countryside," which included the wooden suspension bridge that the principals crossed to get to the temple. The special effects department also created a miniature temple and bridge, which were designed to be destroyed.

Stevens was given a construction budget of $102,400, which he eventually went over by a few thousand dollars. An additional $3,000 was budgeted for maintenance, and another $8,071 was allocated for "standby labor." It took approximately 100 construction workers six weeks to complete the buildings and assorted structures. "The sets are reputedly more expensive, massive, and spectacular than any since *Intolerance*," reported *Motion Picture Herald*.[40]

Stevens entrusted the set design and a $10,000 budget to Van Nest Polglase, who headed the film's art direction department, a group that included Associate Art Director Perry Ferguson, an Art Direction Oscar nominee for *Winterset* (1937). Before joining RKO in 1932, Polglase had worked as an art director at the Famous Players Film Company. Prior to *Gunga Din*, he and his talented art team had worked on nearly 200 films, including such Victor McLaglen films as *The Lost Patrol* (1934) and *The Informer* (1935). Polglase had already been nominated for three Academy Awards: *The Gay Divorcee* (1934), *Top Hat* (1935), and *Carefree* (1938), all Fred Astaire and Ginger Rogers vehicles.

"A glance through the synopsis almost staggered Perry Ferguson," said Polglase. Ferguson was particularly concerned that the art department would have to meet the authentic temple requirements that Stevens ordered. "But not too authentic," cautioned Polglase, who had a cultural concern about the structure. "We don't want to offend East Indian movie audiences with the violent action that takes place there."[41]

Ferguson drew numerous sketches of the sets, including large illustrations that measured nearly two-by-three feet. The military outpost at Muri set was an enormous complex that featured several large barracks, stables for horses and elephants, massive lookout towers, various outbuildings, and perimeter fencing which bordered a huge parade ground. Originally, Stevens believed that part of the complex could be recreated with a matte shot; however, he later insisted that Muri be photographed with actual structures because he needed an impressive pan shot of the fort when the principals return from the fight in Tantrapur.

RKO needed to limit and control Stevens' budget, so the studio transferred sums from one department to another. For example, a mere $250 was reduced from Vernon L. Walker's special effects budget "to help compensate for the above coverage" of "three profile buildings for Long Shot." It was hardly an equitable trade-off. Eventually, the studio spent more on the film than it had originally budgeted.

Despite the additional structures, the large cantonment's $23,000 budget was reduced to $19,325, according to an RKO memo of June 20, 1938. The Muri set became more expensive for the studio when it was filled with soldiers and lancers. Upon the sergeants' return from Tantrapur scene, 410 background performers costumed as Highlanders and lancers were used at a total one day cost of $3,937.50.

Tantrapur, which was set on about eight acres, featured over twenty main buildings—some set alone, some attached—on Bohara Street, the village's main commercial avenue. Polglase gave Ferguson specific information on some of the buildings. "You know, several of the buildings will have to be dynamited, so you'd better specify that the walls be at least eight inches thick," he remarked. Additional out buildings and other structures augmented the set; some were constructed along a nearby ravine. Polglase estimated that his department would have to create "a couple of hundred" drawings "representing the architecture and the scheduled action."[42] Set 6, "Native River Street (1880) Bohara," was budgeted at $31,900. The set also included telegraph poles, a jail interior and exterior with a breakaway capability, and some elephant stalls. A part of the street was recreated at the RKO Ranch for $3,000.

Also, $1,000 was allotted to build Set 21, an interior with stairs, which would be the scene of a fight between the three principals and a group of Highlanders at the beginning of the film. A sum of $3,000 was budgeted to construct Set 4, a companion exterior structure described as an "Ornate Building" with a second floor window.

Darrell Silvera's set decorations department added the appropriate stylistic touches, especially to the Tantrapur and bazaar locations. RKO budgeted $49,218 for "properties & drapery." The completed village sets were filled with baskets, vases, metal containers, furniture, rugs, shelving, and assorted objects that helped create the cultural environment envisioned by Stevens and his writers.

The huge multi-level temple, designated as Set 11, was topped with a "golden" dome made from $1,400 worth of gold-leaf, which "had been discovered through camera tests [as] the only satisfactory substitute for solid gold."[43] The temple included a shrine for Kali, which also served as the headquarters of Ciannelli's Guru character. The imposing structure would be featured in several crucial scenes including the climax. According to a July 1, 1938 RKO construction document, $18,000 was allocated to build the temple, which featured massive pillars and elephant-shaped columns. On the back of one of the production stills, the RKO publicity department exaggerated the cost of the temple by $62,000. The back of the structure's wood-framed exterior, which would never face the camera, was designed to be left open in order to save money and provide shade to the cast and crew during breaks.

Stevens even altered the distinctive Alabama Hills landscape. "The [prop department] produced dynamite and fuses when Stevens decided to blast a rock as big as a room that stood in the way of a new road he wanted built for a column of marching soldiers."[44]

As an additional touch of authenticity, "sprinkler trucks and over twenty-seven thousand gallons of crude oil were used to make the seven acres of light red soil appear like the jet black ground that characterizes northern India."[45]

To those in the cast, the realistic sets looked like India. "It was one thing for a fellow like myself to feel he was actually in India," said Jaffe. "It was another for the Hindu extras— several hundred of them were drummed up— exclaiming that this was just like home."[46]

Chapter Nine Notes

1. *National Board of Review Magazine*, March 1939, 18.

2. Hilda Grenier, "Research Notes," *Gunga Din*, RKO Studio Files, June 1938.

3. Grenier, though, misidentified Jane Tracy as Jane Gracy in her notes.

4. George Stevens, Jr., *Conversations*, 222.

5. Ibid., 223.

6. Lou Shapiro to Hippy Burminister, April 29, 1938.

7. C. E. Potter to Lou Shapiro, May 3, 1938. The railroad suggested an eight p.m. departure with an arrival time of six a.m. for the traveling production company. Breakfast would be served to each passenger at an additional cost of 50¢ per person.

8. RKO Budget of Production Cost, Sheet 3, July 18, 1938.

9. George Stevens, Jr., *Conversations*, 223.

10. Sayre Papers, "You're Better Than I Am," 4. In a taped interview on December 28, 1973, Sayre recalled that Kipling's widow was paid $1,200 for the rights.

11. George Stevens, Jr., *Conversations*, 223.

12. Sayre Papers, "You're Better Than I Am," 2, 4.

13. Ibid., 5. It appears that Sayre was talking about Howard Hawks since the director, Hecht and MacArthur mentioned "thirty elephants" in a December 27, 1936 telegraph message to RKO.

14. *Dialogue in Film: George Stevens*, The American Film Institute, Center For Advanced Film Studies (Beverly Hills, California), May-June 1975, 9. Stevens was aware that there was no "Rover Boys in India" written by Edward Stratemeyer (pen name: Arthur M. Winfield). However, the director was probably familiar with such titles in the series as *The Rover Boys in the Jungle* and *The Rover Boys in Alaska*, among others.

15. George Stevens, Jr., *Conversations*, 224.

16. Lieutenant-Colonel Percy Groves, *History of the 42ⁿᵈ Highlanders –"The Black Watch,"* (Edinburgh & London: W. and A. K. Johnston, 1893), 14; Robert Wilkinson-Latham, *North-West Frontier 1837-1947* (Oxford, UK: Osprey Publishing, 1977), Plate E, 34.

17. Douglas N. Anderson and René Chartrand, "The 78ᵗʰ Regiment of Foot, 1869-1871," *Military Collector & Historian*, Summer 2016, 171.

18. Pagano, *Radio Transcription*, 7.

19. Harry H. Lightig to Pandro Berman, February 24, 1938.

20. Pagano, *Radio Transcription*, 7.

21. *Milwaukee Journal Sentinel*, October 16, 1938, 65.

22. *Evening Star* (Washington D.C.), July 24, 1938, 61.

23. Thomas M. Pryor, "Hollywood's Far-Eastern Problem," *The New York Times*, September 10, 1939, Amusements, 4.

24. *Filmindia*, January 1939, 31.

25. *Pittsburgh Press*, August 14, 1939, 31.

26. *The New York Times*, February 5, 1939, Screen, 4.

27. Turner, "The Making of Gunga Din," 958.

28. *Pittsburgh Press*, August 14, 1939, 31.

29. *Hollywood*, June 1940, 40.

30. *Augusta Chronicle*, June 1, 1939, 4.

31. *Milwaukee Journal Sentinel*, June 4, 1939, 67.

32. *The New Movie Magazine*, April 1934, 16, 46; October 1931, 40. In the 1948 Looney Tunes cartoon, *Bugs Bunny Rides Again*, Yosemite Sam says: "And I don't mean Mahatma Gandhi" when he explains how to pronounce "Rio Grande."

33. *Variety*, December 7, 1938, 13.

34. *Heraldo de Brownsville* (Brownsville, Texas), January 16, 1939, 4.

35. See Pierre Turner, *Soldiers' Accoutrements of the British Army 1750-1900* (Ramsbury, UK: Crowood Press), 2007.

36. "The Wallace Slade Equipment" by J. T. Thompson in Soldiers of the Queen, September 1994. 8-9. The article provides additional details about the items, which are accompanied by illustrations. See also Donald Featherstone, *Weapons & Equipment of the Victorian Soldier* (Poole, Dorset: Blandford Press, Ltd., 1978.) For an overview of the British Army before WWI, see Byron Farwell, Mr. Kipling's Army: All the Queen's Men (New York: W. W. Norton & Co., 1981).

37. Lorrance, *Jaffe*, 182.

38. Musso, to author, November 30, 2016.

39. *Dialogue on Film: George Stevens*, The American Film Institute, May-June, 1975, 3, 11.

40. In 2004, a publicity claim for *The Alamo* stated that the Disney film featured the largest sets every constructed in Hollywood history. Not even counting the non-Lone Pine exteriors sets, *Gunga Din's* three major locations (Muri, Tantrapur, and the temple) constituted the largest set in filmdom's history.

41. Pagano, *Radio Transcription*, 4.

42. Ibid., 5, 6.

43. Ibid., 8.

44. "Better Men Than Gunga Din, Says He," *The New York Times*, February 5, 1939, Screen, 5.

45. Pagano, *Radio Transcription*, 7.

46. Lorrance, *Sam Jaffe*, 183.

Thuggee Temple. © RKO. Courtesy of Craig R. Covner.

Tantrapur Plan.
© RKO. Author's
collection.

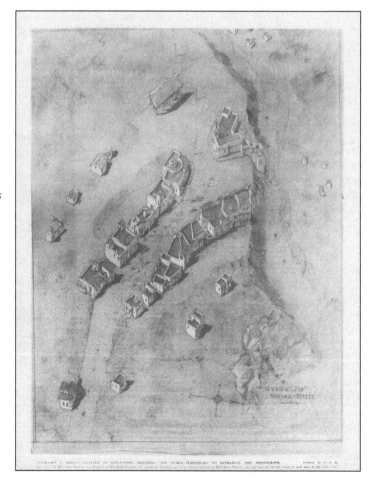

Telegraph Repair Detail at Tantrapur. © RKO. Author's collection.

Production Sketch, Muri Headquarters © RKO. Author's collection.

Highlanders relax at Muri. © RKO. Author's collection.

Gunga Din's (Sam Jaffe) first appearance as he departs Muri. © RKO. Author's collection.

Camera and lighting setup on the bazaar street. © RKO. Author's collection.

CHAPTER TEN
George Stevens: Behind the Scenes

As impressive as the major outdoor sets was the area designated for the cast and crew. "A town complete in every detail with every modern convenience: electric lights, heated rooms, hot and cold running water, shower and toilet facilities," noted *The Hollywood Reporter*.[1] Plumbing, including hot- and cold-running water, pumps, and other related materials, was budgeted at $3,900 (labor alone was $1,200), and electricity carried a $1,500 price tag. In addition, a standby electrician was budgeted at $100 a week for eight weeks. Another $750 was allocated for camp lighting materials, gas, and oil.[2]

Private contractors supplied nearly everything. J. S. Otey of Bishop, California, provided 1,600 feet of two-inch used pipe at a rental cost of $160 for ninety days. RKO rented a water truck from Basich Brothers of Torrence, California, for $30 a week, and the business also supplied diesel trackers, bulldozers, and a Mack truck. The studio utilized Hollywood's Fat Jones Stables for horses, tack, and horse wranglers. Horses weren't used exclusively for the camera; in fact, George Stevens frequently traveled to and from the sets on horseback. RKO also contacted Schanfield Brothers in San Antonio, Texas for "new army bridles with two reins," and the International Sales Company of El Paso, Texas, for "twelve dozen pairs [of] iron stirrups."

Hollywood's Anderson Boarding & Supply Company was contracted to serve thousands of meals at the "Gunga Din Location City" site. An RKO inter-department communication memo, dated September 7, 1938, indicated that the company charged the studio $1 per meal. A rival Hollywood firm, Brittingham Commissary, had offered the studio three meals a day at $8, the price dropping to $4.50 if a minimum number of days could be guaranteed.[3]

RKO budgeted $62,888 for location expenses and $40,295 for transportation. G. W. Dow's Lone Pine Lumber and Supply Company was contracted to supply all the building materials for the film. "Some 400,000 feet of lumber was purchased in Lone Pine for the sets, but dozens of union carpenters had to be imported."[4] Hollywood columnist Jimmie Fidler wrote that "half the population of Lone Pine are members of the Screen Actors Guild qualified to work [as] extras and, ironically, they average twice as many working days each month [compared] to the lot of their Hollywood confreres."[5]

"RKO built a city of 100 tents." The large canvas tents were mounted on wooden frames that were slightly elevated off the ground to help circulate the air and keep unwelcome crawlies out.[6] "The director, principal actors, first cameraman, writer Joel Sayre, and senior technicians either had tents of their own or shared with one another," noted Fairbanks.[7] The best tents included "parlor, bedroom, and bath" sections, which were furnished and equipped with ice boxes. "All tents were floored [and] had sectional sidewalls which opened for ventilation."[8] Imaginative signs were soon created inside the tent city, like

The tent city. © *RKO. Author's collection.*

Vine Street in the tent city. © *RKO. Author's collection.*

Background players line up for transportation to the set. © RKO. Author's collection.

Hollywood and Vine, Sunset, and Olvera Street. The commissary sign was humorously spelled "Gungad Inn."[9]

Transportation was a major undertaking. "A dozen camera and equipment trucks, sixteen studio cars and a number of private ones, six passenger buses each carrying thirty people, and a daily studio car for mail are needed for transportation alone."[10] The buses and cars were in use nearly every day to transport the hundreds of costumed background personnel from the tent city to various set locations.

Of course, everyone needed to be fed. "A commissary staff of thirty-seven—chefs, bakers, waiters, dishwashers, janitors and maintenance men—took care of the preparation of some fourteen tons of meat and vegetables that were trucked in from Los Angeles each week. About 15,000 pounds of ice per week were brought in to keep the food refrigerated."[11]

According to *The Gunga Din Bugle*, RKO "keeps two bakers busy all day long baking, among other items, 100 pullman loaves, 100 dozen rolls, and 60 pies daily. And two more devote their waking hours to the tearful task of peeling 150 pounds of onions every day, squeezing lemons for 80 gallons of lemonade."[12] Furthermore, the daily beverage quantities included 90 gallons of coffee, 100 gallons of iced tea, 80 gallons of milk, and ten gallons of cream.[13] One newspaper reported that "tea was a proper British ritual on the set [because] three of the production's stars are British. So, promptly at four they had tea."[14] Despite the report, Stevens never stopped filming for tea time. On one occasion, though, a meal was interrupted, when a food delivery truck broke down on the way to Lone Pine where some 700 cast and crew members awaited their next meal. "Salads and sandwiches staved off a crisis"

until other vehicles on the set were sent to retrieve the food.[15]

RKO also provided films in "an open air theater to help keep their *Gunga Din* troupe from getting homesick."[16]

An additional expense was added to the film's budget, when Stevens agreed with James Wilkinson, his editor, that a mobile location editing trailer be built for $10,000 and transported to Lone Pine. The two men believed that, in the long run, money could be saved by having the editing done on site rather than having the film shipped to Hollywood and subsequently shipped back to location after being processed.[17]

Sets of a village street and a street bazaar were also constructed at the RKO Ranch at Encino, and a section of Tantrapur "near the river" was built at Lake Sherwood. The most elaborate interior built on an RKO soundstage was the temple, which included sets that featured a dungeon, snake pit, stairways, and a tower. A main temple room was created for the Thug indoctrination ceremony, which used hundreds of background performers. Other interiors (and construction costs) included the Stebbins House ($3,600), the colonel's headquarters ($900), and a "Native Street" stairway ($1,000). Set designer Darrell Silvera requisitioned funds to dress each set. For example, he budgeted $500 for miscellaneous props and $350 for "greens" to adorn the Stebbins House.

Stevens secured the services of cinematographer Joseph H. August, a veteran cameraman, who had an extensive career that began in 1913. He became the principal cameraman for cowboy star William S. Hart, and later joined creative forces with director John Ford. Among August's best-known films prior to *Gunga Din* were *The Informer* (1935), *Mary of Scotland* (1936), and *A Damsel in Distress* (1937). Call sheets frequently identified him as "August Sr." since his son, Joseph A. August, was also part of the camera crew.

Another interesting member of the camera team was William Clothier, an accomplished technician, who had filmed newsreel footage of the Spanish Civil War months earlier. "[He] went through twenty-eight bombings in sixteen days while behind the lines in Madrid," said Fairbanks.[18] James H. Stewart was brought in to head the sound department.

Stevens wanted the production to be properly chronicled, and it was, thanks to still photographer Alex Kahle, a naturalized American citizen, who had fought for Bulgaria in World War I and had earned several battlefield honors, including the Iron Cross, the Bavarian Cross, and the Flanders Cross. "He was one of ten in his entire battalion still alive at the war's end and his recent meeting on the set with a British soldier whom he had bayoneted during the Battle of Mons contained more stark drama than any still he ever took in his present profession," said Fairbanks.[19]

During production, Kahle displayed eighteen of his images from the film in a two-page spread in the October 1938 issue of *International Photographer*. While working on *Abe Lincoln in Illinois* (1940), Kahle said that he "turned in several thousand stills, almost as many as I did for *Gunga Din*."[20] Kahle's unofficial all-time-high figure for creating production stills was challenged when John Wayne's *The Alamo* (1960) was captured by a number of photographers during a location shoot in Brackettville, Texas in 1959. Besides Kahle's photos, Stevens used his own 16mm camera to capture various moments while on location.

Shooting days on location usually began with a wake-up call before six in the morning, sometimes as early as five a.m. [21] After the wake-up call—which was initiated with either a bugle call or an amplified alarm clock over the public address system—breakfast was served. Following the meal, the make-up, costuming, and prop departments went to work. Buses and other vehicles provided by Mac's Auto Tours of Hollywood carried the background players to the sets. D. D. McElroy, the transportation company's chief proprietor, also supplied "De Luxe Parlor Cars" for the principals and key crew members.

On days when the large battle scenes were scheduled, Joseph H. August and his camera team had to wait until hundreds of costumed background performers arrived and were positioned, but with the passing of each morning hour, the temperature began to rise. It was nearly 100° by lunchtime.

Chapter Ten Notes

1. *The Hollywood Reporter*, January 26, 1939, 15. According to a June 16, 1938 telegram sent from the Dow Hotel in Lone Pine to Lou Shapiro, the facility's fifty-five rooms could accommodate no more than 150 guests.
2. Earl O. Miller to Lou Shapiro, June 17, 1938.
3. Albert A. Brittingham to Louis Shapiro, June 17, 1938.
4. *Milwaukee Journal Sentinel*, November 6, 1938, 64.
5. *Oregonian*, August 20, 1938, 11.
6. *Life*, January 16, 1939, 26.
7. Fairbanks Jr., *The Salad Days*, 286.
8. *Silver Screen*, November 1938, 25.
9. *Hollywood*, April 1939, 49.
10. *Milwaukee Journal Sentinel*, November 6, 1938, 64.
11. Turner, "The Making of Gunga Din," 898-899. See also *Silver Screen*, November 1938, 70. Ernest Pagano noted specifically that there were "thirteen waiters [and] six janitors . . . and several men who spend their whole day washing dishes."
12. *The Gunga Din Bugle*, Vol. I, No, 1, July 26, 1938, mentioned in Lorrance, *Sam Jaffe*, 181.
13. *Milwaukee Journal Sentinel*, November 6, 1938, 64.
14. *Evening Star* (Washington D. C.), February 12, 1939, 40.
15. *Columbus Daily Enquirer* (Columbus, Georgia), January 23, 1939, 4.

16. Pagano, Notes, 13.

17. *The Film Daily*, July 8, 1938, 8.

18. *Milwaukee Journal Sentinel*, October 16, 1938, 65.

19. Ibid.

20. *International Photographer*, March 1940, 2.

21. *The Pittsburgh Press*, August 14, 1939, 31; Harris, *Cary Grant*, 91, noted the wake-up call was "at five-thirty." *Silver Screen* magazine, November 1938, 70, stated "5:40 a. m."

CHAPTER ELEVEN
Location Problems

The tent city for cast and crew had been built; the Tantrapur set looked like an actual Indian village; the temple, with its golden dome, shined in the sun; and the recreated outpost at Muri awaited the soldiers, lancers, horses, and elephants. Everything seemed to be ready, except for a finished screenplay that George Stevens would be happy with.

There was, however, something new on paper: a 12-page outline, dated June 24, 1938, taken scene by scene from a previous "Final Shooting Script," which featured the names of Hecht, MacArthur, Sayre, and Guiol. Additional changes were made to the document on June 27.

A title page began with the story's overview: "When an uprising closes the mountains to building [a] telegraph line, the three toughest sergeants in the British Indian Army are put in charge. One, treasure-bound, drags the other two into trouble, whereupon the Lancers, attempting a rescue, walk into an ambush. It is only the heroism of a water carrier, who sacrifices his life. Which summons the Highlanders to the bayonet charge that ends the rebellion."

The latest document included a few character and scene clarifications: Chota's role as a Thug leader is more pronounced; a shootout in the temple, which attracts the Lancers, is more action-packed; and the advance of the Highlanders, while the three sergeants are tied to cannon barrels, is more dramatic. The outline noted that Gunga Din saves the day with his bugle call, but "dies under the hail of bullets, living only long enough to blow up the Thugs' powder room."

According to RKO's call sheet for Friday, June 24, 1938, the first scene to be filmed was located at the studio's Stage 14 Set 5, which featured the interior and exterior of the Stebbins home. Fairbanks, Fontaine, and a designated "Native Servant" were on the set by 9:00 a.m. to begin filming a number of scenes, including part of the punch bowl sequence.

By June 27, all the actors who portrayed British characters were on hand, and thirty-two background performers completed the cast lineup. The filming at Stage 14 continued until Friday, July 1.

On Saturday, July 2, at 7:00 a.m., a number of trucks traveled to the RKO Ranch, where the bazaar exteriors had been constructed at Set 4. Two hours later, at Stage 2B Set 2, Stevens and his crew began filming the exterior telegraph office scene with Montagu Love, Lumsden Hare, and Robert Coote. At 11:30 a.m., Grant, McLaglen, and Fairbanks joined the others at Stage 2B Set 3, where the interior and exterior sets of the colonel's office were located. Filming at Stage 2B lasted until Tuesday, July 5, when the cast and crew worked on the exterior bazaar set.

The fight between the three principals and the Scots was scheduled for July 6, with a call time of 8:15 a.m. The scene, which included stunt men, livestock, and background performers, was concluded the next morning. However, on July 7, the cast and crew returned to RKO Stage 14 Set 21, where the interior fight scene continued. During the next few days, filming took place in the colonel's office and the telegraph office.

In a July 11 note to Stevens, Sir Robert Erskine Holland raised concerns about the language that the non-commissioned officers used when speaking to the colonel. "The last two remarks of the two Sergeants on page five sound a little disrespectful to the Colonel," wrote the advisor. Stevens, though, had a bigger concern: the impending cast and crew departure to the major location site in Lone Pine. He expected the move to be uncomplicated.

On Tuesday, July 12, another script revision was completed. The new screenplay, which only featured the names of Sayre and Guiol on the title page, eliminated Hecht and MacArthur's *The Front Page*-like ending, where Ballantine is brought back into active duty against his will. Instead, Ballantine voluntarily rejoins his mates.

On the evening of July 12, the first equipment trucks left for Lone Pine. The next morning, the rest of the production company departed the studio. "One of the biggest location caravans ever to leave a Hollywood studio started on its way."[1] According to RKO's July 13 call sheet, the crew and the stand-ins departed at 7:00 a.m., and the principals left at 10:30 a.m. "In addition to the people involved, hundreds of horses [were] sent to the location, as well as six elephants, eight camels and nine water buffalo."[2] The move to the location was problem free, and as the sun set Stevens looked forward to the next day's filming. However, he didn't realize what was about to happen.

At 10:30 p.m. on the first night, a "mysterious fire" broke out on the Tantrapur set. Stevens, his crew, the cast members, and hundreds of extras "were routed from their beds." A call was made to Lone Pine for assistance. The three-hour blaze "was brought . . . under control with wet burlap bags, a chemical truck, and a water wagon."[3] An entire block of the Tantrapur village set was destroyed, with a loss estimated at $5,000. In addition to the damaged structures, numerous props were also lost in the flames. However, the cause of the fire was not identified. RKO submitted its first insurance claim for the film. "Lloyds of London paid off what was reported as the largest movie loss in sixteen years. Thirty-one carpenters were rushed in from Los Angeles and rebuilt the damaged structures in ten days."[4]

Sam Jaffe remembered the fire. "We were all called to put it out," he said. "We had a bucket brigade. The next day, in the newspapers, who was given credit for putting out the fire? The three stars. In truth, it was the extras who served as firemen because Stevens wouldn't risk the lives of the stars."[5]

"Forty trucks were sent back to Los Angeles to collect 4,000 pieces of props, lumber, and furniture to take the place of the material lost by flames," said Abdul Hassan, the son of the mayor of Dakuno Kalatare, who served as an unofficial technical advisor on the Hindu sequences. "These were rushed back to location and, whether you care to believe it or not, the village was practically reconstructed within three days from the day of its destruction!"[6]

Stevens moved his initial shooting location to the recreated British military compound. He had an improved script, but it still didn't fulfill his expectations. "There was always a script as far as the spoken word was concerned, at least before we started to rehearse a scene," admitted Stevens.[7] However, the action had yet to be determined.

"The horrible day finally arrived when we got on location up at Lone Pine but had nothing on paper," said Stevens. "So we started with a big parade-ground drill. We didn't have enough horses, and one of the advisors—a sergeant major—told me they used to drill on foot. I knew it would take a good four hours to get this drill organized." In those hours, Stevens worked with Sayre and Guoil to create a scene in which Grant's Cutter confronts Jaffe's title character, who is drilling nearby with his bugle. "The scene was scribbled out and the script girl passed out the three necessary copies, one for herself and two for the actors."[8] It may have seemed to be a rush job, but Stevens wasn't too concerned. "I don't worry about the dialogue until the time comes, and that time is when the actors are on the set ready to speak those certain lines."[9] The scene worked beautifully, identifying Cutter's empathy and Din's humility.

Sir Robert Holland, though, did not like the scene. "Ganga [sic] Din should not be made out to be either a buffoon or a thief or a coward," noted the advisor in a two-page document, which he forwarded to Stevens. "To make Ganga [sic] Din go through the motions of a military exercise with an old bugle is to make him ridiculous," he remarked. Holland also did not like Jaffe's actions when he "cringed and cowered" at the initial sight of Grant's character. "To Indians, it would be very repellent that Ganga [sic] Din, who is to be the hero of the piece, should have been a thief," he warned.

Stevens respectfully ignored Holland's remarks and kept the scene. However, Assistant Director Ed Killy wasn't as diplomatic with the advisor, and he frequently complained about him. "After talk with Sir Holland, find him very difficult," wrote Killy in a telegram

to RKO production manager J. R. Crone. "[He] insists Gunga must be old man with whiskers." More memos from Holland would soon be on the way.

Stevens, Sayre, and Guiol successfully managed their on-the-spot script revisions. "It was like that throughout the picture: writing a day ahead," said the director.[10] Stevens' extemporaneous and improvisational approach proved to be successful; in fact, all the scenes seemed fresh and vibrant. Years later, Stevens made an entry in his diary: "Life is a journey and it's always most interesting when you're not sure where you're going." The comment seemed to perfectly describe the *Gunga Din* production.

Despite the satisfactory progress that was made on the script, Holland offered more critical comments after viewing the Guru's first scene in the temple. "I would suggest that the ceremony of initiation should be simpler," he wrote on July 24. Two days later, Holland suggested that a "more faithful rendering of the Kali chant be used." The advisor pointed out that "a good way to rehearse it would be to get a few of the true-bred Indians together and tell them to do it as realistically as possible in the Indian way."

Stevens, of course, wanted his background performers to be as realistic as possible, but he was more concerned about carefully crafting the relationship among his three principals. Cutter, MacChesney, and Ballantine had distinct personalities but, more than anything, the director emphasized the respect and rugged affection that they had for each other. Stevens' efforts did not go unnoticed. *Motion Picture Herald* observed the trio's obvious "Three-Musketeer friendship" during filming.

"Cutter is a working-class Englishman, unspoilt [sic], principled, and defiantly optimistic," wrote Grant biographer Graham McCann. "He is a creature of the great outdoors, not the smoke-filled drawing room; he provided Grant with the chance, at long last, to emulate his idol, Douglas Fairbanks, Sr."[11] Stevens and the writers provided a soft side to the rugged MacChesney, courtesy of Annie the elephant, and Ballantine's intelligence and wit were refined.

On most days, after the pre-dawn wake-up call, filming began around 9:00 a.m. and lunch was called at noon. "Shooting was resumed at 1:00, lasting until the light failed. Curfew rang at 10:00."[12] Additional activities began when the sun went down. "George, Bob Coote, Cary, Joel Sayre and I would sit up after dinner telling stories, discussing politics, and arguing about and/or rewriting scenes to be done the next day," wrote Fairbanks in his autobiography. "When we boys had got weary of talking and joking, had decided on the details of the next day's shooting, and had taken ourselves back to our own tents for some sleep, Joan would creep into George's place—or vice-versa."[13]

Holland typed four pages of notes on July 15 and sent them to Stevens. Among the advisor's concerns were the office size of a British department ("An Agency Office could not be located in a small, outlying building."), Thug behavior ("There is no tradition that Thugs ever used shovels for excavating graves."), and Thug weaponry ("The strangling cloths were not noosed but were short handkerchiefs."). It appeared that Holland viewed *Gunga Din* as a kind of grand documentary rather than big-screen entertainment.

Holland was particularly concerned that the term "monkey," which had been in the Hecht-MacArthur script, was still in the Sayre-Guiol screenplay. In the Tantrapur scene when the soldiers start leaping into the river below, MacChesney says to Din, "Come on, you monkey. Get over." Holland informed Stevens that "in old days, stupid and ignorant Europeans did openly apply the epithet 'monkey' to Indians, but it is a sin of the past which has now been buried, along with the word 'native,' and I think it would be wise not to resuscitate the painful memory by use of the word in a picture which is to be shown in India." Stevens eventually removed the line from the film.

An unplanned aspect of production was the weather. Everyone knew it was going to be hot in the Alabama Hills during the summer, but hardly anyone could anticipate what 100°+ days felt like; in fact, sometimes the reported temperatures reached approximately 115 degrees, although *Hollywood* magazine writer and part-time extra E. Stimson noted from the set one day: "120 degrees at ten o'clock in the morning."

Dehydration and heat stroke were obvious concerns, but the craft services crew was prepared. Besides water, which was served from large water wagons, a salt and lemon juice concoction was distributed to everyone. "The thermometer climbed as high as 120 degrees; 110 was considered comparatively cool," reported Australia's *Sydney Morning Herald*. Production photographs frequently depicted shirtless cast and crew members, who are seen resting in shady areas in between takes.

The heat had a major impact on the cast. After eight days of filming on location, McLaglen had lost twenty pounds, Grant twelve pounds, and Fairbanks ten pounds. Stevens found it necessary to put the trio "on a fattening diet, lest the weight discrepancies be evident in close-ups."[14]

The cast and crew take a break in the shade. © RKO. Author's collection.

Temperatures became somewhat more bearable in September. Documents from the set at Lone Pine stated that from September 9 to September 17, 1938, the days were mostly sunny with a high temperature of 93° during the day (September 14), and a low temperature of 47° just before dawn (September 9). Temperatures during September 24-27 ranged from a daytime high of 86° to a predawn low of 45°. The heat affected everything. "The ignition switch of my parked car one day melted right off the dashboard, simply drooled down to the floor," recalled Sayre.[15]

The Weather Source's Weather Warehouse Online Past Monthly Weather Data for Lone Pine, California, September and October, 1903-2015, indicates that the highest recorded temperature for both July and August was 101°. Of course, different locations in the Alabama Hills could register different temperatures, and the heat index was probably higher than the recorded temperatures in the town.

"We all sweated like stevedores, drank gallons of bottle water and gulped daily rations of salt pills," recalled Fairbanks.[16] However, he wasn't too concerned over his weight loss; as a matter of fact, he confessed to columnist Sheila Graham that he wanted to lose a few more pounds. "A few weeks ago, I weighed 183 pounds—now I'm 173—but I want to get down to 168." He described his method: orange juice and milk, alternating every two hours.[17]

Hard liquor was forbidden on the set. "Drinking was clearly against regulations except for the weak beer—of which George [Stevens] downed several cans a day—on sale in the commissary tent," said Fairbanks. "However, we kept our smuggled booze well-hidden, and I've little doubt that many of our several hundred-strong company were doing the same and being extra careful about it."[18]

Too much liquid consumption also had its consequences. "Our thirst was quenched by many beers, brought up to us by the prop man," said Fairbanks. "Vic [McLaglen] decided that as the beer had gone through him too quickly and none of us could leave our positions high up in this tower, there was no alternative to lessen his intense discomfort but to unbutton his uniform and relieve himself during the scene! Cary and I didn't know whether to laugh or be furious."[19]

The title character had his own *bhisti* who kept him hydrated. "Jaffe's valet stood by the fountain with a water glass in his hand, waiting to draw his master a drink," stated a press release. The extreme heat statistics were quickly exploited by S. Barret McCormick, the head of RKO's publicity department. "*Gunga Din* Troupe Sizzles Making Picture in Desert," proclaimed *The Pittsburgh Press* on August 14.

Snakes played a prominent role in the script and also presented a real hazard on location. "The troupe also had to fight diamond-back rattlesnakes," claimed an RKO statement.[20] According to the California Department of Fish and Wildlife, the several types of rattlesnakes that resided in the Golden State were most active between April and October, which coincided with *Gunga Din's* production schedule. However, no snake bites were reported to the company's first aid corps.

All of the principals had stand-ins. Malcolm Merrihugh, who had worked previously as Grant's stand-in on *The Awful Truth* (1937), *Bringing Up Baby* (1938), and *Holiday* (1938), explained that his duties were quite demanding. "A lot of people have the idea that a stand-in just goes in front of the lights and the camera while things are being adjusted, while the star gets a breath of fresh air and a chance to relax," explained Merrihugh, who earned a minimum of $35 a week plus bonus cash from Grant for his services. "A good stand-in takes care of his principal's make-up box, his principal's make-up, his clothes, sees that they're pressed and hung properly, checks with the assistant director to find out when the star is working, sees that he's at work, keeps the dressing room orderly, makes and breaks dates on the telephone, does secretarial work, acts as a companion, runs errands, sees that certain people come and go on the set and does everything in general."[21] The other major stand-ins were Art Bruggerman (McLaglen), Gordon B. Clarke (Fairbanks), and Phoebe Campbell (Fontaine). Sam Jaffe had numerous stand-ins, including such Lone Pine locals as Juan Perez.

Besides the heat, the wind also affected the production. "We have up here two types of weather—hot and windy, and sometimes the weather man runs them simultaneously as a double feature," said Fairbanks.[22]

"The wild assortment of weather during our ten weeks on location in the Sierras gave the camera crews the most trouble," said Joseph H. August. "Because of the heavy expense of maintaining a large company so far from Hollywood, it wasn't feasible to shoot the story in sequence. And it wasn't our problem to reconcile the photography to keep the weather cinematically consistent."[23]

On several occasions, the wind became so severe that it threatened the lives of camera crew members, who were working on platforms that stood atop tall wooden parallels. One afternoon, a cameraman and two assistants were on one of the tall structures when a wind storm suddenly developed and started rocking the parallel. "For fifteen minutes the gale raged on, with the three men crouched helplessly atop the thirty-five foot parallel" until the wind subsided.[24] Working as a team, cast and crew members helped stabilize the structure during the storm.

Another unmanned parallel, which was supposedly made secure by four staked corner ropes, collapsed in a strong wind. RKO learned a lesson. In future films, whether indoor or on location, the studio mandated that parallels be constructed of steel. In fact, the studio promptly built a 100-foot-tall steel camera parallel that was used for an imaginative sequence in *The Story of Vernon and Irene Castle* (1939) in which Fred Astaire and Ginger Rogers are seen dancing across a 500-foot-long map of the United States during the title characters' countrywide "Whirlwind Tour" in 1914.[25]

"We had many miserable daytime hours, when the hot desert winds would blow such volumes of sand and dust as to make filming temporarily impossible and cause Joan to suffer recurrences of severe sinus headaches and flooding eyes," recalled Fairbanks.[26]

Conditions made it difficult to film, but Stevens expected the men to handle the elements; however, he made it as easy as possible for his female lead. "Joan Fontaine, her hair dressers, and the wardrobe women, the two script girls lived in a hotel in Lone Pine, traveling to location four miles each morning."[27]

As filming progressed, Fontaine's co-stars continued to act like perfect gentlemen around her. "Apart from these discomforts, Joan's general manner was so shy and maidenly that we all became models of chivalrous behavior in her presence," said Fairbanks.[28]

The first major action sequence in the film was the fight in Tantrapur, where the Thugs attack Cutter, MacChesney, Ballantine, and the rest of the telegraph-repair detachment. The combat took place on the ground, on ladders, and atop buildings, structures that had been solidly built in order to support the weight of dozens of performers, crew members, and equipment. Most of the scene was filmed in late July and early August during some of the hottest days on location.

"It required an awful lot of shooting—lots of setups and explosives—and it took me longer to shoot than anybody imagined," said Stevens. "It took me, I suppose, ten days to shoot it, setup after setup, and it gave Joel Sayre and Freddie Guiol and me time to try and figure a third of our way through the story so we could move ahead."

The Tantrapur fight also has a remarkable upbeat tempo to it, thanks to a simple camera technique: undercranking—a process whereby the camera shoots at fewer than twenty-four frames per second. When projected at twenty-four frames per second, the action is accelerated. "Of course it's possible to adjust camera speed so you expedite things without creating this false choreography of movement," explained Stevens, who slightly overcranked a scene where Cutter dives to knock an ignited dynamite stick away from Ballantine. The resulting effect depicted Cutter's leap in a slower motion, which helped accentuate the drama of the daring leap.[29]

The overall Tantrapur battle sequence also had the pulsating feel of an exciting movie serial. It came as no surprise that upon the film's release one audience member said, "I have a feeling that at any minute they'll flash a sign on the screen saying: 'Will they be saved in time? See the next installment at this theater next week.'"[30]

Holland, though, sent Stevens another critique on August 9, after viewing the previous day's rushes. "I would suggest that the incident of the Sergeant sword-fighting on the roof against a number of Thugs, with one leg sunk to the hip in a hole, comes perilously near clowning, and rather spoils the rather fine and thrilling sequence of the roof struggle," he remarked. Stevens kept the scene.

The fight in Tantrapur included thirty "natives," whose pay ranged from $5.50 a day to $35 a day, the higher amount paid to those who performed special "bits." The scene involved a lot of stunt work, including horse falls, hand-to-hand sequences, roof falls, jumps, and ladder falls (although dummies were used in two falling ladder sequences).

RKO had hired some of Hollywood's best stunt personnel and they performed admirably throughout the film. The base pay for the stunt players ranged from $55 to $75 a day, although adjusted "straight time" pay was higher depending on the stunt. For example, one of the most highly regarded stunt team members, Dave Sharpe, received various additional payments for a "fight on roof" ($35) and "two falls from top of roof" ($70). Stuntman Art Mix's pay was adjusted when he received multiple $35 payments for his work near various explosions, and Mike Lally was paid $50 for doubling Cary Grant in the fight sequence. Ten of the stuntmen were paid $61.25 a day (straight time plus overtime) for "taking falls and being dragged over rocks." In an interview, Charles Levy, director of publicity, exaggerated the pay scale. "Those boys get $100 a fall whether it was two feet or fifty feet."[31]

Of course, no big action movie was without its hazards. Bumps and bruises were expected, but Grant didn't expect to be knocked out

Fight at Tantrapur publicity still. (L to R, standing): Cary Grant, Victor McGlaglen, Douglas Fairbanks, Jr.
©RKO. Author's collection.

Fight at Tantrapur. Douglas Fairbanks, Jr. completes an amazing fight sequence. © RKO. Author's collection.

Fight at Tantrapur. (L to R): Victor McLaglen and Sam Jaffe. Different camera angle scene not used. ©RKO. Author's collection.

Fight at Tantrapur: Gary Grant prepares to toss a stick of dynamite. © RKO. Author's collection.

Fight at Tantrapur. "Over you go!" © RKO. Author's collection.

by McLaglen in a choreographed fight. In the scene, Cutter wants MacChesney to accompany him to the temple, but the senior sergeant refuses and threatens to use force against his alcohol-fueled comrade. "He knocked me out cold," said Grant. "I meant to miss his fist, but my timing was off; instead of moving back, I went right into it. He carried me off the set over his shoulder, not even knowing that he had knocked me out. He could have killed me."[32]

Fairbanks stated that during filming he suffered "two broken fingers, a cracked rib, a bad twist of my already torn knee cartilage, and three knife scars."[33] RKO played down the injuries. "So elaborate were RKO's safety precautions, however, the Company's First Aid Corps found it necessary to treat only a few minor scratches and bruises," noted an official studio document.[34]

RKO provided first-aid personnel on set at all times, and Dr. Howard W. Dueker, a Lone Pine physician, offered his services to the studio. The studio also compensated those who were injured. One background player who "took bumps" when he was "strangled in scene" was awarded an additional $8.25.

The casts' celluloid battle wounds were a source of inspiration for Stevens. "*Gunga Din*, with all the hazards that existed there, had a tremendous excitement about it to me," said Stevens. "It's cavalry-scale improvisation; not knowing just how you're going to do it the next morning really keeps you alive.[35]

Injuries to the horses were very limited, and unlike some earlier films, none were planned. "*Gunga Din* was particularly free from such actual cruelties," wrote film critic W. Ward Marsh. "Because *Gunga Din* spared the horses, I spoke well of it."[36] Marsh was aware of a deadly practice conducted in previous motion pictures called the "Running W." For example, during the filming of *The Charge of the Light Brigade* (1936), a number of horses were killed when they were attached to the "Running W," a wire that was attached to a horse's forelegs and run through slip rings under the saddle. The other end of the wire was connected to a grounded stake. The device was used to simulate a horse and a rider getting shot. When the slacked wire became taught the horse immediately slammed into the ground, which occasionally resulted in an injury or death to the horse and sometimes the rider. The Society for the Prevention of Cruelty to Animals and the American Humane Association brought attention to the practice and it was eventually banned. As a result, select horses were trained to fall on their own without risking serious injury to either the animal or the rider. In time, stunt riding became one of the most sought after specialties offered by stunt personnel.

A few additional events made the set more dangerous. "One of the stuntmen was so affected by the heat, he attacked Eddie Killy, our popular assistant director, with a blackjack," said Sayre. "He was disarmed and sent home. The ex-wife of a member of Joe August's great camera crew appeared with a loaded revolver and the notion of putting some holes in her former husband. She was disarmed and sent home."[37]

Besides the heat, Sam Jaffe only had one unpleasant experience during filming: riding Annie the elephant. "He told me it was very uncomfortable," explained Roxanne Ackerman Spencer, Jaffe's niece. "I do recall Sam saying that the elephant's hair was rough on his bare legs," remarked Bob Ackerman, Jaffe's brother-in-law.[38] RKO described Jaffe's discomforting condition as "elephant burn."

Filming also took its toll on equipment. RKO paid the Fat Jones Stables $157.50 for damaged saddles, reins, bits, bridles, and stirrups. In addition, the studio reimbursed the business for "four army blankets burned in fire."

Stevens, Sayre, and Guiol kept writing and revising the screenplay, and the trade publications continued to provide reports about the motion picture to their readers. One synopsis explained a version of film: "Along India's Northwest frontier there is a native rebellion against the British. Alarmed by the situation, the British authorities send out large bodies of Lancers and Highlanders to cover the district and round up native bands. Sent out with the special detachment are Cary Grant, Douglas Fairbanks, Jr. and Victor McLaglen. They are able to quell the revolt, but not without the aid of Gunga Din (Sam Jaffe), one of the native water carriers [who] blows up a native garrison and allows the British to save Grant, who has been held captive."[39]

Stevens and the writers continued to fine tune the script. They toned down the hostile relationship between MacChesney and Din, accentuated Din's humbleness and nobility, and expanded Cutter's emotional boundaries, which allowed Grant to express a wider range of emotions. "It was stimulating to go to work with George, because he always had another idea when you went in," said Grant.[40]

When he wasn't on set, Grant kept busy. He read the latest newspapers and kept up to date with international markets. "Cary used to do a lot of arbitrage," said Fairbanks. "He would buy Japanese yen and sell English pounds and buy Italian lire or German marks. He did that every morning before work on *Gunga Din*."[41]

Grant received permission from Stevens to attend a special parade held in New York City on July 15, which was to celebrate the round-the-world flight of Howard Hughes and his crew. Hughes had left Floyd Bennet Field in Brooklyn on July 10, 1938, and returned there on July 14, after logging 14,672 miles in three days, nineteen hours, fourteen minutes and ten seconds—a new world record. Hughes invited Grant, his friend, to the event, which not only marked the pilot's record-breaking flight but also promoted the forthcoming World's Fair in New York.

After a two-day absence, Grant returned to Lone Pine. "Observers recalled that Grant appeared uneasy, distracted, and, according to at least one, openly worried. Less than a week later, he asked Stevens for permission to return to New York, and again Stevens let him go."[42] At the time, Grant had much on his mind besides his acting duties. His romance with actress Phyllis Brooks, who visited him on the set of *Gunga Din*, seemed destined to result in marriage. The cast and crew were well aware of Brooks, who made her presence stylishly known in Lone Pine. Gossip columnist Sheila Graham described one of her outfits: "[She wore] a bright red print playsuit, brown Oxfords, white socks, and a blue kerchief round her head."[43] No one seemed to mind her periodic appearances, although, after her arrival, some of the call sheets included a "No Visitors" provision. However, the relationship between Grant and Brooks eventually came to an end.

Grant was also trying to see his mother for the first time in nearly twenty-five years. He had been separated from her when he was a child and believed that she had died; however, he later found out that she was alive. He planned to sail to see her in England as soon as *Gunga Din* wrapped.[44] Grant also traveled back to New York in August to attend

Cary Grant reads the July 17, 1938 issue of New Orleans' The Sunday Item-Tribune. © RKO. Author's collection.

a party David O. Selznick hosted for Alfred Hitchcock. After the event, Grant returned to Lone Pine.

Chapter Eleven Notes

1. Ernest Pagano, *Radio Transcription*, 8.

2. Ibid.

3. Ibid., 9.

4. Turner, "The Making of Gunga Din," 899; Pagano, *Radio Transcription*, 11. Pagano noted that "forty more carpenters were sent up to the location."

5. Lorrance, *Sam Jaffe*, 180.

6. E. Smithson, "Going Native the Hard Way," *Hollywood*, December 1938, 44. In an October 16, 1938 *Milwaukee Journal Sentinel* interview, Fairbanks said that Hassan "has spent the last three years in Hollywood learning the picture business" and was planning to return to India where he would "star and co-direct his own screen story, *Hell Beyond the Khyber.*"

7. George Stevens, Jr., *Conversations*, 225.

8. Ibid.

9. *Arkansas Gazette*, February 18, 1939, 25.

10. George Stevens, Jr. *Conversations*, 225.

11. Graham McCann, *Cary Grant: A Class Apart* (New York: Columbia University Press, 1996), 102.

12. *Silver Screen*, November 1938, 70.

13. Fairbanks, *The Salad Days*, 286.

14. *San Francisco Chronicle*, February 7, 1939, 8.

15. *Evening Star* (Washington D. C.), November 19, 1972, 86.

16. Fairbanks, *The Salad Days*, 286.

17. *Spokesman-Review*, July 21, 1938, 3.

18. Fairbanks, *The Salad Days*, 286.

19. Ibid., 287.

20. Pagano, *Radio Transcription*, 12.

21. Malcolm Merrihugh, "True Story of Cary Grant's Stand-In," *Silver Screen*, September 1938, 30-31. Merrihugh continued to be Grant's stand-in seven more films. At the time of the article, Merrihugh identified himself as "junior member of the Screen Actors Guild." However, union stand-ins only "stand in" for the principals. All of the other tasks mentioned by Merrihugh are conducted by personal assistants, make-up and wardrobe personnel, production assistants, and managers.

22. *Milwaukee Journal Sentinel*, October 16, 1938, 65.

23. Frederick H. Law's *A Guide to the Appreciation the Photoplay Based on Kipling's Gunga Din*, Vol. V, No. 2, 1939.

24. Pagano, *Radio Transcription*, 14-15; *San Francisco Chronicle*, February 8, 1939, 8.

25. *International Photographer*, October 14, 1938, 14.

26. Fairbanks Jr., *The Salad Days*, 286.

27. *Silver Screen*, November 1938, 70.

28. Fairbanks Jr., *The Salad Days*, 286.

29. George Stevens, Jr., *Conversations*, 225-226, 228. Undercranking below twenty-one frames per second results in obvious unrealistic rapid on-screen movement.

30. *Plain Dealer* (Cleveland, Ohio), February 21, 1939, 11.

31. *Charleston News and Courier*, March 11, 1939, 6.

32. Nelson, *Evenings with Cary Grant*, 104.

33. Fairbanks, Jr., *The Salad Days*, 288.

34. Pagano, *Radio Transcription*, 12. According to Pagano, "Cary Grant suffered a bruise only on his fist, which he received during a hand-to-hand encounter; Doug Fairbanks Jr. a small cut on his arm; while Sam Jaffee [sic] got out with only a sprained finger."

35. George Stevens, Jr., *Conversations*, 228. He would use the "cavalry-scale improvisation" expression in a later interviews.

36. *Plain Dealer* (Cleveland, Ohio), February 24, 1939, 8.

37. *Evening Star* (Washington D. C.), November 19, 1972, 86.

38. Roxanne Ackerman Spencer and Bob Ackerman to author, January 14, 2016.

39. *Independent Exhibitor's Film Bulletin*, July 30, 1938, 12.

40. Cary Grant interview, *George Stevens, A Filmmaker's Journey.*

41. Nelson, *Evenings with Cary Grant*, 92.

42. Eliot: *Cary Grant*, 286.

43. *Evening Star* (Washington D. C.), August 4, 1938, 37.

44. Nelson, *Evenings with Cary Grant*, 85; Higham and Moseley, *Cary Grant*, 98-99. Grant's biographers occasionally presented conflicting information about the actor during filming. Higham and Moseley state that Grant was informed of his mother being alive "during the shooting" of *Gunga Din*; however, Nelson provided the text of a letter Grant received from his mother dated September 30, 1937, nine months before he began filming in Lone Pine. On another topic, Eliot states that Grant "was no longer involved with Phyllis Brooks when he went to New York to meet Hitchcock; however, Nelson noted that "as soon as Cary finished making *Gunga Din*, he went to see [Brooks]."

CHAPTER TWELVE
Budget Concerns

Pandro S. Berman was an involved overseer who kept tabs on nearly every aspect of the films under his production domain at RKO, and *Gunga Din* was no exception. He examined the numerous on-the-spot script additions and changes that were made by Stevens, Sayre, and Guiol, and evaluated the rushes sent to him from location. Berman paid particular attention to the shooting schedule and the budget, although, at first, he wasn't too concerned. "George had always been quite economical in most everything he'd done," said Berman. "He never presented us with any large problems on cost."[1] That soon changed.

By the end of July, Berman realized that the production was going over budget. He thought that costs could be better controlled, and the film could be improved, if the screenplay was shortened. On August 5, 1938, Berman sent George Stevens an inter-departmental memo requesting that a number of script pages be eliminated. "It seems to me from the film I have seen to date that the element of mystery attached to the various opening sequences is terribly affected, and that not knowing just what is going on is going to be a lot more interesting to the audience than to have seen the opening episodes, in which we give very clearly away to the audience what all the shooting is all about," wrote Berman, who noted in the communication that 2,100 feet of film was cut from the latest Astaire-Rogers production, *Carefree* (1938). "The picture [*Carefree*] is now in 7,400 feet instead of 9,500 feet, and is twice as good a picture as it was in the first preview."[2]

In the memo, Berman raised the issue of RKO's bottom line. "The picture is running somewhat over schedule in budget, which is of great concern to us all on account of general conditions, but the film looks good," wrote Berman. "And I am hopeful that now that you are acclimated and have been through the early half you will be able to make much better time from here on."[3] Berman expected Stevens to comply with his request; however, Stevens asserted his authority as both producer and director and kept the designated pages. On the next day, *Variety's* Advance Product Chart proclaimed that *Gunga Din* was produced and directed by George Stevens.[4] Berman did not have to be reminded, and considered a more direct way to confront Stevens.

More unexpected weather conditions created havoc in Lone Pine. According to RKO, during one 24-hour period, the temperature reached 115° before dropping to 32°. The mountains became covered in snow, and an emergency request for 2,500 blankets was sent to the studio. One newspaper account stated: "They rehearse in overcoats, shiver during shakes."[5] It was worse for the animals. "The elephants refused to drink the ice water, and so fire pits had to be dug beneath each trough. The cold weather drove the deer down from the mountains, and so consistently did they raid the horses' feed supply that it was finally necessary to keep guards posted to scare them away."[6] Rumbles of thunder, which preceded a mountain snow storm, scared Annie. "On hearing her first crash, she broke her chains, ran amok, and collided with Douglas Fairbanks' car, crumpling a fender and almost throwing Cary Grant and Doug out of the machine."[7]

The scantily costumed Jaffe remembered the low temperatures. "And it was cold; terribly cold," he said. "The snow was on the peaks of the mountain, and the minute we did a scene we had to rush back into the automobile."[8] Of course, the snow-covered mountains presented background continuity problems for Stevens and the camera crew, but everyone carried on.

Berman monitored the ever-changing screenplay and was glad that Stevens eliminated a scene that too closely resembled *The Front Page* (1931). Yet, *Gunga Din's* script featured a couple of brief emotional dialogue passages—one by Fairbanks to Fontaine, delivered in a tongue-in-cheek manner, and one by Ciannelli at the snake pit, which recalled an intense scene from Hecht and MacArthur's script.[9]

Although Stevens had kept earlier script pages that Berman wanted cut, he eliminated a few scenes on his own. "Scenes #155 and #156 in that stuff are out," he wrote in a note to the studio on August 16. "As it is now, Cutter and Din will escape with Annie before Mac and Ballantine get the alarm that Annie has been stolen." In the note, Stevens said that he was ready to leave Lone Pine. "Sure will be glad to get back to the studio," he wrote.[10]

Stevens continued to go over budget, and Berman decided to pay his director a visit on the set. Stevens had been filming during the day and writing at night. "I was looking forward to finishing the day, and then having

Sunday off," said Stevens. "I had sent somebody ahead and got a cabin up the road at Big Pine, back in the hills about four miles, where I could go when I finished work—flee from there, pull myself together a little bit, and come back Monday morning. All of a sudden, I see a studio car drive in while I'm making the last shot. I'm coming down to go to my cabin, and it's Pandro. I say, 'How are you, Pandro?' and get in my car and leave."[11] Berman was surprised at Stevens' quick exit, but expected him to return.

Fairbanks recalled the moment differently. The actor said that Stevens had received a memo from Berman directing that the filming be suspended. "We knew we were on to something good [making the film], so I said, 'Let's just pretend we didn't get the message.' We tore it up and went on working."[12]

Berman had a different take on the incident. "I was waiting for him at 5:30 [a.m.] Monday morning when he got back, and I said, 'Look, you've got x-number of days up here on location with this enormous crowd, and if you don't finish by then, George, you're just gonna have to come home without the rest of the stuff,'" said Berman.[13]

In late August, the production company returned to RKO, where additional interior scenes were filmed. According to the August 29 call sheet, the three principals were filmed at Stage 2B Set 27, where the interior of the sergeants' quarters had been built. The next afternoon, Grant, McLaglen, and Fairbanks were joined by Jaffe, Ciannelli, Biberman, and Olin Francis, who played a Thug Chieftain, at Stage 7 Set 5, where the elaborate temple interior had been constructed. The daily call sheets once again stated: "No Visitors, Please!"

Stevens, Sayre, and Guiol made a few changes to the script on August 31 and

Juan Perez, wearing his Lone Pine Lumber work apron, and Rusty. Courtesy of Juan Perez Collection, National Park Service, USS Arizona *Memorial.*

Two background players escape the sun during a break. Courtesy of Juan Perez Collection, National Park Service, USS Arizona *Memorial.*

Juan Perez and one of the water wagons. Courtesy of Juan Perez Collection, National Park Service, USS Arizona *Memorial.*

Annie lifting a telegraph pole at Tantrapur. Courtesy of Juan Perez Collection, National Park Service, USS Arizona *Memorial.*

September 6.[14] At about the same time, a conversation commenced between Sir Christopher Robinson, Honorary Secretary of The Kipling Society, and RKO about the accuracy of certain historical and cultural details in the film. A letter dated September 4, 1938, that was sent to George Stevens, indicated that the British-based organization confirmed an actual story of an "heroic *bhisti* name Juma, or Jama," who had been issued the Star of the Indian Order of Merit for valor. Robinson also raised concerns about the Gunga Din character not being a Brahman, supposedly the only group of Indians who served as water carriers. The Brahman *bhistis* were recognizable by the "sacred thread" worn over their left shoulder. However, the unsigned letter's author informed Stevens that "a sect of Hindus in the Punjab, called 'Jiwars,' also provide *bhistis* to British regiments. "I rather wish we had thought of making Gunga Din a Brahman, and had given him the 'sacred thread' at the outset, but I fear it is too late now," added the writer. The letter also suggested that a scripted scene with Ballantine, who was disguised as a native approaching the temple with Gunga Din, was "a severe strain on the imagination."[15] The scripted scene was never used.

Filming continued at additional RKO soundstages, including Stage 7 Set 15 and Stage 14 Set 13, where the snake pit interior was created. From September 7 until September 13, the cast and crew worked various scenes, including sequences in which MacChesney and Ballantine are whipped, and the snake pit comes "alive" with the slithering creatures (a mix of real and rubber snakes).

On the afternoon of Tuesday, September 13, filming began in the recreated temple tower exterior on Stage 8 Set 14. The scenes were completed on September 17. On Monday, September 19, and the following day, the call sheets indicated that the action returned to the snake pit set, where the Guru gives his "India farewell" speech before jumping to his death.

The next day, Stevens started filming additional exterior temple tower scenes. On September 26, the call sheet surprisingly listed Fred Guiol as the director for the day's shoot, which included interior temple and tower room scenes filmed at two different RKO soundstages.

On September 27, some exterior camp scenes were filmed at RKO's Tenfield Avenue, Chalk Hills location, better known as Set 31. The call was for 7:00 p.m. and the first meal was served at 11:30 p.m. The call sheet noted: "This call works if not raining." The next day, Reginald Sheffield joined the cast at the funeral scene.

"In September, a rough cut was assembled and shown to the studio executives," noted *American Cinematographer*. "Only the climactic battle and some post-production work remained to be done. So impressed were the officials that they decided to authorize another two weeks of shooting at Lone Pine to permit the battle to be filmed on an even larger scale than was envisioned originally."[16] Of course, everyone realized that the film would go over budget once again, but there was a sense that *Gunga Din* was going to be an outstanding motion picture.

Chapter Twelve Notes

1. Berman interview, *George Stevens: A Filmmaker's Journey*.

2. Berman to Stevens, August 5, 1938. RKO Studio Records reproduced in the 1995 *Gunga Din* laser disc.

3. Ibid.

4. *Variety*, August 10, 1939, 19.

5. Times-Picayune, (New Orleans, Louisiana), October 19, 1938, 18.

6. Pagano, *Radio Transcription*, 14.

7. *Omaha World-Herald*, October 21, 1938, 23.

8. Lorrance, *Sam Jaffe*, 182.

9. "I'm an anarchist," cries George E. Stone's Earl Williams character. "It's got nothing to do with bombs. It's a philosophy that damages every man's freedom. All of those poor people being crushed by the system. And the boys – the boys that were killed in the war. And in the slums – all of those slaves to the crust of bread. I can hear them cryin.' Go on! Go on; take me back! Hang me! I got my bet!"

10. RKO Studio Files.

11. George Stevens, Jr., *Conversations*, 226-227.

12. *Gadsden Times*, Alabama, March 5, 1992. Fairbanks made the comment while visiting a veterans hospital.

13. Berman interview, *Gunga Din*, directed by George Steven, DVD, Turner Entertainment Co., 2004.

14. This screenplay can be read in its entirety on the 1995 *Gunga Din* laser disc.

15. Robinson to Stevens, RKO Studio Records.

16. Turner, "The Making of Gunga Din," 961.

CHAPTER THIRTEEN
The Final Battle

The biggest scene in the movie was the final battle at the gold temple. "The job was to use 1,500 men, several hundred horses and mules—to say nothing of four elephants—most effectively for scenes of utmost confusion, and still plan the action to obviate accidents and possible injuries," said George Stevens. "To do this, we first fought on paper the entire battle, the charge, and the headlong retreat of the Thugs. [We] rehearsed the cast in small detachments and in 'slow motion' until the mechanics of the action were established. Just beyond the range of the cameras were posted first-aid facilities as well as wranglers to capture frightened, riderless animals."[1] Stevens was ably assisted by cinematographer Frank Redman's second unit in creating the final battle.

The climactic battle was big in every way, but it wasn't big enough for S. Barret McCormick's publicity department, which overstated the number of background performers. An exaggerated caption attached to *Gunga Din* still GD-Pub-A-263 stated: "Two thousand extras were used for the battle scenes." However, a production document noted that a maximum number of 410 background performers were used in the battle on any given day.

The concluding battle was shot during the first weeks of autumn, and it was no longer hot in the Alabama Hills; in fact, some mornings were quite cold. In 1938, the lowest recorded temperature in Lone Pine in September was 47°, and the lowest temperature in October was 30° (the highest in October was 78°).[2] Cold morning wind chills added to everyone's discomfort.

Unlike the freakish cold spell that caught everyone off guard weeks earlier, the production company was somewhat better prepared. In the mornings, the wardrobe department distributed hundreds of blankets to the Thug extras, but for most of the time the recreated Highlanders had to do without, since their legs were partially protected by their kilts. "Why is it that we always have to . . . wear kilts in the mountain[s]," quipped Carl Voss.[3]

Near the end of principal photography, Grant reportedly "blew up when George Stevens ordered him to stay over another day or two" after McLaglen had developed a black eye in a fight, which "prevented him from working in scenes with Grant that day." Grant came up with an idea. He proposed that Stevens proceed with the scene because the camera could be re-positioned without showing the bruised side of the actor's face. "Stevens followed Grant's suggestion exactly, saving RKO the $10,000 it would have cost to cancel production for the day."[4]

Joan Fontaine appreciated Stevens' directorial approach. "I felt quite at home with his meticulous technique, his camera shooting from every conceivable angle."[5] Joel Sayre also praised Stevens. "Stevens was the most pleasant guy to work for," said the writer. "Stevens took personal interest in writers and had some realization of problems."[6]

Sam Jaffe also respected him. "Stevens really understood," said the actor. "You do the

Preparing for the final battle. © RKO. Author's collection.

best for him; you bring your nuggets, so to speak. He puts you at ease."[7]

Douglas Fairbanks also enjoyed his relationship with Stevens. "He frankly tried to make his team feel that they were his trusted partners rather than hired puppets, unlike such tyrannical directors as C. B. DeMille and Fritz Lang," noted the actor.[8]

On October 14, Stevens filmed Gunga Din's dramatic climb to the top of the temple. The scene also included two risky actions: a moment when the devoted *bhisti* loses his grip and almost falls (which was filmed earlier on an RKO soundstage), and another when he falls off the top after being mortally wounded. Bryan "Slim" Hightower was called on to double for Sam Jaffe in both shots, although it appears that Jaffe did the actual fall. Hightower also replaced Jaffe atop the temple in a long shot. Hightower had acted and performed stunts in a number of films prior to *Gunga Din*, including *The Plainsman* (1936), *Thunder Trail* (1937), and *The Texans* (1938). Like the other stunt players, Hightower was earning $55 a week, but he requested an increase in pay for doubling the title character in the film's climax. His dated Players Adjustment Memo was approved by Ed Killy.

"Principal photography was completed on October 15, 1938, after 104 working days, of which ten weeks were at the Lone Pine locations. The negative cost was $1,909,669.28— about a half-million over budget."[9]

Although William Faulkner had not been actively involved in the project for nearly two years, he chronicled some of the scenes in a typed memo dated October 4, 1938. In his random notes, Faulkner noted a scene which described an "elephant's shimmy" and another in which a big rock hits Higginbotham during the final battle. On the back of one of the pages, the writer made a note in his own hand about shots #301 (Din blows the bugle) through #328 (end).[10]

A revised 194-page script, dated October 25, 1938, appeared to be the final screenplay. An accompanying cover page with the words "all changes," and dated October 27, seemed to clarify the script's "final" status. However, two days later, RKO staffer William Koenig read an edited 188-page version, and summed it up in a memo: "When one of three close friends, all Sergeants in the British army in India, is captured by native fanatics, his friends go after him. Eventually, it is the heroism of a native water-carrier that saves the lives of all three and the rest of the regiment as well. One of the Sergeants who had meant to leave the army and marry, changes his mind and reenlists to stay with his pals."

On November 18, 1938, *Gunga Din's* Dialogue Continuity, primarily a transcript of lines spoken in the film, noted that the motion picture was contained in nineteen reels totaling 14,074 feet of film, which ran for two hours, thirty-six minutes, and twenty-three and one-third seconds. However, the document noted that Reel Five was eliminated and no status was given to Reel Eleven. Editing would reduce the number of reels.

As *Gunga Din* approached its completion, another British-in-India period film debuted in November: Republic Pictures' *Storm Over Bengal* (1938). The Sidney Salkow-directed film about the fight between the British and rebellious Indian tribesmen was seemingly capitalizing on *Gunga Din's* advance promotional press. Coincidentally, the film included a few early *Gunga Din* script elements (the primary Indian antagonist is called Khan, a British soldier disguises himself as an Indian holy man and later blows up the Khan's ammunition supply, and another soldier sacrifices himself to save the regiment from an ambush), and featured a musical score that would earn a Best Music Scoring Oscar. However, the film's story line was set in the twentieth century and included sequences featuring aircraft of the Royal Air Force. Emphasizing its *Lives of a Bengal Lancer-Gunga Din* connection, the B-movie production's main poster substituted mounted lancers instead of the airplanes.

The RKO publicity department provided magazines and newspapers across the country with the latest *Gunga Din* news. The *Richmond Times-Dispatch* published a large article, complete with an illustration of the film's major sets, in its November 29, 1938 issue. The article, written by Edith Lindeman, overestimated the price of the gold-leaf on the temple by $1,000 and incorrectly stated that the wooden bridge that Cutter and Din first cross was actually constructed over "a formidable chasm." The studio's publicity department, no doubt, must have loved the article.

The *Independent Exhibitor's Film Bulletin* reported that the film's post-production was slightly ahead of schedule and stated that *Gunga Din* would open on Christmas day, 1938. However, the trade publication's report was inaccurate. Post-production had yet to commence; as a matter of fact, additional scenes were filmed—although without sound—at RKO's Lake Sherwood property, which was also known as Set 20. This exterior Tantrapur river location was used to depict the fighting between the British troops and the Thugs after MacChesney commanded his men to "get to the river." In the existing footage, there is no transitional scene showing the Sepoys boarding the inflated bullock hides,

only a long shot of them on the makeshift devices as the three sergeants jump into the water. No cast members were involved in the multi-date shoot, which was completed on December 6, 1938, under the direction of Syd Fogel. The call sheet noted that lunch would be provided for seventy-five crew members and background performers.

The primary post-production tasks included breaking down the tent city; returning the equipment, costumes, props, weapons, and animals; editing the footage; and scoring the film. The sets, however, remained. "The fantastic sets of *Gunga Din* will not be forgotten," reported the *Richmond Times-Dispatch*. "The present plan is for Lone Pine business men to purchase the three big movie sets from the studio at salvage prices, keep them in repair, station guides at each, and publicize their locality to America's touring millions as the 'Home of *Gunga Din*,'"[11]

Lone Pine entrepreneur-rancher and veteran film liaison Russ Spainhower became the primary "business man" in the area. He hired some locals to remove portions of the Muri, Tantrapur, and temple sets and establish them on his nearby property, Anchor Ranch, where he created a mission-hacienda movie set. Spainhower also had another property, the Lucas Ranch, which had been used since the early 1920s for a number of Western films.

In 1947, a false-front Western town was built next to Spainhower's mission-hacienda set. The site was renamed "Anchorville" and served as the site of numerous productions. Unfortunately, Anchor Ranch's majestic backgrounds were not extensively used by TV studios in the 1950s, because the small-screen Westerns were produced primarily on Hollywood soundstages and outdoor properties closer to Los Angeles. "The last picture

Russ Spainhower worked on was *From Hell to Texas* (1958)," just a year after *Gunga Din's* re-release in theaters.[12] "Anchorville" was eventually abandoned and fell into disrepair. The mission-hacienda part of the set lasted longer, but was eventually removed in 1975.

Henry Berman and his team did a masterful job editing *Gunga Din*, especially the battle sequences during the fight at Tantrapur and the attack on the temple. In particular, the cutting during Gunga Din's climb to the top of temple while the soldiers advanced and the Thugs waited was particularly suspenseful.

Max Steiner, who had composed numerous memorable scores for RKO, including *King Kong* (1933), *The Lost Patrol* (1934), and *The Informer* (1935), which earned him an Oscar for Best Music, Score, would have probably been the studio's first choice for composing *Gunga Din's* music. However, Steiner left the studio in 1937, and moved to Warner Bros, where he maintained his busy schedule; in fact, he helped create music for over a dozen films in 1938.

RKO considered Erich Wolfgang Korngold, who was also at Warner Bros. The talented composer's resume included four Errol Flynn films: *Captain Blood* (1935), *The Prince and the Pauper* (1937), *Another Dawn* (1937), and *The Adventures of Robin Hood* (1938). Korngold originally declined to work on *The Adventures of Robin Hood* because of time concerns and his disapproval of the film's story. "Robin Hood is no picture for me," said Korngold. "I have no relation to it and therefore cannot produce any music for it. I am a musician of the heart, of passions and psychology; I am not a musical illustrator for a 90% action picture." However, Leo Forbstein, the head of Warner Bros.' music department, convinced him to score the film with the promise of giving him a flexible time schedule.[13] Despite his initial reluctance to score the motion picture, Korngold composed *The Adventures of Robin Hood* soundtrack and won a Best Original Score Oscar for it.

RKO approached Korngold without knowing about the composer's time requirements. "The deal was made, but when Korngold learned he would have only three weeks to compose and record a score with the scope of a symphony, he refused the job." [14] According to film historian Rudy Behlmer, George Korngold, the composer's son, said that his father "did compose a theme for the water carrier before seeing the film."[15]

RKO was eager to finish the film and needed a composer who could work fast. On December 7, 1938, *Variety* announced that Alfred Newman "resigned after nine years as head of Samuel Goldwyn's music department."[16] During his years with MGM, he had also created a number of scores for other studios, including United Artists' *The Count of Monte Christo* (1934) and 20th Century Fox's *Island in the Sky* (1938). He also created 20th Century Fox's signature opening fanfare theme in 1933. Among Newman's film scores were two that were set in India: *Clive of India* (1935) and *Wee Willie Winkie* (1937). Newman was nominated for two Oscars, *The Hurricane* (1937) and *The Prisoner of Zenda* (1937), and won the Best Music, Scoring Academy Award for *Alexander's Ragtime Band* (1938).

The New York Times stated that "RKO has borrowed Alfred Newman from United Artists to prepare the music score for *Gunga Din*." The timing couldn't have been better for RKO, which hired him on November 25, 1938.[17] For *Gunga Din*, Newman utilized the orchestration skills of Robert Russell Bennett,

Edward B. Powell, Conrad Salinger, and a 32-piece orchestra, which delivered a wonderfully diverse score of melodramatic moments, rhythmic action sequences, sentimental passages, and stirring thematic refrains. Newman also successfully integrated original Scottish bagpipe tunes, which were recorded outdoors at Bronson Canyon, within his score.

"The score has two basic themes," wrote film historian Tony Thomas. The first is the sprightly tune for the rollicking sergeants and the second is the more reflective and rather poignant theme for the brave water-boy."[18]

Within the few weeks he had to complete the score, Newman worked tirelessly, examining every frame of film and creating appropriate musical passages for each dramatic moment.[19] RKO also contracted forty singers, a voice coach and supervisor, a rehearsal pianist, and a drummer for additional musical parts. On December 29, 1938, RKO hired thirty-five musicians, at $50 each, to travel to a designated location for supplemental music. Newman's completed score was superb and helped elevate the film's status among the other great motion pictures of the year.

At the end of the year, *Independent Exhibitor's Film Bulletin* added *Gunga Din* to its "Recently Completed" roster. RKO began making prints of the film for distribution worldwide.

Upon its completion, *Gunga Din* included twelve reels of film totaling 10,523 feet and 119 minutes.[20] The film was previewed at three theater locations in the Los Angeles area: Whittier, Huntington Park, and Englewood. "*Gunga Din* preview drew a brilliant gathering, most striking couple being Irene Castle on Antonio Moreno's arm," stated *The Hollywood Reporter*.[21] Audience responses were favorable enough for Stevens, who only clipped a few of the final battle scene shots.

One sequence, which ended up on the cutting room floor, featured a mounted Higginbotham being hit on the head with a rock as he awkwardly ordered the Thugs to surrender. Stuntman Horace Brown doubled for Robert Coote in the scene. "At the preview, the audiences roared at it," said Sayre. "The squashing of Higginbotham was immediately followed by the solemn and gulpy funeral of Gunga Din. But the previewers never heard a word because they were still roaring at the squashing. Guess which sequence won out."[22]

A number of post-release previews were held at various theaters throughout the country and some involved RKO publicity personnel. At Charleston, South Carolina's Gloria Theater on March 11, 1939, Charles Levy of the RKO publicity department supervised the showing, which included the distribution of feedback cards. "Seventy-nine persons marked the picture excellent, nineteen said that it was good and one woman gave this reply: 'War is hell, and I don't like war. That's why I didn't like this picture.'"[23] A number of movie theaters, like Dallas' Melrose Theater on May 13, 1939, simply ran *Gunga Din* as a late night preview a day before the film began its scheduled run.

Joel Sayre was satisfied with the film and described it as a "Three Musketeers-One for All type of epic."[24] For his efforts, Sayre was paid $14,750 (through September 3, 1938); Fred Guiol received $7,400 (through September 3, 1938). Past payments for *Gunga Din's* writers went to William Faulkner ($5,166.67), Lester Cohen ($16,750), John Colton ($2,975), Ben Hecht and Charles MacArthur ($40,000), Vincent Lawrence ($2,000), Dudley Nichols ($9,208), and Anthony Veiller ($4,583.33).[25]

Over five years had passed since *The Film Daily* reported that *Gunga Din* was going to be produced by Reliance for United Artists release—and a decade had gone by since MGM expressed interest in the project. Nevertheless, despite changes in studios, directors, writers, and casting, the RKO film was finally ready for its release.

Chapter Thirteen Notes

1. Turner, "The Making of Gunga Din," 962.

2. Weather Source Weather Warehouse Online Past Monthly Weather Data for Lone Pine, California, September and October, 1903-2016.

3. *Modern Screen*, September, 1940, 87.

4. Harris, *Cary Grant*, 91.

5. Fontaine, *No Bed of Roses*, 41.

6. Sayre Papers, "You're Better Than I Am," 8.

7. Lorrance, *Sam Jaffe*, 183.

8. Fairbanks, Jr., *The Salad Days*, 1988, 284.

9. Turner, "The Making of Gunga Din," 962. The principals' biographers provided different shooting day totals: 108 days (Lorrance, *Sam Jaffe*), 104 days (Harris, *Cary Grant* and Wansell, *Haunted Idol*), 114 days (Eliot, *Cary Grant*) and 115 days (Higham and Moseley, *Cary Grant*). Another source noted that principal photography was completed on October 19, 1938.

10. Notes and Screen Treatments by William Faulkner.

11. *Richmond Times-Dispatch*, November 29, 1938, 9.

12. Dave Holland, *On Location in Lone Pine: A Pictorial Guide to Movies Shot in and Around California's Alabama Hills*, (Santa Clarita, California: Holland House, 2005), 23.

13. Behlmer, *Behind the Scenes*, 84. Korngold was later nominated for two Academy Awards for two other Flynn films: *The Private Lives of Elizabeth and Essex* (1939) and *The Sea Hawk* (1940).

14. Turner, "The Making of Gunga Din," 963. Max Steiner composed the *King Kong* (1933) soundtrack in less than two weeks.

15. Behlmer, *Behind the Scenes*, 99.

16. *Variety*, December 7, 1938, 13.

17. Behlmer, *Behind the Scenes*, 99.

18. *Historical Romances: The Charge of the Light Brigade – Gunga Din – Devotion*, Potsdam, Germany: HNH International Ltd., 1995, 4.

19. RKO Studio Records, Music Files, Boxes #107M, 108M, 109M, and 252M.

20. *The Kinematograph Year Book of 1940* stated that *Gunga Din's* film length was 10,202 feet. *Motion Picture Herald* (January 28, 1939) stated that the film's screen time was 135 minutes; *Harrison's Reports* (February 4. 1939) indicated the screen time was 116 minutes.

21. *The Hollywood Reporter*, January 26, 1939, 1. The publication did not identify which of the three theaters the couple appeared at.

22. *Evening Star* (Washington D. C.), November 19, 1972, 86.

23. *Charleston News and Courier*, March 12, 1939, 10. A day earlier the newspaper incorrectly reported that "England was chosen as location for the movie at first."

24. Sayre Papers, "You're Better Than I Am," 2.

25. RKO Studio Records, "Labor and Material." On the same page were two interesting expense entries: "H. Hawks Expenses to New York" ($4,449.31) and "H. Hawks Secretary" ($1,579.49). It appears that RKO still maintained a relationship of sorts, or an outstanding obligation, with its former *Gunga Din* director.

CHAPTER FOURTEEN
The Completed Film

Following the iconic image of the RKO radio tower and the sound of its pulsating Morse Code delivery, *Gunga Din's* opening credit sequence begins in a dramatic and original way. The first shot centers upon the Victoria Memorial in London. Alfred Newman's score quickly segues from the opening bars of The British National Anthem ("God Save the Queen") to a poignant strings-led orchestral piece as a row of unfurled British regimental flags pass the camera. On the audio track, an uncredited Montagu Love reads an edited-for-clarity passage from *Gunga Din*: "Now in India's sunny clime, where I used to spend my time a-servin' of 'Er Majesty the Queen. Of all them black-faced crew, the finest man I knew was our regimental *bhisti* . . . ." Immediately, Newman's score rises as the film's title appears on a giant gong.

A native Hindu, dressed only in minimal clothing and a turban, wields a mallet against the gong. Each time he strikes it, the credits appear and subsequently disappear in a series of dissolves. According to studio documents, the man was paid $71 for his services. The rippling shimmering effect of the metal gong's vibrations is vivid and "strongly resemble[s] the later trademark of J. Arthur Rank Productions: a muscular man striking a large gong. Optical photography expert Lin Dunn, ASC, created the effect by reflecting the title letters in a pan of mercury."[1] Years later, Stevens had second thoughts about the opening sequence. Instead of the man's multiple gong hits, Stevens would have "let him hit it once,

bring the other titles in and let him hit it the last time, once for the director, of course, and then get on with it."[2]

As Newman's main theme plays, the opening credits read as follows on the big screen:

RKO
RADIO PICTURES
PRESENTS
GUNGA
DIN

Starring
Cary Grant • Victor McLaglen
and
Douglas Fairbanks, Jr.

with
SAM JAFFE
EDUARDO CIANNELLI
JOAN FONTAINE
MONTAGU LOVE
ROBERT COOTE
ABNER BIBERMAN

PANDRO S. BERMAN
IN CHARGE OF PRODUCTION

SCREEN PLAY BY
JOEL SAYRE & FRED GUIOL
•
STORY BY
BEN HECHT & CHARLES MacARTHUR
from
RUDYARD KIPLING'S POEM
GUNGA DIN

MUSIC BY
ALFRED NEWMAN

•

TECHNICAL ADVISORS
SIR ROBERT ERSKINE HOLLAND
CAPTAIN CLIVE MORGAN
SERGEANT MAJOR
WILLIAM BRIERS

Photographed by JOSEPH H. AUGUST ASC.
Art Director .. VAN NEST POLGLASE
Associate .... PERRY FERGUSON
Special Effects by VERNON L. WALKER
ASC.
Set Decorations .. DARRELL SILVERA
Gowns by ... EDWARD STEVENSON

Recorded by
JOHN E. TRIBBY & JAMES STEWART
Edited by
HENRY BERMAN & JOHN LOCKERT
Assistant Directors
EDWARD KILLY & DEWEY STARKEY

PRODUCED And DIRECTED
BY
GEORGE STEVENS

•

THOSE PORTIONS
OF THIS PICTURE DEALING
WITH THE WORSHIP
OF THE GODDESS KALI
ARE BASED ON
HISTORIC FACT

•

The ominous final credit panel provides the set up for the opening scene in the film (based upon the 188-page script of October 26, 1938): a vulture flies off the top of a tele-graph pole before Chota (Abner Biberman) climbs to the top of the pole and destroys a glass insulator with a pickaxe. Chota and his nefarious henchmen, posing as a group of innocent civilians seeking protection, soon join a small mounted British detail headed by Lieutenant Markham (Roland Varno).[3] That night, Chota and his followers strangle Markham and his men while they sleep.

Forty-eight hours later, at British military headquarters in Muri, Colonel Weed (Montagu Love) and Major Mitchell (Lumsden Hare) discuss Markham's failure to report his whereabouts. A telegrapher informs the officers that the telegraph wires are down.[4] Suddenly, a telegraph message comes through from Burgess House in Tantrapur, a small village fifteen miles north of the fort.

The scene shifts to Tantrapur, where a telegrapher is confronted by Chota and a pair of Thuggees. The messenger frantically sends an emergency signal. "Wire's gone dead, sir," says the telegrapher at headquarters. Meanwhile at Tantrapur, a large force of mounted Thuggees invades the town. Chaos erupts among the hapless civilian population. Although the script says "they run in terror," one fleeing woman and a young girl don't seem to be too frightened by the attack; in fact, they both display exciting smiles as they run past the camera.

Colonel Weed expresses concern and questions why the telegraph lines are down in the village. As he exits the telegrapher's room, the officer sees Sergeant Higginbotham (Robert Coote) and orders him to find sergeants MacChesney, Cutter, and Ballantine. Coote quickly establishes his character's priggish-ness and states that the three missing soldiers are on leave together, participating in an ill-advised "mysterious mission."

The first dozen pages of script—and the opening minutes of the film—are replete with suspense, drama, and mystery. However, Stevens alters the tone of the film in the next scene, when Higginbotham and a detachment of military police arrive at the nearby town bazaar and locate the three missing non-commissioned officers. With Newman's lively music setting a light-hearted adventurous mood, Higginbotham finds the trio engaged in a fistfight with a squad of Scottish Highlanders, who are conveniently being dropped out of a second floor window by MacChesney (McLaglen) and Ballantine (Fairbanks).

Inside the building, the two sergeants criticize Cutter (Cary Grant) for foolishly buying a treasure map. Cutter realizes that one of his kilted antagonists was the one who sold him the map, and promptly knocks him out. He holds the unconscious Scot over the window ledge. The final script included a line in which Cutter tells him, "Sell me a map, will you?" The scene was cut; however, the shot (minus Grant's dialogue) appears in one of the film's re-release trailers. Higginbotham commands Cutter, "Take your hands off that man!" Cutter literally obeys the order and drops the Highlander out of the window. The suspenseful mood of the opening scenes has been replaced with frivolity, humor, and a sense of style. Stevens is just getting started.

The scene establishes Cutter, MacChesney, and Ballantine as comrades-in-arms who are one for all and all for one—the Three Musketeers disguised as British Royal Engineers. A few pages of additional fisticuffs between the principals and the military police were cut from the film.

The next scene opens with Cutter, MacChesney, and Ballantine standing at attention in front of an angry Colonel Weed, who questions their behavior. Cutter explains that they unsuccessfully searched for a barge filled with emeralds, which had "sunk in the year 241." Several lines about an attack by Holy men against the sergeants were edited out of the scene. The no-nonsense commanding officer succinctly describes the characters: "Ballantine, a man of your intelligence. And MacChesney—at your age." Later, the script included a line in which MacChesney notes his twenty-two years of military service, but the dialogue never made it to the final print.

Cutter, clearly not a man of discriminating intelligence, justifies his purchase of the map by explaining that the precious stones were "the spoils of a maharajah." Weed dismisses his remarks with a gentle "thank you." Anticipating the inevitability of the colonel's punishment, the three prepare for the worse. "But fortunately for you," says Weed, "I need all three of you at Tantrapur." The three sergeants are relieved, particularly Ballantine.

A scene involving the three sergeants discussing Ballantine's letter writing and another sequence, which included Ballantine, Emmy Stebbins (Joan Fontaine), and her father (Cecil Kellaway), were eliminated. In another cut scene, Emmy questions her fiancé about the Tantrapur mission, his upcoming retirement from military service, marriage, and future employment in the tea business. In the omitted scene, Emmy presents Ballantine with a bowler hat, a symbol of his upcoming civilian status. The scene was apparently sacrificed because Stevens wanted to pick up the pace.

The next scene shows the three mounted sergeants leading an infantry work detail out of the fort. The camera follows the column of soldiers as they march by and focuses on the

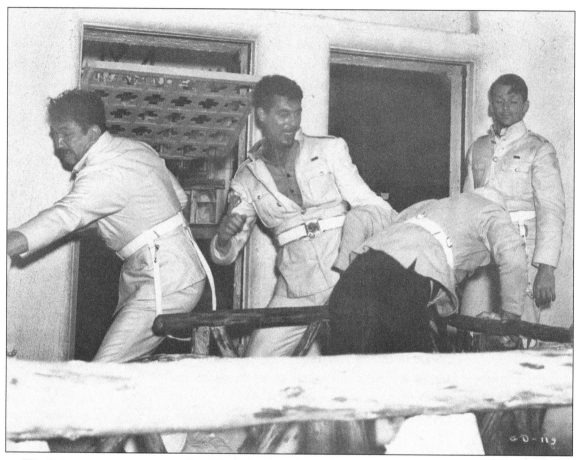

The fight over a treasure map. (L to R): Victor McLaglen, Cary Grant, Douglas Fairbanks, Jr. ©RKO.
Author's collection.

handful of *bhistis* who trail the group. The last water carrier becomes the camera's character of interest, and Newman's score—with its signature eleven-note "Gunga Din" melody—associates a melodic tone of humility with the unidentified Hindu.

The soldiers arrive at the seemingly abandoned mountain village, which is brilliantly displayed on the screen in bold contrasting shades, courtesy of August's cinematic skills. A vulture flies away as the group advances. Cutter, MacChesney, and Ballantine enter the officers' quarters and find a dining table filled with untouched cold and stale food. Cutter removes a pickaxe that had been thrust into a wall map of India.

MacChesney orders ten men to stand guard duty while the rest are assigned to repair the telegraph poles and wires. As the men toil in the hot sun, some call out for Gunga Din (Sam Jaffe), who promptly brings his water-filled gourd to them. The *bhisti* says nothing as Newman's simple but poignant melody underscores the scene. Some of the Hindu soldiers' dialogue doesn't match their respective mouth movements. It's the first of a few minor technical goofs in the film.

"I couldn't find a trail or a single footprint leading in or out," says Cutter to MacChesney. Ballantine explores the town. He walks down the main street, but fails to see an armed Thug crawling on a nearby rooftop. Ballantine looks at one of his guards who is positioned on another rooftop. As the sergeant turns and walks away, a Thug places a strangling cloth around the guard's neck and pulls him out of sight. A superb deep-focus camera shot of Cutter at street level and a guard, positioned atop a nearby hillside, suggests that all is well, but Grant's character doesn't see the sentinel get strangled by another Thug.

Ballantine enters another building and sees Chota exiting a room. "The village isn't quite deserted," quips Ballantine. Chota identifies himself as Pandoo Lal, "a miserable seller of trinkets," and explains that a raiding band of dacoits, which had attacked Tantrapur the night before, has taken his wife and six children.

The sergeant enters the room and discovers six adult Hindu men. "Well, the children are looking bonney," he says, and orders them out of the room. One of the men, armed with a strangling cloth, follows Ballantine and attacks him. The sergeant quickly flips him over. It's not the smoothest transitional edit, though, since the Thug is already being tossed before Ballantine gets a proper grip on him.

Ballantine begins fighting all of them. Outside, Cutter hears the commotion. Newman's rollicking score begins and quickly builds. Cutter walks in nonchalantly, shakes his head back and forth as if to suggest that what he sees is nothing more than child's play, and promptly joins the fight.

MacChesney walks in and casually joins the mayhem. After one Thug escapes by diving through a window, MacChesney quickly subdues Chota with an arm twist. With the fight over, the senior sergeant asks about the identities of the "playful subjects." Ballantine says that "toad face"—Chota—is their leader.

Taken outside, MacChesney interrogates Chota, but the prisoner is an unwilling participant. Ballantine, who understands Hindustani, questions Chota, who responds in his native language with several "I don't know" replies. (Ballantine's mastery of the language originated in Hecht and MacArthur's March 24, 1937 script.) MacChesney informs Chota that he and his men will be taken back to the outpost at Muri. Chota stands firm and informs his captors—in English—that he will not accompany them. Chota begins to chant "Kali!" "You will never leave here," threatens the Thug leader. "Already your graves are dug." Chota continues to chant, and voices from afar join him. It's an eerie moment.

The sergeants escort their captives away, but a Thug on a roof fires his rifle and hits one of the enlisted men in the leg. At that moment, Newman's score shifts into high gear as one of filmdom's all-time great street battles begins.[5]

Thug riflemen fire from atop buildings as hand-to-hand struggles erupt in the street, but Cutter, MacChesney, and Ballantine remain cool and in charge. MacChesney holds a Thug in a headlock, and yells out a command to "form a square," an inappropriate order that would have resulted in greater casualties in a closed street fight. Somehow, the advisers missed this military error in the script. MacCheshey punches the Thug, and the battle continues. Cutter throws a pickaxe at Chota, but he catches it and promptly charges the sergeant; Cutter delivers an effective uppercut and takes the weapon away from his adversary.

A three-man hand-to-hand stunt sequence, which was seemingly inspired by Hermes Pan, Fred Astaire's legendary choreographer at RKO, develops as Ballantine delivers a salvo of blows to a Thug. Instantaneously, Ballantine pulls the man back by his own garment and finishes him off with an uppercut. Another attacker closes in on Ballantine, but the inventive soldier sets him up with a jab. Ballantine pulls the first Thug back again and promptly tosses him over his shoulder on top of the second Thug. Without skipping a beat, Ballantine shoots a Thug off the top of a nearby roof. It's martial Terpsichorean brilliance, and more is on the way—but on a bigger scale.

"It all has to do with this choreography of a fist fight in which everything worked and all the punches are valid and the right people are hit and laid unconscious and the other people stand upright no matter how the blows are," explained Stevens. "That's part of the pageant of this film at this time."[6]

The battle escalates. Dozens of mounted Thugs gallop toward the town and join the fight. A few loyal Hindu soldiers are stranded atop the telegraph poles, but their expected fate is never seen. Greatly outnumbered, the British detachment reforms and makes a stand in a courtyard. MacChesney orders everyone to the rooftop. As the rugged sergeant is being lifted to the roof, a Thug attempts to shoot him, but Ballantine promptly shoots the attacker. A smiling and caring Gunga Din, who has miraculously survived the fight, gives a drink of water to the wounded Thug.

Ballantine jumps down to a wagon and shoots open a box of dynamite. He tosses the dynamite sticks up to Cutter, who conveniently places them in his tunic pockets. The fight gets more destructive as Cutter throws ignited dynamite sticks against the Thugs. One scene features a non-congruent edit in which Cutter's hands appear in two different positions against a wall as he waits for a stick to explode.

The battle gets more exciting, when the three sergeants initiate a counter attack on the rooftops. "Charge!" shouts MacChesney. A camera shadow can be seen on Cutter at the beginning of the charge, but it's another minor flaw. The surprised Thugs stop, turn, and run for their lives. During the charge, Gunga Din gives a wounded soldier a drink. It's a spectacular scene, marvelously composed by Stevens, and Newman's spirited score provides the perfect musical backdrop.

The fight continues as dispatched Thugs roll off the slanted roof tops. Ballantine takes on four Thugs and escapes by jumping to another building, but his left leg goes through the roof and gets caught—just as one of Cutter's dynamite sticks is about to explode near him. Ballantine tries to reach the ignited explosive with his sword but he can't quite get to it. Cutter leaps to his friend's aid and knocks the stick down a flight of stairs. A Thug picks up the dynamite stick and prepares to throw it back, but MacChesney quickly shoots him, and the dynamite explodes in the attacker's hand. It's another outstanding scene.

The battle tempo continues its frantic pace. The remaining soldiers seek protection behind a short wall and continue to fight. A helmetless MacChesney attempts to retrieve his headgear, but a jump cut depicts him wearing it in the next shot. Gunga Din emerges from seemingly nowhere and offers a drink to a surprised MacChesney. "You're a funny bloke, Din, but I'll admit, you're a good *bhisti*," says the sergeant. "Could be first class soldier, sahib," replies Din, who holds a broken sword. "Don't make me laugh," shrugs MacChesney, who takes the weapon from Din. Stevens shot this scene two ways: once with Din standing below MacChesney and the other with him emerging behind the sergeant. The script included Din's explanation about three generations of his family who served as soldiers, but it was cut from the final print.

A fine use of miniatures is seen when Cutter pushes away a tall ladder filled with Thugs. MacChesney orders the soldiers on the ground to "get to the river." One quick camera shot reveals the modern-day tent city camp in the distance. The temporary camp for cast and crew will be seen again in the far background when the troops return to Tantrapur.

The surviving Indian soldiers seek an escape at the river's edge. According to RKO Studio Records, special safety instructions were provided to all who worked in the scene: "These men have to run down bank to river, jump on bullock hides [and] paddle out to middle of lake. Must know how to swim in case of tipping over."

Outnumbered, the soldiers and Gunga Din escape by jumping off a roof into the river below. Although RKO records indicate that stunt men were scheduled to "work on 100-foot tower" nothing indicates that they jumped into the water outfitted as the principals. Veteran stunt man Harvey Parry was offered $500 to fall 105 feet off a high cliff into a lake. "He noticed a man in a canoe paddling about the lake. Every time the paddle swept the water, mud appeared on the surface." Parry was concerned and dropped his life-sized, weighted dummy into the water, but it promptly disappeared into the lake's muddy bottom and never surfaced. "He turned down the job and held firm even when the studio doubled its offer."[7] The scene eventually utilized full-size dummies. However, during an interview years later, Stevens claimed that "they weren't really dummies, they were guys."[8] As the last figure hits the water, Newman concluded 300 memorable musical measures that marked the fight at Tantrapur.

Back on land, the decimated column (sans shoulder arms) marches back to Muri. Cutter questions Ballantine's mournful look and begins a conversation, but nearly half of the dialogue was eventually cut. "My time is up on May the fourteenth," notes Ballantine, about the upcoming end to his enlistment. "You can sign up for another nine years, can't you?" asks MacChesney.[9] "I'm leaving the service," states Ballantine. "I'm getting married and I'm going in the tea business." MacChesney and Cutter are astounded; they can't imagine what they have heard. The trio's ensuing debate is cut short as the detachment approaches the outpost.

They march into the fort as the pipers play a spirited version of "Bonnie Dundee," a classic Scottish tune written by Walter Scott in 1825. Stevens' elevated main camera, which casts a brief shadow at the bottom of the frame, opens up to view the enormous compound and its breathtaking lineup of hundreds of Highlanders, Hindu lancers, and support personnel. Newman's music track increases in volume. It's a majestic scene.

MacChesney reports, "Eight killed, three wounded." After the column is dismissed, the three sergeants report to Colonel Weed and Major Mitchell. The commander compares the pickaxe the men brought back with another one positioned on his wall and concludes that Thugs are responsible for the recent deaths and destruction.[10] MacChesney asks about the Thugs. "A murder cult Colonel Sleeman crushed fifty years ago," replies Weed. The scripted statement is accurate. Lord William Bentinck, the Governor-General of India from 1828 to 1835, appointed Colonel William Henry Sleeman to command the East India Company's Thuggee and Dacoity Department from 1835 to 1839. Sleeman became Commissioner for the Suppression of Thuggee and Dacoity in early 1839. During his tenure, British authorities crushed the murderous band. Based on the historical record and Colonel Weed's explanation, it appears that *Gunga Din* takes place in the late 1880s—although Hecht and MacArthur had set the film's story in 1880.

"Thugs were the most fiendish band of killers who ever existed," notes Mitchell. "There were at least 10,000 of them in India, and they murdered 30,000 people a year," explains Weed. "The order was religious and they worshiped Kali, the goddess of blood."[11]

Weed informs Mitchell that action must be taken to "stamp this out immediately," and the three sergeants get excited as they await their orders. Weed dismisses Ballantine since the sergeant's enlistment is about to expire. When Weed informs Cutter and MacChesney that Higginbotham will be their new companion in arms, the two cringe.

Outside, Cutter and MacChesney witness Ballantine and Emmy in an embrace; the soldiers wince. Stevens relies primarily on close-ups to depict both the affections shared by the betrothed couple and the disgust displayed by the sergeants. It's a splendid scene that recalls the plot of *The Front Page* (1931) in grand fashion. This scene originally contained more dialogue and was positioned to be placed before the aforementioned scene with the three sergeants, Colonel Weed, and Major Mitchell.

A high mounted camera shot positioned above the outpost's massive courtyard shows approximately 400 unmounted lancers participating in a drill. The group's martial choreography is being mimicked by Gunga Din, who carries a bugle. Cutter approaches the *bhisti.* Din sees the sergeant and recoils in embarrassment and humiliation. He drops the bugle and anticipates his punishment. However, Cutter orders him to attention as if he were a soldier. The *bhisti* slowly smiles, stands erect, and awaits the next command with gleefulness. "Thank you, sergeant," says Din. A couple of Cutter's lines, which too obviously suggested Din's ultimate fate and the film's climax, were cut: "Well, just keep at it Bugler, and some day you'll blow us all on to glory" and "I tell you, you save it for some time when things get really hot."

On the drill field, Colonel Weed orders the lancers to be drilled until sundown. The camera shifts back to Cutter, who questions the *bhisti* about how he acquired the bugle. "Please, sahib," pleads a worried Din, "I find when nobody looking." Cutter gently admonishes him for his "naughty" behavior. "Please, sahib, don't take away," asks Din. "Bugle only pleasure for poor *bhisti*." Cutter sympathizes with Din and hands the bugle back to him. Cutter assesses the nearby marathon drill session and decides to play a prank. He pretends to only command Din but shouts: "Company, dismissed!" The entire drill collapses and the guilty sergeant promptly exits the area. The script also included dialogue in which Cutter informs Din to be on the lookout for gold upon their return to Tantrapur, but the lines were eliminated.

The next scene is completely offbeat—a quirky, comedic, and touching moment involving MacChesney and Annie the elephant in the animal stalls. It appears that Annie isn't feeling well. MacChesney feels her forehead with his hand and then checks his own. It's obvious that this rough and tumble veteran soldier has a weak spot—and it weighs several tons and has a trunk. The animal's Hindu caretaker suggests that a powerful elixir may help the pachyderm, and the sergeant agrees that a "very old Indian remedy" be administered to the animal. Annie refuses to take the elixir from the handler. MacChesney interrupts with language that sounds as if he were talking to a baby. "Oh, I know you want your daddy to give it to you, don't you?" says MacChesney. However, Annie remains reluctant to consume the medicine.

Cutter enters and offers a suggestion: "Now, if daddy took a spoonful first himself baby might do a paddy cake for him." MacChesney likes the idea and makes believe that he is taking the elixir. The trick works. Annie opens wide and MacChesney delivers a tiny amount of the substance on a wooden spoon. Annie suddenly drops to the ground but quickly stabilizes herself, much to MacChesney's relief. Additional dialogue and action featured MacChesney chasing after the caretaker, but it was trimmed from the scene.

Higginbotham arrives and delivers betrothal dance invitations to the two sergeants. One of the invitations is addressed to Archibald Cutter, an amusing acknowledgment to Grant's real first name. A scene involving a conversation about "some theories on military matters" between the sergeants and Higginbotham was cut.

Later, the two sergeants, attired in their formal dress uniforms, which are adorned with impressive service decorations, eavesdrop on the engaged couple at the social gathering.[12] Ballantine notices them and dismisses the pair with a tall tale about MacChesney's leg being sawed off. Undeterred, the two sergeants have a plan: they want to delay the marriage by making Ballantine ill. The two carry out their stealthy idea in a wonderful scene in which Cutter empties the bottle of elephant elixir in a bowl of punch. Grant's delightful facial expressions provide yet another look at his evolving mastery of big-screen comedy. A scene in which Cutter tries to discard the empty bottle while dancing with Miss Fowler (Ann Evers) was eliminated.

The two sergeants want Ballantine to drink the punch, but their plan gets thwarted when Mr. Stebbins, Colonel Weed, and Major Mitchell arrive. The two officers approach the punch bowl, but MacChesney provides excuses for the quality of the punch. Unconvinced, Weed and Mitchell look to fill their cups, but MacChesney immediately places both of his hands in the bowl, searching for a make-believe fly, which might have contaminated the beverage. Disgusted and perplexed, the officers promptly walk away. This part of the scene was later removed from re-release prints and the version that initially aired on television decades later.

On the dance floor, Cutter and Fowler make a charming couple. Cutter gets an idea, excuses himself, approaches Higginbotham, and escorts him to the punch bowl. MacChesney asks about Ballantine's whereabouts. "Never mind that civilian," says Cutter. "I've got Bertie Higginbotham, his replacement." Cutter's eyebrows rise, and MacChesney understands; a new plan is underway. The two sergeants believe that if Higginbotham gets sick, Ballantine will be needed to fight the Thugs. With Ballantine back in the ranks, they reason, the wedding will not take place—or, at least, it might be delayed until they can implement another plan. Surprisingly, Higginbotham drinks the first glass without displaying any discomfort. Cutter glances behind Higginbotham as if to witness the impending effect. Higginbotham's second drink doubles him over and creates the necessary results.

The next day, Cutter and MacChesney arrive at a draper's shop in the bazaar where Ballantine and Emmy are shopping for curtains. MacChesney tells her that Ballantine is marching out to Tantrapur in twenty minutes. Emmy reminds them that Higginbotham is replacing her fiancé, but the two sergeants inform her that Ballantine's substitute has been hospitalized. Ballantine knows what's going on but he has to obey orders; however,

he threatens to knock their "heads together" when his enlistment expires in five days.

As Newman's score plays "The Barren Rocks of Aden," a traditional bagpipe tune, two large columns depart from the outpost at Muri. The three sergeants and their squad return to Tantrapur. At the deserted village, a disgruntled Ballantine drives the enlisted men in their tasks and scolds his fellow sergeants. A long tirade, delivered by Ballantine, was eliminated from the film.

Later, Ballantine reminds Cutter and MacChesney that his enlistment expires in twenty-four hours. "Cutter, we've got to do something," says MacChesney. Cutter, a bit drunk, suggests that they start a war by blowing up the Taj Mahal in order to keep Ballantine in the ranks. MacChesney rejects the outrageous idea, but Cutter offers another. "Three hours from where we're sitting by a secret trail there's a gold temple waiting to be sliced away and carried off in a wheelbarrow," says Cutter, who credits Gunga Din as the source of the information. MacChesney has heard this before. Cutter suggests that when Ballantine sees the gold he will forget marriage and the tea business. MacChesney is rapidly losing his patience. He threatens Cutter, who reacts by throwing shadow box punches at his comrade. MacChesney promptly knocks him out with an uppercut and sends him to the village jail. A number of shots were also edited out of this scene when the film was re-released.

Gunga Din visits Cutter in the jail and tells him that he has seen the gold temple again. Cutter gets excited and asks Din to help him escape. Din promptly brings Annie who destroys the jail. Cutter and Din flee on Annie's back.

"I spent hours on Annie," said Grant, years later. "She was a wonderful elephant. I even

The Bridge to the Temple. Courtesy of Juan Perez Collection, National Park Service, USS Arizona Memorial.

had my lunch pitched up to me because it was so damn difficult to get down off that blinking thing."[13]

Guards inform MacChesney about Annie's alleged kidnapping, and the sergeant, believing Thugs took her, immediately sets out to rescue the animal. However, Ballantine assumes that this activity is just another trick.

Cutter and Din reach an old wooden suspension bridge and dismount. "In the scene with the elephant, we crossed a very shaky bridge and we wondered whether the whole thing would topple down," recalled Jaffe.[14] Out of the camera's view, the two ends of the bridge were set in concrete bases, and a temporary ramp was situated next to one end of the elevated structure in order for Annie to walk upon it. Elephant trainer Barlow Simpson, who was close by, made sure Annie didn't take any unnecessary destructive steps. Although the actual bridge was only about ten feet above the ground at its lowest point, a superb matte shot created by Vernon Walker depicts a deep chasm with a river flowing several hundred feet below. Despite Annie's attempt to follow, Cutter and Din manage to cross the bridge. Fortunately, this scene was considerably edited because it contained too much Laurel and Hardy-like confusion on the bridge, and it still included a non-matching soundtrack moment with Cutter moaning in fear.

The pair view the gold temple and enter the structure after they see a long line of torch bearers heading toward them. Hiding behind a large stone column, Cutter and Din witness a Thuggee initiation rite supervised by the Guru (Eduardo Ciannelli), whose fanatical induction speech creates a frenzy. "Rise our new-made brothers," commands the Guru, whose menacing countenance is accentuated

by torch light. "Rise and kill. Kill lest you be killed yourselves! Kill for the love of killing! Kill for the love of Kali! Kill! Kill! Kill!" Newman underscores each of the Guru's final words with orchestral bursts which make the cult leader seem even more ominous. At the same time, Stevens emphasizes the Guru's intensity with a close-up of the character's threatening eyes, which almost seem to glow.

"The colonel's got to know," whispers Cutter to Din. However, the two can't escape; Thugs are everywhere. Cutter slips behind a column and strangles a Thug. He gives Din part of the dead man's garment, but the disguised *bhisti's* path is blocked. Cutter boldly clears a way out for Din when he walks into the center of the temple and begins singing "The Roast Beef of Old England," an early seventeenth century English patriotic ballad, written by Henry Fielding. While the Thugs gather around Cutter, Din escapes.

Brought before the Guru, Cutter, with hands on hips, confidently states, "You're all under arrest." Chota appears and Cutter calls him "young toad face." The Guru is incensed and demands that Cutter "grovel" before his son. When Cutter refuses, the Thug leader orders him to be taken away and tortured.

The next scene shows Higginbotham and Emmy on the road to Tantrapur, where they meet MacChesney and Ballantine. Higginbotham says that he is ready to replace Ballantine, and Emmy presents MacChesney with her fiancé's discharge papers. The group returns to Tantrapur, where Gunga Din is standing next to Annie. Din admits that he helped Cutter escape with Annie. MacChesney orders a firing squad to execute Din. "You lazarushian beggar!" shouts the sergeant. Ballantine intervenes, and Din explains what happened to him and Cutter. Once informed, MacChesney prepares to depart alone in the rescue operation, but Ballantine wants to join him. It's obvious to Emmy that her relationship with her fiancé isn't as strong as she had hoped. The senior sergeant reminds Ballantine that his service to Her Majesty is "over and done with." MacChesney delivers a sarcastic farewell to Ballantine: "I'm saying goodbye, Ball, and I wish you luck in the tea business and your matrimony both."

Ballantine insists on joining the rescue effort, but MacChesney tells him that he cannot—unless he signs a reenlistment form. Ballantine is suspicious. MacChesney assures him that once Cutter is rescued the document will be destroyed. Ballantine reluctantly agrees but demands to hold on to the paper. As Ballantine signs the document, MacChesney's plotting Cheshire cat-like grin fills the scene with a unique charm that underscores his devious scheme and the respect he holds for his friend.

Ballantine informs Emmy about the rescue effort, but she protests: "Why don't you come right out and say you don't want to get married?" Ballantine assures her that he loves her very much, but states that he won't "run out on his friends when they're in danger." Ballantine, MacChesney, and Din ride off. Surprisingly, the prop crew allowed Fairbanks and McLaglen to depart wearing empty cartridge belts.

The three men cross the bridge, approach the temple, and pause to look around. The camera focuses on Ballantine, and then circles around to MacChesney. It's a captivating shot that shows the false tranquility of the area. They enter the temple but are immediately surrounded by Thugs. MacChesney blames Din: "Why didn't you tell me they was Thugs?"

Surprisingly, Din asserts himself and criticizes MacChesney's "roarings." The trio is promptly imprisoned with Cutter, who is shackled to a column inside a large chamber. The Guru, Chota, and some armed henchmen enter the area and prepare to sacrifice "three soldiers and a slave." Din steps forward and proudly states: "Who is slave? I am a soldier, too, please!" "You're what?" responds MacChesney. "Well, regimental *bhisti*," replies Din meekly. Din's brief confrontation with MacChesney and his claim of being a soldier represents an indication of his inner strength, a condition that will soon manifest itself.

MacChesney and Cutter engage in a verbal argument about their situation. MacChesney calls Cutter a "white-livered elephant stealing treasure hunter." Cutter calls him a coward who hid "behind . . . telegraph poles." Although they both face death, each one wants to blame the other for the predicament that they are in. The animosity disappears when the whip wounds on Cutter's back are revealed (a crew member, just out of frame, gently pulls the sergeant's tunic off of his shoulders).

When MacChesney refuses to reveal information about the British forces to his captors, the Guru orders that he be whipped. Despite several lashings, MacChesney remains steadfast. MacChesney is escorted to the edge of a snake pit, which is filled with real creatures and rubber impostors. One imitation reptile on a string can be easily spotted. MacChesney appears to crumble at the thought of falling in the pit and agrees to tell the Guru about British Army troop movements. MacChesney tells the Thug leader that the information he seeks is located in Ballantine's tunic pocket. However, the alleged information is nothing more than Ballantine's reenlistment document.

MacChesney quickly secures the paper after using it as a ploy to capture the Guru.

MacChesney, Ballantine, and the Guru climb to the top landing of the temple. Gun shots are immediately fired at them from below and from the nearby hillsides; the soldiers duck for cover. However, the Guru stands, knowing that his men will not fire at him. By the time Cutter and Din emerge from below, the scene is noticeably an indoor set. Furthermore, the bullet holes don't match up from the previous shot, and the rocky hillside soundstage backdrop appears flat and lifeless.

Cutter is elated that the gold stands before him. The five remain atop the temple through the night. At sunrise, MacChesney offers to free the Guru if the Thug leader will allow them to get safely to the bridge. The Guru refuses. Later, Cutter and MacChesney, exhausted from a lack of sleep and water, lose their composure and threaten each other over the topic of gold. In this brief exchange, which was filmed in a tight close-up, Grant displays an animosity that is dramatically unnerving. "Preserve your courage, gentlemen," says the Thug leader. "You are not forgotten. They will come to save you."

The Guru sees the approaching British column. "Two come to rescue one and the others follow," he says. The Guru speaks about Chandragupta Maurya, the ancient Indian emperor, and then explains his plan to destroy Colonel Weed's command.[15] The Guru confronts his captors with a feverish speech, "I see it in your faces: who is this ugly little savage to snarl so boldly at the British lion?" Cutter calls him mad. "Mad?" replies the Guru. "Hannibal was mad. Caesar was mad. And Napoleon surely was the maddest of the lot. Ever since time began they've called mad all the great soldiers in this world. Mad? We shall see what wisdom

lies within my madness." It's another powerful delivery by Ciannelli.

The Guru yells commands to his followers below, but the sergeants threaten to kill him if the Thugs march to their battle positions. The Guru escapes and runs down to the edge of the snake bit where he delivers a poignant message to his captors: "You have sworn as soldiers if need be to die for your faith which is your country, your England. Well, India is my country and my faith and I can die for my faith and my country as readily as you for yours. Go Chota. India, farewell." His delivery seems hardly the message of a bloodthirsty fanatic; in fact, he sounds more like a moderate politician attempting to win over the other side.

The Guru leaps into the snake pit; Chota, who makes an amazingly fast run from the temple's grounds to the area outside the chamber, screams in agony. A Thug fires a rifle through an opening in the door and the gunshot hits Cutter in the leg. The Thug is accused of warning the approaching soldiers and is promptly strangled, although in the script, Chota stabs the Thug. A wounded Cutter nearly falls into the snake pit but is caught by his comrades.

They realize they have to return to the tower level in order to warn the oncoming British column, but several Thugs—one of whom conveniently carries a bugle—have already climbed to the lookout area and block the path at the top of the stairs. Ballantine shoots one of them and the Thug drops his rifle. Gunga Din picks up the weapon with its attached bayonet and charges up the stairs; the three sergeants follow and join the fight. Newman's pulsating orchestral score adds to the action. After Din bayonets a Thug, Cutter says "good work, soldier!" Din responds with

Victor McLaglen and Cary Grant inside the temple. © RKO. Author's collection.

Montagu Love (wearing helmet) looks on as Douglas Fairbanks, Jr. prepares for a scene inside the temple. © RKO. Author's collection.

Temple scene exterior on location. (L to R): Victor McLaglen, Douglas Fairbanks, Jr., Eduardo Ciannelli. ©RKO. Author's collection.

*Temple scene exterior on soundstage. (L to R): Cary Grant, Eduardo Ciannelli, Victor McLaglen, Douglas Fair-
banks, Jr., Sam Jaffe. ©RKO. Author's collection.*

an accomplished smile. "Thank you, sahib," says Din. But another Thug bayonets the *bhisti* in the back, and Din collapses. Cutter is clubbed and bayoneted (slightly warped parts of the mountain and sky backdrop are visible). MacChesney and Ballantine are overwhelmed. Chota has the two bound and gagged, and forces them to watch as their fellow British soldiers march towards their apparent doom.

The approaching infantry appear confident and relaxed; in fact, the men sing "Will Ye No Come Back Again," a traditional Scot song. Stevens had the original lyrics produced on a single-sided sheet of paper which were distributed to the background performers:

> Bonnie Charlie's now awa'
> Safely owre the friendly main
> Mony a heart will break in twa
> Should he ne'er come back again
> Will ye no come back again?
> Will ye no come back again?
> Better le-od ye canna be
> Will ye no come back again?

Newman arranged the music in the advance-to-the-temple scenes by alternating passages between the drums and pipers and the singing soldiers.[16] His simple but effective musical arrangement adds to the mounting tension and suspense in the next scenes.

Cutter hears the song, but is too weak from his wounds to act. Wounded but unguarded, Din tells Cutter, "The colonel's got to know." Stevens shifts the camera's view between shots of the approaching soldiers and the Thugs who await them. The expressive George Regas, who plays one of the Thug Chieftains, maintains an intense blood-lust expression as he anticipates the slaughter that is about to take place.

Din crawls to the dead Thug who had carried the bugle. He secures the instrument and begins his memorable climb to the top of the gold temple. Stevens uses two and one-half minutes of screen time, in twenty-seven shots, to trace Din's dramatic and suspenseful ascent to the top of the cupola:

Medium Shot (MS): Gunga Din retrieves bugle from dead Thug.

Close-Up (CU): Gunga Din with bugle.

Wide Shot (WS): View from top of temple towards mountain pass.

CU: Gunga Din with bugle crawls away.

MS: Chota and three Thugs restrain Ballantine and MacChesney.

MS: Gunga Din at base of temple tower.

CU: Gunga Din begins ascent.

CU: Cutter looks at Gunga Din.

MS: Gunga Din continues climb.

CU: Gunga Din continues climb.

CU: Cutter looks at Gunga Din.

WS: Thug forces in position.

CU: Cutter looks at Gunga Din.

MS: Gunga Din continues climb but nearly loses his grip.

MS: Cutter looks at Gunga Din.

WS: Thugs await four British advance scouts.

WS: Thugs strangle two other British advance scouts.

CU: Ballantine and MacChesney.

MS: Gunga Din's hands reach temple cupola's rim.

MS: Gunga Din reaches top (British troops in background).

CU: Gunga Din sees the approaching British.

MS: Six Thugs hide behind boulders.

WS: Dozens of Thugs hide behind boulders.

WS: Dozens of Thugs hide behind boulders.

CU: Gunga Din sees the Thugs about to fire.

WS: Thugs prepare to fire.

MS: Gunga Din blows bugle call.

The longest shot in the sequence—twenty-six seconds—is primarily devoted to a medium shot of Din's fingers as he grasps the ledge of the temple tower's gold rim. Despite almost losing his grip, Din manages to reach the top, which provides him a brief opportunity to be out of the Thugs' immediate reach.

Four advance Scots approach on one path, and in the next shot, two other soldiers are accosted by a pair of Thugs armed with strangling cloths. A careful examination of this shot shows that the second soldier fails to react to his comrade's assault before he is also taken down in a similar fashion.

The Thugs are seconds away from initiating their surprise attack on the British when Din stands and blows "Alarm," an actual bugle call "for troops to turn out under arms." For a moment, the Thugs are stunned in disbelief. Colonel Weed hears the call and orders his bugler to sound off. The British column immediately halts and reforms into counterattack units. The Guru's grand plan is collapsing, and Din is beyond the Thugs' grasp. The Thugs start shooting at Din, but he continues to sound his bugle call until he is fatally wounded and falls. His body rests among a pile of rubble caused by an artillery shot that had yet to be fired at the temple. Cutter says, "Good work, Bugler."

Newman's score shifts into a powerful piece of music that is stirring, energetic, and exciting. As Chota departs, he orders one of his men to chop the heads off MacChesney and Ballantine, but the Thug is shot by Cutter. The three avoid a cannon shot, which smashes into the temple, and then Ballantine shouts, "Mac, look! Here they come!" Stevens opens up the screen with an epic shot of the attacking Scots. Newman's score escalates again with rousing verve, beginning with strings and then expanding to full orchestration. It's a magnificent spectacle of sight and sound.

The vast battle scenes feature frames full of action. At times, nearly every rock seems to feature an armed antagonist. A handful of dummies dressed as Thugs fall from rock formations, and other artificial cultists are blown into the air as artillery casualties. "We used lots of dummies," said Stevens. "Where those rocks were in the battle scenes, wherever we had an area we were going to use, we'd arrange dummies on wires so that when the shooting was going on, every now and then, some bolt of gingham would fall off part of a rock cliff in the middle distance or background."[17]

Newman even manages to successfully integrate elephant-like sounds from his brass section into the score when the pachyderms appear transporting Gatling guns. In one masterful shot, two elephants exit the left side of the frame as the Gatling gun crews begin to fire against the Thugs. Six Scots quickly enter the frame behind the guns, providing an additional layer of action. The shot lasts a few seconds but it displays Stevens' skill as a director who has mastered the multi-dynamics of choreographed battle action.

Despite the seriousness of combat, Stevens injects a comedic scene in which MacChesney believes that Ballantine has been killed by an artillery shell. MacChesney seeks revenge by throwing large chunks of stone at the Thugs below. Almost immediately, Ballantine seemingly

British field camp. © RKO. Author's collection.

rises from the dead and joins in the rock throwing. Ballantine' dead possum act was just a ploy that allowed him to retrieve his reenlistment papers from MacChesney. It's another offbeat moment that works.

Stevens returns to the battle with a spectacular cavalry charge of the Indian lancers. The horsemen fill the entire screen in two successive attacking lines; the rock formations of the Alabama Hills provide the impressive backdrop. Newman adds the perfect martial orchestration to the scene as strings, woodwinds, brass, and percussion underscore the sounds of hundreds of hooves. Chota becomes one of the casualties when he is lanced in his chest.

The next scene shifts to the wooden suspension bridge. As a group of Highlanders approach, the structure's ropes snap and the suspended Thugs fall to their deaths—in a classic miniatures shot. The remaining Thugs surrender and the battle ends.

The film's final scene location is the British field camp at night. The bagpipers play a poignant "Lord Lovat's Lament," and a funeral pyre burns in the distance. Major Mitchell was scripted to deliver a prayer, but it was eliminated from the final print. A ceremonial firing squad performs at a grave.

Kipling (Reginald Sheffield) is featured in a close-up, writing something in his tent as Colonel Weed looks over the writer's shoulder. A restrained musical passage is heard. The two depart and walk to Gunga Din's body. MacChesney, Ballantine, and Cutter, recovering from his wounds, are already there. A *bhisti* stands nearby. A wounded Higginbotham, who was positioned on a stretcher, was edited from the final print. After Weed congratulates the sergeants for their "fine"

soldiering, Ballantine hands the officer his reenlistment papers. MacChesney exhibits a contented smile.

Weed looks at Din. "And here's a man whom the regiment will always be proud," he says. "According to regulations, he had no actual status as a soldier. But those of us who had the privilege of serving with him today know that ever a man deserved the name and rank of soldier it was he. So I'm going to appoint him a corporal in this regiment. His name will be written on the rolls of our honored dead."[18]

Weed fumbles for more words and asks Kipling for the document he had been writing. A bugle is heard playing "The Last Post (tatoo)," and the colonel begins reading the end of Kipling's epic poem as Newman's "Gunga Din" theme plays, "So I'll met him later on at the place where he is gone—where it's always double drill and no canteen. He'll be squatting on the coals, giving drink to poor damned souls and I'll get a swig in hell from Gunga Din."

Weed pauses and adds an emotional tone to his reading: "Yes, Din! Din! Din! You Lazarushian-leather Gunga Din! Though I've belted you an' flayed you, by the living God that made you. You're a better man than I am, Gunga Din! Newman interrupts his theme with an inclusion of "Auld Lang Syne," which raises the emotional level yet again.[19] A tearful Ballantine looks upward; MacChesney, shamed at how he mistreated Din, tries to hold back the tears; a teardrop falls from Cutter's eye. Gunga Din's body is carried towards the funeral pyre. Colonel Weed salutes the deceased *bhisti* with a poorly executed American hand salute, another action which seemingly missed the watchful eyes of the military advisors.

The scene shifts to another part of the camp, where a ceremonial pipe and drum unit plays "Pibroch of Donald Dhu," a splendid traditional jig. A faint image of Gunga Din in a soldier's uniform suddenly emerges as "Auld Lang Syne" augments the pipers' tune. The music builds and Din's appearance becomes clearer. He salutes—and then slowly smiles. His ghost-like image, content that he has become a "first class soldier," dissolves away until the end of the shot. It's one of the most moving and emotional film endings in Hollywood history.[20]

Chapter Fourteen Notes

1. Turner, *American Cinematographer*, 963. The RKO Studio Records indicate the payment for the gong-striking man.

2. *Dialogue on Film: George Stevens*, 9.

3. "[Thugs] commonly follow each other in small parties of ten or twenty. [When] the Thugs determine to attack a traveler, they usually propose to him, under the specious pleas of mutual safety, to travel together." Edward Thornton, *Illustrations of the History and Practices of the Thugs*, (William H. Allen and Company, London, 1837), 5, 7.

4. The telegraph became the essential communication device in British-held India. In 1854, sixteen years after Samuel F. B. Morse first demonstrated the telegraph to the public in Morristown, New Jersey, an officer stationed at Fort Murdan in India, marveled at the invention. "We are in an age of wonders," wrote Maj. W. S. R. Hodson in *Twelve Years of a Soldier's Life In India: Being Extracts from the Letters of Major W. S. R. Hodson* (Boston: Ticknor and Fields, 1860). "Ten months ago, there was not a telegraph in Hindostan [sic], yet the news which reached Bombay on the 27th of this month, was printed at Lahore, 1,200 miles from the coast, that same afternoon."

5. Newman's annotated sheet music for "Reel 3 – Battle Part 1" features sixty-three detailed notes in red pen which designated such specific on-screen actions as "man grabs leg," "falling," "soldiers and prisoners march," and "fighting," and 180 measures of accompanying orchestration.

6. *Dialogue on Film: George Stevens*, 9.

7. *Milwaukee Journal Sentinel*, April 23, 1939, 83.

8. *Dialogue on Film: George Stevens*, 13.

9. According to The Kipling Society: "For the period covered by Kipling's writing about the army in India, the regular army was entirely volunteer and infantry soldiers could serve for terms of six, twelve or twenty-one years."

10. The Thug pickaxe was constructed according to strict rules and later consecrated in an elaborate multi-step religious ritual that includes "three further absolutions."

11. The Thugs were actually hereditary assassins who utilized the *Pugree*, a strangling cloth. The word Thug can be traced to the Hindi and Urdu word *thag* which means swindler or thief, and

is derived from the Sanskrit word *sthagati,* meaning "conceal" or "sly." The group dug the graves of their intended victims in advance. According to Law's *A Guide to the Appreciation the Photoplay Based on Kipling's Gunga Din*, "Bentinck...imprisoned 1,562 Thugs, hanged 382 for murder, and imprisoned for life or exiled from India 986 others." The most important contemporary account of the Thugs is Edward Thornton's *Illustrations of the History and Practices of the Thugs*. "Between the years 1826 and 1835 (both inclusive), 1,562 [Thug] prisoners were committed by various magistrates," wrote Thornton. "Of these 328 were punished by death, 999 by transportation, 77 by imprisonment for life; from 21 security was required; 71 were sentenced to limited periods of imprisonment – making a total of 1,450 [sic] convicted." Of the remainder, 21 were acquitted, 31 died before sentences, 11 contrived to escape and 49 "were admitted evidence for the prosecution." On page 468, Thornton warned that "though the practice of Thuggee has received a serious check, it must not be supposed that the whole of its followers have been apprehended." See also Sir Walter Roper Lawrence, *The India We Serve* (London: Cassell and Company, 1928), 45-46. Lawrence served in the British Civil Service in India from 1879 to 1896. Gary Grant had a first-edition copy of Lawrence's book in his library. Another interesting account is *Confessions of a Thug*, a novel written by Captain Meadows Taylor, which was published in London by Richard Bentley and printed by Richard and John E. Taylor in 1839. The novel, which was utilized by the studio researchers, is set in 1832, but contains some historical information in its introduction about the fate of 1,727 Thugs who were apprehended by British authorities from 1831 to 1837: transported, 1,059; hanged, 412; imprisoned for life with hard labor, 87; imprisoned in default of security, 21; imprisoned for various periods, 69; released after trial, 32; escaped from jail, 11; died in jail, 36. Over one thousand more were imprisoned awaiting trial or sentencing.

12. According to Dan Allen of the Victorian Military Society, the one common medal that each of the three principals wear is the Indian Service Medal. "General Service Medals were awarded for active service in campaigns that were deemed too small to merit a medal of their own," noted Allan on December 11, 2016. "The ribbon should have at least one 'bar' on it with the name of the battle or action for which it was awarded engraved on it. Presumably, the wardrobe department couldn't come up with one of those – or did not know about it. Queen Victoria issued two Indian General Service Medals. The pre-1895 version had a red ribbon with two dark blue stripes; the post-1895 version had a crimson ribbon with two dark green stripes." In the punch bowl scene, MacChesney wears three medals. "The middle one that he wears is the campaign medal for the Second Afghan War of 1878-80 – green with crimson edges," said Allen. "In a black and white photo it usually comes out as being of one colour, but if you look closely you can make out a slightly different shade on one edge of the ribbon. The medal on the left is a puzzle. The ribbon has a single broad stripe, which means it could be either a New Zealand Medal awarded for the Maori Wars, fought between 1845-66 (dark blue with a red stripe), or the Cape of Good Hope General Service Medal, 1880-1897, awarded for service in South Africa. British troops serving in India also served for a spell in South Africa, either on their way out of India or on their way back. So, there's nothing impossible about a soldier having medals for service in both places."

13. *George Stevens: A Filmmaker's Journey.*

14. Lorrance, *Sam Jaffe*, 182.

15. Chandragupta Maurya (340 BC-297 BC) established the Maurya empire, and as emperor unified most of what is now greater India. His forces conquered much of Alexander the Great's eastern empire and defeated efforts by Seleucus I Nicator (358 BC-281 BC), one of Alexander's successors, during the 305 BC-303 BC war.

16. The scene utilized 147 measures of music, the 148th being eliminated due to the interruption commanded by Colonel Weed after he hears Din's bugle call. "Routine of Tune 'Will Ye No Come Back' in work print – reel eleven" in RKO Studio Records.

17. *Dialogue on Film: George Stevens*, 15.

18. Din's actions, as an enlisted man, would have qualified for a Victoria Cross, Great Britain's highest military honor since the regimental bhisti demonstrated the "most conspicuous bravery, or some daring or pre-eminent act valour or sacrifice, or extreme devotion to duty in the presence of the enemy." A legendary tale during the Indian Mutiny (1857-58) describes that a British cavalry officer recommended his regiment's *bhisti* for the Victoria Cross. Since he was not an actual soldier, the award could not be given. As a result, the officer refused to recommend another man from his regiment.

19. Notwithstanding those motion pictures which included scenes of New Year's Eve celebrations, *Gunga Din* was not the only film to incorporate "Old Lang Syne" in its ending. Prolific stock music composer Heinz Roemheld used "Old Lang Syne" during a sensitive concluding scene between Errol Flynn's Jim Corbett and Ward Bond's John L. Sullivan in *Gentleman Jim* (1942). The song was also used as introductory music for the film's opening credits sequence. Roemheld's resume has some indirect *Gunga Din* connections: he provided musical passages for *The Werewolf of London* (1935), which was written by John Colton, and added musical pieces to *Hopalong Rides Again* (1937), which was filmed in the Lone Pine area. Composer Sol Kaplan also utilized "Old Lang Syne" in several scenes as well as the ending of *Mr. 880* (1950), a heartfelt comedy starring Burt Lancaster and Dorothy McGuire.

20. *Gunga Din* was one of a several films in the late 1930s and early 1940s which featured endings where the major character or characters appear as heavenly apparitions or in flashbacks. Among the films which used the ghost-like technique were *The Story of Vernon and Irene Castle* (1939), *Wuthering Heights* (1939), *The Man in the Iron Mask* (1939), *They Died with Their Boots On* (1941), and *The Sullivans* (1944).

CHAPTER FIFTEEN
Holland's Comments and Suggestions

Sir Robert Erskine Holland not only provided technical support during filming, but after a preview, he wrote two detailed documents to George Stevens on November 22, 1938: a fifteen-page collection titled *General Observations and Comments and Suggestions* and a six-page entry titled *Preview of Gunga Din,* which included sections on "Observations" and "Comments."[1] These writings went beyond the scope of his original duties, which were to provide technical assistance regarding the British Army in late nineteenth century India—before and during production, not after it.

In the documents, Holland commented on nearly everything, from actors' performances and scenes to technical details and potential audience reactions. Holland was expanding his prescribed responsibilities to that of writer and director. For example, he suggested that the Guru jump to his death from the top of the temple, not into the snake pit. "The snake pit could have been used for the extinction of some lesser Thug in the scrap when the Guru was seized," he pointed out. Furthermore, Holland described Gunga Din's "progress up the dome [as] endlessly slow."

He also said that the rock that hit Higginbotham was too large. "It might have killed him." Holland suggested that a subsequent scene in which Colonel Weed awakens the injured sergeant be eliminated.

Holland was especially concerned about Montagu Love's reading of Kipling's poem at the end of the film, and requested that it be shortened. "This seems to me of great importance," he noted, without explaining why. Furthermore, Holland recommended that the "though I belted you and flayed you" line be eliminated, since Colonel Weed never performed any acts of cruelty on the title character. "And having regard to the sensitiveness of Indians at the present time, the less reference made to such happenings the better," he added.

Holland's comments about the cast were direct and unambiguous.

Sam Jaffe: "Gunga Din was of course outstanding. I feel sure that no one better could have been found for the part, and I feel his rendering of it ought to make *Gunga Din* a household word among film fans. I feel sure that he will gain the sympathy and interest and laughter of the audience at once, and that he will have their tears for his heroic and moving death and farewell ceremony."

Cary Grant: "Cutter is surprisingly good throughout. I did not expect that he would come out so well, from what I saw of his earlier work."

Victor McLaglen: "Mac has a peculiar never-failing appeal, is always thorough and hard-working, and dominates the scene in which he appears by his brutal vigour and the set of his jaw. His 'brutality' or perhaps 'vitality' is a little overpowering at times."

Douglas Fairbanks Jr.: "Ballantine was admirable in his love scenes, but never seemed really comfortable in a helmet. He made a pretty pair with Emmy, and played a good part in the fighting."

Joan Fontaine: "Emmy was very attractive and fetching in her rather thankless part."

Montagu Love: "I regard the colonel as disappointing. He seemed worried and flurried, and had not the restraint or the air of command which mark a leader of men."

Eduardo Ciannelli: "The Guru struck me as being a particular success. He was dignified, forceful and venomous, a fine actor."

Abner Biberman: "Chota was also disappointing, being rather too clownish for the part and hardly worthy of being the Guru's son."

Robert Coote: "Higginbotham worked hard and seemed to succeed in being the comic character which he was intended to represent."

Lumsden Hare: "The Major was colourless."

Cecil Kellaway: "Stebbins was decidedly good in a small part."

Holland appreciated the closing scenes but thought that Gunga Din's body be embellished with the Indian Order of Merit, an award given for valor. "That decoration was earned by Gunga Din's prototype, the *bhisti* called Jumma, whose exploits at the Siege of Delhi was Kipling's inspiration for the poem," he noted. "The story of Jumma is told in Sir George Younghusband's book, *Forty Years a Soldier*."

He also criticized a few of the characterizations. Holland thought Emmy was selfish. "If she really loved Ballantine, she would be quite content to be a sergeant's wife," he remarked, in neo-Victorian style. However, Holland did not offer a comparative comment concerning Ballantine's selfishness about wanting to remain in the army with his buddies.[2]

In another memorandum, Holland raised concerns about passages from the poem and their potential impact on audiences in India and Great Britain. "I think that great care is needed not to show any part of it which might be unpalatable to Indian sentiment at this present time, e.g., such epithets as 'black-faced' or 'eathen,'" he noted. He also suggested that the poetic line about getting "a swig in hell" be dropped.

Holland was also troubled about the portrayal of the Thugs. "It seems a pity that anything should be said in the picture which might seem to suggest that Thuggee was aimed against the British, particularly since some modern secret societies in India, quite unconnected to Thuggee, but working through assassination, have taken Kali as their patron goddess," he stated. He recommended that "the sight of Cutter's back lacerated by stripes" be eliminated. "I think that Indian censorship might object to it," said Holland. "I would omit all reference to the lash, and especially the lashing of Mac and Ballantine, as shown. I think that the Indian authorities would take exception to it."

Holland also criticized the Guru's comments about Chandragupta Maurya. "[He] did not as a matter of fact slaughter all the armies left in India by Alexander the Great, although his Empire was erected to some extent on the ruins of Alexander's conquests." He cautioned Stevens again: "The speech seems to inculcate racial hostility, and suggests the Guru was trying to inject nationalist sentiment into Thuggee. I have continuously advised against this, and regard the point as very important having regard the present condition of affairs in India." Holland added, "I have, at earlier stages in the picture, suggested the elimination of matter which might seem to suggest anti-British sentiment." Ironically, during production, Holland had been criticized by Indian journalists for his lengthy "high-born services in India [as] one of [its] rulers" and his inability to speak "two words of Hindustani correctly." Yet of all those involved in the production, he had expressed more sympathy and concern for India's reaction to the film than anyone else. Nevertheless, it was practically impossible to satisfy both British and Indian audiences.

Of course, even if Stevens had approved any of Holland's suggestions, additional re-shooting would have had to take place. Stevens, already over budget, dismissed the advisor's recommendations. After the film's release, Holland may have believed that his remarks, not the preview audience's reactions, were the reason for the elimination of the Higginbotham rock scene.[3]

Chapter Fifteen Notes

1. Sir Robert Erskine Holland, *General Observations and Comments and Suggestions*, and *Preview of Gunga Din,* RKO Studio Records. Holland died in 1965, at the age of ninety-two.

2. Otis Ferguson, *The New Republic's* film critic, condemned the script's depiction of the three sergeants' friendship in a 1939 review: "They play up the undying beauties of the comradeship, and then have two of the buddies scheming to wreck completely the honeymoon plans of the third." See Robert Wilson, ed., *The Film Criticism Of Otis Ferguson* (Philadelphia: Temple University Press, 1971), 246.

3. Robert Coote's final dialogue: "Surrender, surrender. All of you. You're all my prisoners." As a result of the edit, Higginbotham is last seen with Emmy Stebbins in Tantrapur after she delivered Ballantine's discharge papers.

CHAPTER SIXTEEN

The Promotion and Exploitation Campaign

S. Barret McCormick, Chief of the Publicity, Advertising, and Promotion department at RKO, characterized the campaign for *Gunga Din* as "punch and general all around high pressure and ballyhoo."[1] It was more than that; in fact, the campaign was organized like a military operation, complete with strategies and tactics designed to guarantee victory for *Gunga Din* at the box office.

The campaign "took over three months in planning and preparation" before McCormick set his crew in motion.[2] His advance team was composed of fifteen veteran promo men, who were scheduled to target 665 newspaper editors in 445 cities during a five week period. RKO estimated that the promotional brigade would cover 40,000 miles while on active duty.[3]

While McCormick and his team went into action, RKO planned a special radio program about the making of the film. The studio hired Ernest S. Pagano to write the script. Pagano had penned dozens of short subjects, and had co-written the screenplays for such RKO Astaire-Rogers hits as *Shall We Dance* (1937), the George Stevens-directed *A Damsel in Distress* (1937), and *Carefree* (1938). Pagano also wrote the George Stevens-directed *Vivacious Lady* (1938) and *Having Wonderful Time* (1938), which co-starred Douglas Fairbanks, Jr.

On January 11, 1939, Pagano produced a 22-page radio transcription for *Gunga Din*. Although a first draft, Pagano wrote the planned national radio program as if it were a script, complete with narration and cast and crew dialogue (featuring, in order: Pandro Berman, Van Nest Polglase, Perry Ferguson, George Stevens, Edward Killy, Victor McLaglen, Douglas Fairbanks, Jr., Cary Grant, Eduardo Ciannelli, Sam Jaffe, Lumsden Hare, and Montagu Love). He also included sound effects, music cues, and assorted directorial notes.[4]

Early in the radio transcription, Pagano stated that on February 3, 1936, at a general meeting at Berman's office, an announcement was made that RKO had "finally secured the screen rights to Kipling's *Gunga Din*." Pagano indicated that, at the time, a report noted: "George Stevens has been signed as Producer-Director [and] Ben Hecht and Charlie MacArthur will develop the ballad into story form." However, Pagano's writings ignored much of what had transpired since April 1936, when the trade publications announced that producer Edward Small had hired William Faulkner to write the *Gunga Din* screenplay.

In various publicity releases, the studio pointed out that the title character's name was pronounced "Gunga Deen," and that the first name was "the Hindu name for the Ganges River and 'Din' was an Arabic word meaning 'faith.'"

Some local exhibitors started their *Gunga Din* campaigns early. Bill Johnson, the manager of the Opera House in Millinocket, Maine, printed hundreds of stickers with "You're a better man than I am Gunga Din" printed on them. According to *Motion Picture*

Herald: "These were plastered on doors and windows all over town several weeks ahead of opening, and by the time the picture opened, the line was a real catchword."[5]

The promotional guidebook for theater owners and managers was the *Gunga Din* campaign pressbook, an impressive, oversized (12"x18") 28-pager in four colors, which featured production stills, mat images, posters (which were printed by Cleveland's Morgan Litho Corporation, Hollywood's major supplier of posters), give-away paper mache sun helmets, automobile bumper stickers, radio announcements, and over three dozen suggested newspaper articles, ranging from full-page stories to short teasers. RKO left no one out of its wide-scale publicity effort. The pressbook even promoted an educational group discussion guide and included a quiz contest that was designed for teachers and school children.

The pressbook also featured numerous exploitation stunts that theater managers were encouraged to implement. Most were rather conventional, but others were quite imaginative. The recommendations included the following activities:

"Feature a special Indian dinner . . . Gunga Din's Menu at a local restaurant. Suggest the following Indian dishes to the restauranteur: Bedami soup, Indian rice, Chappati, lamb curry."

"Obtain the services of public officials to attend [*Gunga Din*] street-naming ceremonies."

"Borrow a horse-drawn gun carriage—perhaps one equipped with a Gatling gun—as used in the picture—[and] use it for a street ballyhoo."

"[Have] eight men in costume marching in perfect rhythm along the main streets to the strains of a military band! What a traffic stopper!"

"Have your film delivered to you by an airplane."

"You can borrow an elephant from your local zoo."

Obviously, RKO's promo department believed that just about anything was possible when it came to exploitation. The pressbook, in typical Hollywood promo style, provided higher figures for the publicity team's visits: "More than 1,000 newspapers in nearly 500 cities!" Even some of the promotional items were pure fiction. One movie still featured Sam Jaffe positioned behind a Gatling Gun, and the accompanying caption read: "Crouched behind the muzzle of a machine gun, Gunga Din helps repel the attack of fierce tribesmen."

The pressbook also provided different figures for the cast and crew. On one page, "2,000 players and technicians" were mentioned, but on another, "a corps of 3,000" was identified. The publication also stated that it "took all of 1938 to make" the film.

"Some $200,000 is being spent [on] national magazines and papers, billboards, and cooperative advertising," said McCormick.[6] The billboards were different from the standard roadside variety. "The biggest picture of the year brings the first new thing on the billboards since Barnum first plastered a town!" noted the studio's publicity department. McCormick explained that the new billboards, made with a new "lifeographic" process, depicting six different life-sized highlight images taken from the film, would be a unique part of the campaign. Approximately 5,000 billboards, featuring huge 24-sheet color poster images, were planned to be strategically placed in thirty-seven principal cities in the United States and Canada.[7]

Although McCormick specialized in the large-scale promotions, he never ignored the small-scale details. He and his staff even infiltrated the crossword puzzle market by suggesting *Gunga Din* connections to the game makers. For example, "Major Mitchell in Gunga Din" appeared in a *Hollywood* magazine crossword puzzle, and "Author of *Gunga Din*" was a common crossword question in several newspapers. And Cleveland's *Plain Dealer* offered monetary prizes ($5 to the first place winners) and free movie tickets for readers who could complete the newspaper's "Complete The *Gunga Din* Limeric" contest.

The top twenty magazines, including *Life*, *Look*, *The Saturday Evening Post*, *Liberty*, and *Colliers*, which had a combined circulation of nearly 16 million subscribers, featured full-page advertisements and stories about *Gunga Din*. Trade publications and movie magazines also celebrated the film in grand style.

Life, with its 1,891,789 subscribers (according to figures supplied by McCormick), had a *Gunga Din* promotion in its January 16, 1939 issue. The magazine's main story was about President Franklin D. Roosevelt ("He Would Save Democracy For the World"), but the weekly's film focus was on *Gunga Din*, in a lively three-page story that included six black-and-white photos.[8]

On January 19, 1939, the film received an indirect promotional boost when the HMS *Kipling*, a "K" Class Destroyer in the Royal Navy, was launched in Scotland. Mrs. Elsie Bambridge, Kipling's daughter, attended the ceremony at the Yarrow and Company shipyard based in the Scotstoun district of Glasgow.[9]

On the same day as the ship's launching, RKO staffer William Nutt produced "Notes, Comparisons and Synopses of All Material on *Gunga Din*," a studio research document that was used, in part, to confirm when specific story elements were written. The document's creation coincided with a legal issue that the studio would soon address.

On January 23, *Life* featured one of McCormick's primary full-page ads that proclaimed "Kipling's heroic lines inspire Hollywood biggest movie!" The ad hyped the film's "war elephants, its bandit hordes, its terror Temples and mystic mountains of India." The advertisement stated confidently: "Out of the drumbeat of Kipling's most famous 85 lines rises a picture that may well become known as the one great movie of the year!"

Harrison's Reports provided an optimistic assessment of the film: "This should make an exciting melodrama. Considering the players listed, it should do very well at the box office." The *Independent Exhibitor's Film Bulletin* noted: "*Gunga Din* is expected to be one of the most impressive pictures ever turned out by this studio. It has a top cast and will require ninety production days. Sixty of those will be spent on getting location shots."

RKO's president George J. Schaefer said that McCormick's publicity campaign was "the most comprehensive ever given a picture."[10] The studio waited for *Gunga Din*'s early box office results to see if everyone's efforts paid off.

© RKO.

Chapter Sixteen Notes

1. *The Film Daily*, June 21, 1939, 4.

2. *Motion Picture Daily*, Jan. 13, 1939, 2.

3. Ibid., Jan. 1, 1939, 10; *The Film Daily*, January 1, 1939, 3.

4. Pagano, *Radio Transcription*, 1939, RKO Studio Records.

5. *Motion Picture Herald*, April 29, 1939, 75.

6. Ibid., February 25, 1939, 50.

7. Ibid., January 21, 1939, 54. The large billboard designs had previously been used with great success to advertise the Ringling Brothers Circus, the Morgan Litho Corporation's biggest customer.

8. *Life*, January 16, 1939, 26-28.

9. *The Kipling Journal*, April 1939, 4-5. The periodical, an official publication of The Kipling Society, reported that Kipling's daughter said that "since her father died, some three years ago, many places, works, etc. had been named after him, but was certain that had he known, nothing would have given him such immense pride and pleasure than that a ship of the Royal Navy would one day bear his name." In 1898, Kipling wrote *The Destroyers*, a poem dedicated to the fighting ships. The HMS *Kipling*, which featured six 4.7-inch guns and two quintuple torpedo tubes, was active during World War II, serving in the Atlantic Ocean and the Mediterranean Sea. It was sunk, along with two other Royal Navy ships, in a fight against an Axis convey sailing to Benghazi, Libya in May 1942, by German Junkers JU88 aircraft. During WWII, "Gunga Din" was painted on the fuselage of aircraft #41, a B-26 Marauder medium bomber, in the United States Army Air Corp's 320th Bomb Group.

10. *The Film Daily*, February 1, 1939, 1.

CHAPTER SEVENTEEN
Release, Reviews, and Reactions

The year was only three weeks old, but the RKO publicity department was promoting *Gunga Din* as one of 1939's "great movies." Additional exploitative slogans filled newspaper and magazine ads:

"Out of the stirring glory of Kipling's seething India they roar—three fighting, loving, swaggering sons of the British Battalions ... in the picture that's too big for words!"

"Red-blood and gunpowder heroes roaring from Kipling's storied India."

"Armies and elephants! Love and laughter! Breathless adventure inspired by Kipling's heroic odyssey of fighting in India!"

"Here they come! The reckless, lusty, swaggering sons of the thundering guns of Kipling's storied India!"

"Epic of sublime heroism: war elephants ... fighting troops ... martial daredevils!"

"Romance and thrills for a thousand movies plundered for one mighty show!"

"Love in a lawless land, where terror stalks through brooding hills—and a woman is sure of nothing!"

The promotional hype for *Gunga Din* would be joined by publicity campaigns for other noteworthy motion pictures, and during the next eleven months, so many other great movies were released that some would claim 1939 as Hollywood's greatest year. Other films of note included *Goodbye, Mr. Chips*; *The Hunchback of Notre Dame*; *The Wizard of Oz*; *Drums Along the Mohawk*; *Dodge City*; *Ninotchka*; *Stanley and Livingstone*; *Young Mr. Lincoln*; *Only Angels Have Wings*; *The Women*; *The Roaring Twenties*; *Jesse James*; *Mr. Smith Goes to Washington*; *Destry Rides Again*; *Stagecoach*; *The Four Feathers*; *Beau Geste*; *Union Pacific*; *Dark Victory*; *Of Mice and Men*; *Son of Frankenstein*; *Wuthering Heights*; *The Rains Came*; *Babes in Arms*; *The Private Lives of Elizabeth and Essex*; *Gulliver's Travels*; *Man of Conquest*; *Juarez*; *Love Affair*; and *Gone with the Wind*.

Gunga Din made its debut on Tuesday, January 24, 1939, in Los Angeles at the RKO Hill Street and Pantages theaters, where Ginger Rogers, Jeanette MacDonald, and Gene Raymond were among the celebrities who attended the event. General admission tickets cost $2.20. The film also debuted that same day in Miami at S. A. Lynch's Sheridan theater.

However, the film's "World Premiere" was held two days later at New York City's Radio Music Hall, a grand entertainment venue with 5,874 seats, which had opened to great fanfare on December 27, 1932. On January 26, *The Hollywood Reporter* promoted the premiere with twelve of its eighteen pages devoted to *Gunga Din*. On hand for the premiere were George Stevens, Douglas Fairbanks, Jr., Joel Sayre, Katherine Hepburn, and W. G. Van Schmus, the managing director of Radio City Music Hall.

Following the premiere, *Gunga Din* was shown daily at 11:40 a.m., 2:21 p.m., 5:03 p.m., 7:50 p.m., and 10:31 p.m. The regular showings of the film were augmented by "The Waltz King," an elaborate stage program produced by Leon Leonidoff. *Showplace*, Radio City Music Hall's program-magazine, indicated that a grand organ presentation by Richard Leibert began the show. Next, the Music Hall's Symphony Orchestra, under the direction of Erno Rapee, performed the "immortal melodies of Johann Strauss." The Choral Ensemble, the Rockettes and the venue's Corps de Ballet were also on the bill. According to a *New York Times* advertisement, the entertainment extravaganza also included performances by Paul Remos and Company, Kay Katya and Kay, Ruby Mercer, and Nicholas Daks. It was a grand New York-styled spectacle, and *Gunga Din* was the main attraction.

Kate Cameron, the chief film critic of the *New York Daily News*, awarded *Gunga Din* a five-star review, one of five films released in January that received the highest rating. "A rousing screen spectacle that keeps Music Hall audiences glued to their seats for two thrilled-packed hours," said Cameron.[1]

Variety gave high praise to George Stevens: "[He] has employed superb change of pace, first going from action army combat to character close-ups and then tossing in a bit of humor [and a] romantic touch. He directs with fine discernment, both in the sweeping episodes of long range, and the less hectic indoor scenes." *The Washington Post* was particularly enthusiastic: "There is nothing stereotyped about *Gunga Din*. It is beyond question the most impressive production that RKO-Radio had ever brought to the screen."

Sam Jaffe was the focal point of *The Wall Street Journal's* highly favorable review: "But it is Sam Jaffe as the wistful, faithful Gunga Din, who seeks to be a soldier but never becomes one until after his death, who, rightfully, is the outstanding character. And it is

only because he is so believable and appealing, that the closing scene where Kipling's poem is read at his burial service does not appear maudlin or out of place—as it easily might." Jay Carmody, writing in Washington D. C.'s *The Evening Star*, also lavished praise on Jaffe: "Sam Jaffe gives a remarkable performance as the title character. His Gunga Din is an adroit admixture of loyalty, humility, high patriotism, intelligence and bravery." In the *San Diego Union*, critic Maurice Savage wrote, "Credit Sam Jaffe with one of the finest acting jobs of the new movie season."

Although the entire cast and crew received accolades from the *Los Angeles Times*, one cast member's talents were noted: "Grant is very persuasive in his work [and] is especially clever in the comedy [scenes]."

"Recommended most enthusiastically," wrote Bland Johaneson in the *New York Daily Mirror*. "A striking pageant of frontier warfare . . . stretched to the breaking point with suspense," stated Howard Barnes in the *New York Herald Tribune*. William Boehnel of the *New York World-Telegram* was particularly generous in his review: "Just about one of the finest films I have ever seen." Rose Pelswick of the *New York Journal-American* called the film an "impressive action drama." A *San Francisco Chronicle* ad for the Golden Gate Theater called *Gunga Din* "the most important picture to ever play this theater." Interestingly, the Golden Gate was one of the theaters in the RKO chain that also included a Vaudeville review. Another unusual presentation was at Seattle's State Theater, a burlesque house, which promoted "Seattle's Gay Girl Show" and two features: *Gunga Din* and *Boy Trouble*.[2]

"All movies, as a matter of fact, should be like the first twenty-five minutes and the last thirty minutes of *Gunga Din*, which are the sheer poetry of cinematic action," noted B. R. Crisler in *The New York Times*. "At its best it is an orchestration, taught with suspense and enriched in the fighting scenes with beautifully timed, almost epigrammic bits of 'business' and a swinging gusto which makes every roundhouse blow a thing of beauty. Although *Gunga Din* is not an adult picture, when it gets going you might as well try to question the ideology of a parade of Seaforth Highlanders."[3]

"What a wow of a picture this is!" proclaimed *Silver Screen* magazine. "There's suspense galore, and believe me, there's many a scene where your hair will stand up right on end. The photography is breath-taking."

"This is one of the bigger pictures, so if you are seeing only a few, put it on the must list," reported *Hollywood* magazine.

"[The writers] have skipped lightly from melodrama to slapstick to sentiment to genuine thrills mingled with theatrical heroics, sticking to only one discernibly resolute aim, to break away conspicuously from the conventional boy-and-girl theme: the girl is brutally abandoned by her fiancé for the presumably greater pictures of life in Her Majesty's service," wrote James Shelley Hamilton in *Photoplay* magazine.

The Film Daily reported that 148,000 admissions had been sold during *Gunga Din's* first six days at Radio City Music Hall. George Stevens was so pleased at the success of the film and the positive press that he remained in New York for six weeks before returning to Hollywood. [4]

A half-page ad that celebrated *Gunga Din's* third week at Radio City Music Hall in the February 8, 1939 issue of *Variety* proclaimed: "Every new date a new demonstration of terrific box office power! Everywhere the biggest money picture the industry has seen in months!" The film had "played to approximately 310,000 admissions in its first two weeks," and generated over $100,000 at the box office nationwide. *Motion Picture Herald* stated that the film established "new all-time box office records in Hollywood and Los Angeles."[5] By February 17, *Gunga Din* had been released in nearly every motion picture market in the United States. Despite winter weather conditions across the United States, *Variety* reported that the film was "able to prosper in the face of frigid blasts" in Minneapolis, performed a "strong three weeks in Boston," did "smash-up business at the Paramount" in Portland, received "major attention" in Seattle, was a "life-savor in a week socked" by weather in Philadelphia, and "chalk[ed] up one of the big weeks in the history" of Baltimore theaters. "*Gunga Din* . . . is expected to prove one of the most important engagements of the screen," reported Washington's *Ellensburg Daily Record*. Since most theaters were charging 15¢, 20¢, 25¢, and 35¢ admissions, *Gunga Din's* box office figures were impressive. Of course, all other Hollywood films' ticket sales were based on the same admission prices.

"Big, beautiful, boisterous, and bursting with thrills," claimed the *Richmond Times-Dispatch*. "It's the sort of show for which moving pictures were invented—all action, excitement, panoramic backgrounds, and bang-up entertainment."

Richard E. Hays, the film critic for the *Seattle Daily Times*, said that the film was "one of the greatest in all the exciting history of motion pictures." He added that "*Gunga Din* is a triumph in motion picture art that will thrill any audience to its marrow."

Cary Grant and Douglas Fairbanks, Jr. caricature by Abe Hirschfeld.

The Denville Theatre in Denville, New Jersey placed a prominent full-page *Gunga Din* ad ("The picture that sweeps the screen like a cyclone!") in its four-page program during the film's three-day run in March. *The Spokane Daily Chronicle* stated that *Gunga Din* is "nearly sure to be included in the year's 'best ten' films, and Quebec's *St. Maurice Valley Chronicle* noted that the film would "rank among the great offerings of recent years." The Canadian newspaper also printed a different ending to the film: "When the regiment parades to witness the conferring of the decoration (Victoria Cross) on the humble Hindu's surviving friends, sergeants Cutter, MacChesney, and Ballantine, the trio hold a hurried consultation as to who shall wear

the Cross. Their decision is to pin it on the breast of an old native water carrier as a proxy for the beloved *bhisti* who died so gallantly." The newspaper utilized an excerpt from the pressbook, which featured part of an undated outline that was never used in the film, and a closing scene where MacChesney tells the old *bhisti*: "We present this to you for one of your kind, a brave man and one of the most heroic, regardless of creed or color, that has ever served her Majesty in India."

One American reviewer took exception with *Gunga Din's* overall positive press. Otis Ferguson, *The New Republic's* film critic, writing through a socio-political prism, assessed *Gunga Din* as a "miscomprehending lark." "I regret to say that Sam Jaffe was persuaded to play Gunga Din, a part to which he brings everything, including the apparent belief that East is South and that Little Eva was the natural son of Uncle Tom," wrote Ferguson in the publication's February 22, 1939 issue. "But the whole mood is irresponsible and wrong, as though there were nothing left in the world to do but try on other men's hats by pulling them down over your ankles." Ferguson was incorrect about Jaffe needing to be persuaded to take on the title role, but his other views would be expanded upon by writers in India.

Joseph H. August's majestic cinematography did not go unnoticed by the press. "The photography is breathtaking," stated *Silver Screen* magazine. "The camera work by John [sic] H. August enhances the production values," reported *Variety*. *The New York Times* mentioned his camera's "panoramic sweep," and the *Los Angeles Times* remarked that the "magnificence of the outdoor scenes . . . has never been rivaled in the history of pictures." Ironically, a year later, August was commended for not featuring memorable images on screen. Critic Vernon Steele admitted that he "didn't see" August's photography in *Primrose Path* (1940). "It must have been good beyond question," said Steele. Another writer was more supportive. "But that is Joe August's way of doing things—he did that in sunlit *Gunga Din* and he did it in low-lighted *Primrose Path*," wrote George Blaisdell in *American Cinematographer*.[6]

August admitted that his skills behind the lens had little to do with careful calculations; as a matter of fact, he said that he avoided using exposure meters when preparing a shot. "I am not against meters, by any means," explained August. "They just don't fit into my plan of taking pictures. The meters I lean on are my eyes."[7]

Motion Picture Herald gave *Gunga Din* a glowing review, but was one of the few publications that included comments on Great Britain's status in the world. "The film is fast, furious, and fascinating, a blunt, hard statement of the imperial policy that was and may yet be England's, a powerful account of masculine adventure under arms."[8]

Despite the numerous positive reviews and healthy box office returns, RKO received some bad news when it received a formal request from Rudyard Kipling's widow and members of his family about the inclusion of the poet's character in the film. Kipling's descendants stated that the poet should not have appeared during the final battle scene, since the fictitious conflict did not inspire him to write *Gunga Din*, especially on site in a post-battlefield tent. As a result of the complaint, Reginald Sheffield was cut from the film in all shots where he was identifiable (his character survived in a long shot riding with the troops), including an important scene where Kipling stands near Gunga Din's body during the film's conclusion. An awkward matte shot of a wagon was substituted for Sheffield's position in the scene, and the resulting effect wasn't smooth; in fact, the edited prints showed a slight herky-jerky movement of the wagon. As a result of the actor's removal from several scenes, *Gunga Din* was reduced from 10,523 feet of film to 10,453 feet. The movie's running time was reduced by about a minute and a half to about 117 minutes.

Thanks to S. Barret McCormick's publicity campaign and the innovative promotions created by individual theaters owners, *Gunga Din* generated lots of public attention. Many theaters displayed such basic movie promotional items as banners, full-sheet posters, lobby cards, and large cardboard standee signs, which graced the entrances; however, many movie houses created imaginative publicity stunts for the film. Some of the promotions were interesting, some were novel, and some were bizarre.

The RKO Orpheum in Kansas City, Missouri, staged a *Gunga Din* night at a local ballroom the night before the film opened. A "gold" loving cup was awarded to the best dance couple and "immediately following the dance, several hundred colored balloons were released, among which were 50 [which] included complimentary tickets to see the picture."[9]

At the Durfee Theatre in Fall River, Massachusetts, a display "of uniforms of original Black Watch Scots soldiers with complete regalia" was set up and provided by British war veterans. And one of the town's beauty parlors offered a "Joan Fontaine coiffure" to its customers.[10]

In Brooklyn, New York's Alba Theatre, a "lad dressed as a water boy blew a bugle at intervals during the day."[11] The Duffield Theatre in Brooklyn constructed a New York World's Fair-like trylon and perisphere out of compoboard and decorated it with cast members' names and glossy production stills.[12]

Marcel Brazee, the manager of the Avalon Theater in Chicago, distributed 5,000 envelopes containing "mystic wishing sand from the desert." Inside each envelope were instructions: "Place the contents of this envelope on the palm of your left hand, make a wish, close your eyes, and slowly allow the sand to trickle through your figures; no greater wish could be made than to see *Gunga Din*."[13] Milwaukee's World Theater took a more direct approach to generate box office activity: the venue distributed free dishes to ticket buyers, a common practice during the Great Depression.

A mounted troop of Boy Scouts, wearing pith helmets and carrying lances, appeared at Schine's Hippodrome in Gloversville, New York.[14] In Bridgeport, Connecticut, Matt Sanders loaned his sixteenth century Indian armor collection to the Loew's Poli theater during *Gunga Din's* run. A "mammoth sign painted in soft coal dust over snow-capped mountains in Denver drew attention to the opening of *Gunga Din* at the Orpheum. The sign was seen by thousands." In Nashville, Tennessee, large advertising cards were placed on the city's street cars.[15]

In Peoria, Illinois, a theater showcased the film with a large 41x10-foot sign, which featured raised four-foot high letters containing colored lamps that changed colors every five seconds. Forty mirrors positioned at the sign's base reflected the colors at night, making it the most eye-catching promotional event of all.

In New Orleans, press agent Gary Moore "lined up contestants at a prominent downtown bar and had them recite Kipling's famous poem while imbibing drinks, free on the [Orpheum] Theatre." Later, "judges decided the best emoted performance while speakers were well imbibed with grog."[16]

The promotions and positive reviews helped *Gunga Din's* domestic box office receipts, but popular word-of-mouth praise from those who had seen the film also helped increase theater attendance figures. Repeat business at many venues was common. "*Gunga Din* is continuing to break records in every key situation so far," stated *The Film Daily*. "It has been booked for a third week at Keith Memorial, Boston, and Keith's Washington. Now in its third week at the Hillstreet and Pantages, Los Angeles, the picture will be held for a fourth week in both houses. In all other spots the picture is being held for an additional week."[17]

Advance publicity campaigns in other nations were also innovative. A simulated army tank, decorated with the title of the film and a list of the principal cast members, toured the streets of Guayaquil, Ecuador.[18] At the newly built Panama Theatre in Panama, the entire staff wore *Gunga Din*-styled British soldier helmets to promote the opening of the film.[19] The management of the Roma Theatre in Warsaw, Poland, heralded the film by hiring horsemen dressed as Sikhs, who rode around town. Sign carriers on foot accompanied the riders.[20]

J. J. La Fave of the F. P. Tivoli Theatre in Walkerville, Ontario, promoted the film by outfitting his ushers with cadet uniforms, which were acquired from a nearby vocational school, makeshift pith helmets ("Gunga Din" was hand painted on them), and boots, which were borrowed from a nearby riding academy.[21]

Gunga Din was released worldwide a few weeks after its North American premiere. On February 23, 1939, France was the first foreign nation to debut the film, and one French publisher produced an attractive 26-page pressbook-story program, which mixed handsome illustrations with publicity stills. Another French publisher produced a 54-page photo novel. *Variety* reported on March 15 that the film had broken house attendance records at the Le Paris Theater.

Gunga Din had a special multi-week early release opening in England on February 28, at the Gaumont Haymarket in London. The entire country would have to wait until September 18 for the film's general release.[22] The RKO office in London helped promote the film by stamping its printed invoice envelopes with "Too Big For Words: *Gunga Din*."

Argentina debuted *Gunga Din* on March 2, and Ireland, Sweden, the Netherlands, Denmark, Yugoslavia, and Mexico showed the film over the next several weeks. Finland opened the motion picture on April 9, and Portugal debuted the film on April 11. Czechoslovakia's *Kinorevue* magazine celebrated the film with a beautiful color-tinted cover image of Fairbanks and Fontaine, and the main cast members were featured on the cover of Yugoslavia's *Magazin*.

"The most successful recent American picture in Prague has been *Gunga Din*," reported *Motion Picture Herald*, but that was soon to change, as world events influenced theater attendance throughout Europe.[23] Nazi forces entered Prague, the capital of the Czechoslovak Republic, on March 15, 1939. Adolph Hitler's regime soon banned nearly 200 non-German films shown in the country, but allowed *Gunga Din* to be shown since the United States had remained "neutral" at the time. However, once the United States went to war with Germany and the Axis Powers, American films were banned throughout Nazi-controlled lands in Europe.

The trade publications reported that the film was particularly successful in Poland, Panama, France, Canada, and Australia. "It provides plenty of fighting and many thrills which made the life of a Bengal Lancer so popular," reported Melbourne's *The Age*. A translation problem occurred in Cuba when the movie was initially publicized in the trade papers as *Cunga* [sic] *Din*.

The film was released in Germany as *Aufstand in Sidi Hakim (Uprising in Sidi Hakim)*. *Illustrated Film-Stage*, a German entertainment publication, printed a four-page pressbook that prominently featured Joan Fontaine on the cover, along with photos of Douglas Fairbanks, Gary Grant, and Eduardo Ciannelli. The rear cover featured a close-up of Abner Biberman and a background image of Fairbanks. Sam Jaffe is nearly lost in a two-page centerfold of assorted stills, which centered on Joan Fontaine and Fairbanks. The publication's photographic emphasis on the film's love story is ironic, considering Germany's assault on the world later in the summer.

World War II began on September 1, 1939, and it had an immediate impact on motion picture theater attendance. According to *Variety*, attendance in British theaters fell 50% during the first month of the war. During that time, *Gunga Din* took in $33,000 at the box office instead of the $110,000 to $140,000 it was expected to generate.[24]

"I made it just in time," said Stevens. "Another year later and I'd have been too smart to do it, because the film is delightfully evil in the fascist sense. It celebrates the rumble of the drums and the waving of the flags. No

German pressbook. Author's collection.

one in modern times has done that as well or as with as much grace as the British with their uniforms and stiff salutes and all of that. I really got that film done just before it would have been too late."[25]

Gunga Din was targeted at general audiences but "the gents were imperiously partial to *Gunga Din*," reported *The Film Daily*, which later tagged the film as "a lusty he-man picture." *The National Board of Review* magazine noted that the film was especially favorable for boys nine to thirteen years of age, and the *Boys Cinema* annual included a picture story of *Gunga Din*. *Variety* reported that Ohio's Cleveland Theatre reported "crowds nearly exclusively male."

B. R. Crisler, the film critic of *The New York Times*, championed the motion picture's emphasis on rough-housing over romance: "Another thing we like about it is the way it shoves romance resolutely aside when the bugles blow and the stallions begin to whinny. Who cares all about the mush stuff when there's a good battle in prospect somewhere beyond Cuckoo Cloudland and the Khyber Pass?" However, there was a price to pay at some theaters over the film's masculine posture. L. A. Irwin of the Palace Theatre in Penacook, New Hampshire, pointed out that "the women turned thumbs down" on the film after a two-day run.[26] One newspaper characterized *Gunga Din* as a "woman chasing man" movie.[27]

One institution of higher learning attempted to scientifically explain the impact of *Gunga Din* on certain members of the audience. At the Oklahoma University School of Medicine, "a blonde, brunette, and red-head were used in an experiment to test the thrill reactions of the various female types to *Gunga Din*." No results were reported, though.[28]

The film and its promotions continued to pay off, especially in the domestic market and Canada. In its April issue, *Photoplay* named *Gunga Din* as one of the "best pictures of the month" and one of the "outstanding pictures of [1939]." The publication, which also hailed Cary Grant and Victor McLaglen for the "best performances of the month," recommended that *Gunga Din* be nominated for its readers' "Best Picture of the Year" poll.

The film still had box office legs in the spring, when it began its run in secondary and rural markets. In May, *The Film Daily* called *Gunga Din* an "outstanding money pix."[29]

Everyone associated with the film was pleased—except Joan Fontaine and a few small town movie houses. "The *Gunga Din* mistake" is how *Modern Screen* magazine described Fontaine's experience making the film. She was supposedly told that she had been cut out of the film, which disappointed her, but was later informed that her scenes were restored. However, when Fontaine previewed the film, she felt as if she had merely "walked in and out of a few scenes." She allegedly left the screening "sick and disheartened."[30] In her autobiography, Fontaine admitted that "on location [her] days were lonely," and the only enjoyment she had was "daydreaming about George Stevens, too infatuated to do anything but quake as he directed me on the set."[31]

H. M. Gerber of the Roxy Theatre in Hazleton, North Dakota, reported: "My customers just don't appreciate these historical pictures and show it by staying away." P. G. Held of the Strand Theatre in Griswold, Iowa, noted: "Very good picture that failed to draw. I guess the title was the fault of that." Sammy Jackson of the Jackson Theatre in Flomaton, Alabama, commented: "[The usual] business, nothing extra."[32] B. C. Brown of the Temple and Vernon Theatres in Viroqua, Wisconsin, noted: "As a box office draw, it is not up to standard." C. L. Niles of the Niles Theatre in Anamosa, Iowa, complained: "Did not gross the guarantee."

Immediately after finishing *Gunga Din*, Sam Jaffe was cast in *The Gentle People*, which opened at the Belasco Theatre in New York on January 5, 1939. During the play's 141-performance run, Jaffe went to see *Gunga Din* at Radio City Music Hall. At the conclusion of his stage performance one evening, he and Sidney Hillman, leader of the Amalgamated Clothing Workers of America and a key leader in the creation of the Congress of Industrial Organization (CIO), walked to the theater and "waited forty minutes outside" in line to catch a late night showing of the film. When asked why he didn't use VIP treatment to gain entrance, Jaffe replied: "I've got the same right to stand in line and pay my money as the next man."[33]

After he completed his scenes, Fairbanks traveled to New York for a winter vacation. "A man lives longer in this kind of climate," he said. "I like cold weather and wouldn't mind going to Norway. There's too much sameness of climate in certain parts of California and the tropics, which weakens a man physically and mentally."[34]

Unlike modern big-screen epics that have merchandising campaigns built into their promotional budgets, films made in the 1930s rarely had any commercial items produced, but there were a few exceptions. Cowboy star Tom Mix had an assortment of collectible items for sale—from badges and rings to pocketknives and flashlights—but the products weren't associated with a specific film. Shirley Temple had a considerable amount of merchandise manufactured in her image, especially dolls, some of which were modeled after characters she played on screen. Walt Disney also produced toys and dolls, especially those featuring Mickey Mouse.

In 1939, only a few insignificant items were produced for Gunga Din and its cast, and none of the products were offered through deals made with the studio. Following the film's release, Cary Grant was used in an ad for a Gruen Curvex wrist watch, Joan Fontaine was featured in a Max Factor face powder ad that appeared in *Radio Mirror* magazine, and photos of Grant and Douglas Fairbanks, Jr. were placed on Dixie Ice Cream container lids. The Strathmore Paper Company in West Springfield, Massachusetts, produced a print ad promoting its quality letterhead paper with a scene from the film and a sample of the Gunga Din letterhead, which RKO used in its correspondence.

The film was featured as a cover story in the first issue of *Movie Comics*, which was created by Max Gaines' All-American Publications. The 10¢ 64-page comic book (No. 1, April 1939) traced *Gunga Din's* story line (and three other movies) with colored film stills that were accompanied with dialogue-text. During the film's 1941 re-issue run, the Keasbey & Mattison Company of Ambler, Pennsylvania promoted its asbestos-cement pipe lines with an illustration of a *bhisti* and the headline: "Even Gunga Din's profession is invaded by asbestos!" Not counting a few promotional items included in the pressbook, there was no "official" *Gunga Din* merchandise.

In a twenty-first century incarnation, toy store shelves would perhaps be filled with boxed *Gunga Din* action figures, toy bugles, rubber Thug pickaxes, assorted games, miniatures of Annie the elephant, and Tantrapur playsets, complete with tin buildings, accessories, and plastic 54mm figures.

At the end of the year, *Gunga Din* was selected as one of the top films of 1939, and included in the Showmen's Hall of Fame "in recognition of meritorious performance at the box office." Despite its impressive ticket sales, RKO had yet to cover all its production and promotional costs.

Nine motion pictures received multiple Academy Award nominations for the 12th annual Oscar ceremony, which was held at the Coconut Grove in Los Angeles' Ambassador Hotel on February 29, 1940, but *Gunga Din* received only one nomination: Joseph H. August was nominated for Best Cinematography, Black and White. Gregg Toland, however, won the cinematography Oscar for *Wuthering Heights*. A new category for color cinematography was introduced at the 1940 Academy Awards ceremonies, and the award was presented to Ernest Haller and Ray Rennahan for *Gone with the Wind*, which also took the Best Picture Oscar, among other categories.

A number of *Gunga Din's* specialists were nominated for their work on other pictures at the Academy Awards ceremony. Van Nest Polglase received an Art Direction nomination for *Love Affair*; Alfred Newman earned Music Scoring nominations for *The Hunchback of Notre Dame* and *They Shall Have Music*; and Ben Hecht and Charles MacArthur received a Screenplay nomination for *Wuthering Heights*.

Sam Jaffe was awarded a "Best Character Performance" by *Modern Screen*. "Another gem of character work," noted the magazine. "He brought a simple heart-felt sincerity to the role that made the British soldiers' feeling and respect for him credible in every way."[35]

Winning Academy Awards was important to the studios, but box office revenue was more important. A year earlier, the January 26, 1939 issue of *The Hollywood Reporter* noted that two seasoned public relations men had made a wager concerning the box office fate of *Gunga Din* and another film. Milt Howe bet Perry Lieber "a tidy sum" that *Jesse James* would outgross *Gunga Din*. Howe won. The 20th Century Fox outlaw film topped *Gunga Din* by at least $1 million.[36]

Still, *Gunga Din* had one of the biggest box office grosses in 1939, although it did not generate any black ink for RKO until the film was re-released in the early 1940s. At the conclusion of its initial run, the motion picture was still $193,000 short from matching its production costs.[37]

It is difficult to ascertain the film's exact box office status compared to other motion pictures in 1939, since no single source for the information is definitive. For example, *Gunga Din* is listed as the 24th top-grossing film of 1939, according to the Internet Movie Data Base. Another Internet site states that the film was the 2nd biggest money maker of the year, yet another site claimed it was the 7th biggest box office champ of year (sixth, if *Gone with the Wind's* receipts for only 1939 are counted). However, *Gunga Din* was ranked 10th, according to *Box Office Digest* in 1940.

The Internet's Ultimate Movie Ranking estimated that *Gunga Din's* box office returns in current dollars would total approximately $242 million, but that figure is exaggerated since an estimation based upon *Gunga Din's* $8.05 million domestic ticket sales (accumulated from 1939 to the present) and applicable Consumer Price Index (CPI) calculations would result in a figure totaling about $140 million in today's dollars. Another internet source stated that the film "was the second biggest money-making film of the year, next to *Gone with the Wind*."[38]

Chapter Seventeen Notes

1. *Motion Picture Daily*, February 10, 1939, 2. The other "five-star" films were *Jesse James, The Great Man Votes, Heart of Paris,* and *The Green Hell.*

2. *Seattle Daily Times*, July 23, 1939, 32.

3. *The New York Times*, January 27, 1939, Amusements, 17.

4. *Motion Picture Daily*, March 1, 1939, 2.

5. *Motion Picture Herald*, February 4, 1939, 68; *Motion Picture Daily*, February 2, 1939, 43.

6. *American Cinematographer*, April 1940, 149.

7. William Lewin's *Group Discussion Guide,* 1939, quoted in George E. Turner, "The Mighty Spectacle of Gunga Din," *The Cinema of Adventure, Romance & Terror* (Hollywood, California, ASC Press, 1989), 226.

8. *Motion Picture Herald*, January 28, 1939, 32.

9. *Motion Picture Herald*, March 4, 1939, 72.

10. Ibid., April 8, 1939, 82.

11. Ibid., 78.

12. Ibid., April 22, 1939, 60.

13. *Showmen's Trade Review*, June 3, 1939, 15.

14. *Motion Picture Herald*, April 15, 1939, 80.

15. Ibid., February 25, 1939, 69.

16. Ibid., February 18, 1939, 47.

17. *The Film Daily*, February 21, 1939, 7.

18. *Motion Picture Herald*, March 16, 1940, 58.

19. Ibid., July 1, 1939, 52.

20. Ibid., May 6, 1939, 61.

21. Ibid., May 13, 1939, 65.

22. *Motion Picture Daily*, February 24, 1939, 4:

23. *Motion Picture Herald*, January 13, 1940; *The Kinematograph Year Book 1940*, 104.

24. *Variety*, October, 11, 1939, 3.

25. George Stevens, Jr., *Conversations*, 228.

26. *Motion Picture Herald*, June 10, 1939, 49.

27. *Milwaukee Journal Sentinel*, February 19, 1939, 56.

28. *Motion Picture Herald*, March 11, 1939, 57.

29. *The Film Daily*, May 17, 1939, 3.

30. *Modern Screen*, August 1940, 29, 72.

31. Fontaine, *No Bed of Roses*, 89.

32. *Motion Picture Herald*, July 1, 1939, 52; August 19, 1939, 61.

33. *The Film Daily*, Feb. 16, 1939, 3.

34. *Milwaukee Journal Sentinel*, March 5, 1939, 64.

35. *Modern Screen*, January 1940, 62. Maria Ouspenskaya also received the award for her performance in *The Rains Came.*

36. According to Ultimate Movie Rankings, *Jesse James* outgrossed *Gunga Din* by more than a million dollars. Comparatively, Susan Sackett's *The Hollywood Reporter Book of Box Office Hits* (New York City: Billboard Publications, 1990), states that *Jesse James* grossed $3 million.

37. Richard B. Jewell, "RKO Film Grosses, 1929-1951: The C. J. Tevlan Ledger," *Historical Journal of Film, Radio and Television,* cited in H. Mark Glancy, *When Hollywood Loved Britain: The Hollywood "British" Film 1939-1945,* (Manchester, Great Britain: Manchester University Press, 1999), 232.

38. *Gone with the Wind* debuted on December 15, 1939, and it's box office returns for the remaining sixteen days of the year were insignificant compared to its all-time accumulated world-wide gross. Long term, of course, the epic MGM film became the all-time box office champion, adjusted for ticket price inflation (via the CPI), according to Box Office Mojo.

CHAPTER EIGHTEEN
Reading, Writing, and *Gunga Din*

Besides *Gunga Din's* basic commercial campaigns, RKO promoted the film for its educational benefits, since it was based on writings of a Nobel Prize in Literature recipient. The film's pressbook suggested numerous ways that movie theater managers could generate business by contacting local schools and libraries. *Gunga Din* poem recitation contests, school assembly programs, and library displays were among the recommended activities. The pressbook also featured a demanding "School Quiz Contest," which included challenging questions about the location, length, and width of the Khyber Pass; Hindu terms; and India's population. The studio suggested that tickets be awarded to qualifying students who not only answered the pressbook questions correctly, but also wrote a "fifty-word descriptive composition of a topic pertaining to the picture, such as the Khyber Pass, the caste system, India, etc." For many school kids, it was probably easier just to purchase tickets.

Theater managers around the country quickly picked up on the promotional ideas, and alerted schools, colleges, and other community organizations about forthcoming showings of the motion picture.

Ralph Tully, the manager of the Central Theatre in Biddeford, Maine, sent letters to area high school teachers, informing them about the showing of *Gunga Din*. "As a result, English teachers took the children to the show in a body in conjunction with the history classes."[1]

A number of theaters printed special programs that included the classic poem as an educational promotion. The Texas Theater in Palestine, Texas, distributed an "Easter Greetings Souvenir Copy of Rudyard Kipling's Famous Poem 'Gunga Din'" to its preview audience at a Saturday night April 8, 1939 showing of the film. The four-page program featured film images on the front and back covers, and the poem was printed on its two interior pages.

Frank Shaffer, manager of the Warner Dixie in Staunton, Virginia, created a quiz contest that he sent to "the weekly magazine of Mary Baldwin College, the weekly publication of the Staunton Military Academy, and a daily paper printed by high school students." Tickets to *Gunga Din* went to the first fifteen winners.[2] In Detroit, a special screening of the film was provided to more than 350 public and technical school representatives, educators, and local officials to help promote the educational aspects of the film.

Gunga Din received an important endorsement from the National Legion of Decency when the influential American Catholic Church organization classified the film with its highest rating, "Class A-1," which meant "morally unobjectionable for general patronage."[3] The other ratings were A-II ("morally unobjectionable for adults and adolescents"), A-III ("morally unobjectionable for adults"), B ("morally objectionable for adults"), and C ("condemned"). *Gone with the Wind* (1939), for example, was classified as

"B," and the future cult classic, *Reefer Madness* (1938), was labeled "C."

Gunga Din was selected as one of fifty feature films to have a classroom study-guide created for it. "Over 6,000 high schools will use the booklets in motion picture appreciation classes," noted an article in the February 24, 1940 issue of *Motion Picture Herald*. "The motion picture companies cooperate by . . . supplying scripts, stills and other material" to the educational organizations which published the guides. The guides also had a commercial tie-in to the film. "These guides foster the study of photoplay appreciation in schools," said Leon J. Bamberger, RKO's sales promotion manager. "And with the children of today being the adults of tomorrow, better pictures are assured more success through interest aroused by these guides."[4]

Although RKO's educational promotion was also designed to increase theater attendance, it cautioned local theaters to limit their advertising efforts. "Do not under any circumstances send teachers the Study Guides with play-dates stamped across them," stated the pressbook.

An article titled "Electrifying English," written by Walter Ginsburg of the English Department of Columbia University's Teachers College, in the May 1939 issue of *The Educational Screen*, praised the "educational derivatives obtainable from theatrical productions" like *Gunga Din*, especially when study guides and other materials were supplied by the studios and educational organizations. The publication's review stated: "Excellent, picturesque thriller of British army life in India, informative in sets, costumes, customs and routine. But action bristles with absurdities and burlesque heroics, with actors striving to be box office attractions, not British soldiers."

It recommended the film to "discriminating adults" and awarded it a "very good" rating for "youth."[5]

The film was also featured in the February 17, 1939 issue of *Young America*, the "National News Weekly for Youth." The publication specialized in stories about military leaders, industry and transportation, philanthropic organizations, famous United States cities and landmarks, sports figures, motion pictures, and movie stars.

Photoplay Studies, a publication of the Motion Picture Committee of the Department of Secondary Education of the National Education Association, produced *A Guide to the Appreciation of the Photoplay Based on Kipling's Gunga Din*, a title that was both informative and challenging. New York's Educational and Recreational Guides, Inc. sold the guides for 10¢ each (orders of 100 or more cost 3¢ each). Prepared by Dr. Frederick H. Law, chairman of the English department at Stuyvesant High School in New York City, the guide included a capsule history of India, a description of the Thugs, a short biography of Kipling, and a suggested reading list, which included Alfred Lloyd Tennyson's *The Defense of Lucknow* (1879) and Alexander Dumas' *The Three Musketeers* (1844), among others. One of the recommended titles was Katherine Mayo's controversial *Mother India* (1927). The Pennsylvania-born writer, who supported White Anglo-Protestant policies and was anti-immigrant and anti-Catholic, opposed the growing Indian independence movement. Mahatma Gandhi and other Indians criticized her book. "The book presented a sensational picture of the most degenerate aspects of Hindu society and advanced the case for continued British rule in India. [It was] famously dismissed by Gandhi as a

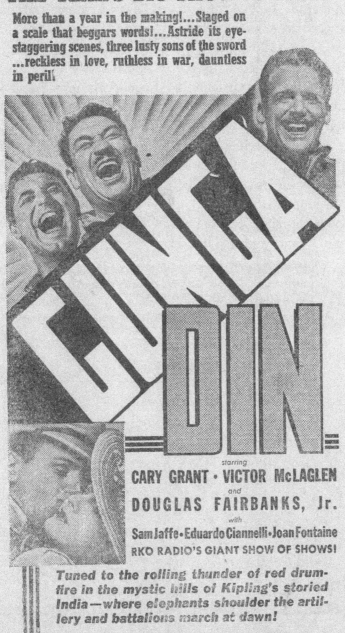

Texas Theatre, Palestine, Texas program. Author's collection.

'drain inspector's report,' [but] the book sold an astonishing 256,697 copies, making it the biggest best-seller in India."[6]

In *Photoplay Studies*, Law posed classroom questions that seemed more appropriate for college students, who were majoring in cinematography, rather than school kids. Among the challenging questions were: "How do scenes of 'mass action' aid in producing heightened dramatic effect?" and "Can you describe some particularly good uses of background? Of foreground? How does each contribute to motion-picture values in *Gunga Din?*"

An interesting trivial footnote in the publication was the naming of Cecil Kellaway, who portrayed Mr. Stebbins, and Charles Bennett, who played the headquarters' telegraph operator, in a limited cast roster that identified a dozen performers, yet Bennett and Kellaway's names were never listed in the film's credits.

New York's Schools Motion Picture Committee, "a voluntary organization composed of teachers and parents of pupils in local public and private elementary and high schools," endorsed *Gunga Din* as a film "suitable for children fourteen years and under." The film was given a special weekend showing at the Translux (Lexington Avenue), Translux (Madison Avenue), Waverly, and Manhasset (Long Island) theaters on March 31-April 2, 1939.[7]

Many students, no doubt, enjoyed their field trips to see the film. To be sure, it was an enjoyable break from their classroom routine. Unfortunately for Empire State students, the Regents Examination, a statewide standardized test given in New York high schools, included questions about several films with literary associations, including *Gunga Din*.[8]

Chapter Eighteen Notes

1. *Motion Picture Herald*, May 17, 1939, 66.
2. Ibid., June 3, 1939, 68.
3. Ibid., February 4, 1939, 68.
4. Ibid., February 24, 1940, 32.
5. *The Educational Screen*, February 1939, 70; May 1939, 150.
6. Srinath Raghavan, *India's War: World War II and the Making of Modern South Asia* (New York: Basic Books, 2016), 212.
7. *The New York Times*, March 30, 1939, 19.
8. The *Gunga Din* question was included in the Regents Examination's "American History" section, which had gone through three updatings between 1934 and 1969.

CHAPTER NINETEEN
The Plagiarism Accusation

Several writers had contributed to the *Gunga Din* story outline and screenplay, but on March 30, 1939, an Associated Press story stated that an additional contributor added his name to the roster of writers via a legal challenge. "RKO Pictures, Inc. was named defendant in a copyright infringement suit by Harry Gould, who charged that the film *Gunga Din* was pirated from an original story he submitted to the company in 1934."[1] A few days later, *Variety* reported that "Harry Gould filed a damage and injunction suit here [Los Angeles] claiming copyright infringement on the story of *Gunga Din*. Named as defendants are RKO-Radio, George Stevens, Pandro Berman, Ben Hecht, Charles MacArthur, Fred Guiol and Joel Sayre."[2]

The studio initially disregarded the lawsuit, since it claimed it didn't have rights to the film at that time. RKO argued that in 1934, Rubeigh J. Minney had been assigned by Reliance Pictures to do the screenplay for *Gunga Din* as an Edward Small production, which was planned to be released a year later though United Artists. Despite the studio's assertion, two months later, a judge allowed the suit to "go to trial."[3]

Variety later identified the writer making the claim. "Harry Gould, assignee for Alfred Goulding, author of the story, asks for an injunction and an accounting of profits."[4] Goulding, a forty-three-year-old Australian director and writer, who began in the movie business in 1917, had over 200 credits (mostly silent short subjects) by the time he brought the lawsuit against RKO. Known in Hollywood as Alf Goulding, the prolific director had collaborated with Hal Roach and Mack Sennett, and had even worked on a number of RKO silent two-reelers in the 1920s.

The studio was prepared to counter any argument proposed by Goulding. As evidence, RKO had William Nutt's notes on all of the outlines, synopses, and scripts that had been written by the various RKO-contracted writers. Among the specific information in Nutt's documents was such detailed historic data as "a list of the material, with dates and authors, in which the business of Gunga Din blowing the bugle from the top of the temple."[5] Goulding's name was not mentioned in the notes. RKO's legal department rejected the claim and asked that the suit be dismissed.

The court had another view. "Federal judge Paul J. McCormick denied RKO counsel's motion to dismiss copyright infringement suit brought by Harry Gould, assignee of Alfred Goulding, New York writer, claiming *Gunga Din* infringed Goulding's story submitted to, and rejected by, the studio in 1934," reported *Motion Picture Daily* on June 28, 1939. "After viewing the film and reading Goulding's script, the judge ruled that the suit must go to trial on its merits."[6]

Goulding had written an 84-page script, dated July 21, 1931; a four-page, nineteen-scene outline; and a two-page synopsis.[7] The documents contained information that looked similar to writings created by some of the RKO-contracted writers listed in Nutt's records.

Goulding's outline for *Ghunga Din or Paw-nee Wallah* begins in a London pub, where Buck O'Neill tells his cronies about his "adventures in India." The story begins with Buck and his three fellow soldiers engaged in a fight with a cart driver. The companions "annex a street water-carrier boy, Ghunga Din." Yvonne, "a charming English girl who runs a tea garden," falls in love with O'Neill; however, the Rajah Joudmapour is attracted to her and is "jealous of Buck."

Later, as Buck proposes to Yvonne, his three friends eavesdrop on the couple. Meanwhile, Joudmapour plans a "native uprising," while deceiving the "stupid and self-complacent General Watkins."

Buck and his comrades expel "a crowd of hostile worshippers at a Burmese temple" and loot some of its jewels. Buck brings a sacred diamond bracelet to Yvonne, who has just refused a similar bracelet from Joudmapour. Buck and Yvonne marry. Later, some fakirs steal Yvonne's bracelet. They believe Joudmapour stole the sacred bracelet and kill him.

A native force initiates a surprise attack against the British, but the soldiers prevail, although Buck is wounded. "Din is fatally wounded, gets the water to Buck and dies." In the nineteenth and concluding scene, Buck completes his story in the pub.

Goulding's synopsis sets the opening pub scene in Calcutta "about 1900." The story begins at a bazaar with a fight between Buck and a cart driver. After the soldier knocks the driver out, Din arrives with water for the fallen man. Buck later meets Yvonne, who is stranded in Calcutta, following the sudden death of her father, an entrepreneur who operated a tea garden.

The couple plan to marry but the regiment is quickly called out. While Buck is away,

Rajah Joudmapour tries to "win the girl" with the "replica of a famous bracelet in a Burmese temple." Din serves as a messenger between Buck and Yvonne. Following a skirmish, Buck smuggles the original sacred bracelet from the temple and presents it to Yvonne when he returns to Calcutta. Buck and Yvonne get married. "Though Buck has but one day of enlistment left, he is forced to go out with the regiment to Khyber" where a battle takes place. The rebellious locals, who subsequently kill the Rajah because they believe he stole the sacred bracelet, hurl boulders down at the British. However, the soldiers win, "the faithful Ghunga Djin [sic] is killed," and "his enlistment over, Buck takes Yvonne to London."

Goulding created a poignant death for the faithful water carrier. Din runs back with a ration of water but an Afghan sniper shoots him. Though wounded, he manages to reach Buck, who is wounded and thirsty. "I hope you liked your drink, sahib," says Din, who "crumbles dead with his head in his master's lap." Buck puts "his arms around the poor Pawnee Wallah's head and says to Din: "I belted yer . . . I flayed yer . . . by the livin' God that made yer . . . you're a better man than I am—Ghunga Din." Buck begins to cry and his "tears drop one by one" on Din's face.

The script ends in the Peacock Bar, where Buck tells the misty-eyed group that Din was given a military funeral, and a statue of the fallen *bhisti* was placed on his grave. Buck says that the bracelet was returned to a "pagoda God in Mandalay," and that he and Yvonne have five children: "Three Jacks and a pair o' Queens." After he departs, Flossie, the bar maid, tells the group that Buck didn't pay for his drinks. In the conclusion, "Little Charlie taunts her by cawing like a crow," but

Flossie "squirts him in the face with a bottle of syphon."

Goulding even suggested a cast list and some brief character descriptions:

James Cagney (Buck O'Neill) soldier of fortune.

Al Austin (Gloomy Gus) a bar fly

Clyde Cook (Little Charlie) a smaller bar fly

Joan Blondell (Queenie) a "Broad" barmaid

Billy Bevans (Mike) a British Tommy Atkins

Bobby Dunn (Muckey) another Tommy

Vic Portel (Splinter) a bean pole Tommy (or Charlie Chase)

Warner Oland (Hindoo Performing Man)

Ivan Lieberdorff (Rajah Joudmapour) a potential

William V. Mong (Rajah Batgahl) a decrepit old prince

Frank Hagney (Sergeant Mulligan) of the British Army

Albert Gran (General Watkins) a passe general

Noah Berry (Hindoo Fakir)

Evelyn Knapp (Yvonne) the belle of Calcutta

Matilde Comont (Simba) her Hindoo ayah (maid)

Georgie Stone (Ghunga Din) a pawnee walla[h]

Parts of Goulding's writings (a group of feisty soldiers, a romance between one of the men and a woman with a tea business connection, the looting of treasure, a native uprising, the expiring enlistment, the stone throwing, the courageous death of the faithful water car-

rier, and the use of Kipling's closing line from the poem) were similar enough to various elements in the final *Gunga Din* screenplay that RKO decided to reach a settlement instead of challenging the claim in a court of law.

"Harry Gould's plagiarism suit against RKO over *Gunga Din* was settled by stipulation in federal court here today [June 28, 1940]," stated *Motion Picture Daily*. The stipulation decision simplified the litigation, eliminated unnecessary court time, and saved additional costs for both parties. "Gould was said to have been paid a substantial sum on his claim that he owns a story written by Alfred Goulding which RKO is alleged to have used without authorization."[8] At the time, Goulding was basking in the success of *A Chump at Oxford* (1940), one of Laurel and Hardy's best Hal Roach comedies, which he had directed for United Artists.

Although the legal issue was resolved, RKO was involved in another controversy over *Gunga Din*.

Chapter Nineteen Notes

1. *Richmond Times-Dispatch*, March 31, 1939, 14; *Motion Picture Daily*, April 3, 1939, 6.

2. *Variety*, April 5, 1939, 6.

3. *Motion Picture Daily*, June 28, 1939, 8.

4. *Variety*, July 5, 1939, 22.

5. Nutt to Lillie Messenger, RKO Studio Records, Inter-Department Communications, March 1, 2, 1939. On June 26, 1940, the studio's legal department also prepared a Plot Structure Analysis document that compared and contrasted seventeen common elements shared by both *The Front Page* and *Gunga Din*, but it is not clear as to the value of that information with regard to Goulding's writings. Perhaps, RKO wanted to show that certain elements in Goulding's works possibly originated in *The Front Page*, but that could not be substantiated.

6. *Motion Picture Daily*, June 28, 1939, 8.

7. RKO Studio Records.

8. *Motion Picture Daily*, June 28, 1940, 5.

CHAPTER TWENTY
The Reaction from India: Protests and Murder

When *Gunga Din* was first released, B. R. Crisler of *The New York Times*, called Kipling "the Peter Pan of imperialism," since the writer's poetics underscored the glory associated with Great Britain's world-wide empire.[1] However, that empire greatly diminished in size during the twentieth century as nationalist movements erupted around the globe. Indian nationalism was championed by Mahatma Gandhi, who led the movement for an end to British rule.

The United States had maintained a marginal interest in India since the late eighteenth century. Even in the early twentieth century, America's economic relationship with the Asian subcontinent remained limited. "American investment in India in the late 1930s amounted to less than $50 million, with over half of this accounted for in missionary schools, hospitals and other non-commercial activities."[2]

On the other hand, the United States had a long standing political and economic association with Great Britain. Following the War for American Independence and the War of 1812, the two nations developed a lasting international friendship; however, Anglo-American ties would be tested by India's quest for independence. Although the United States was a strong ally of Great Britain, it was sympathetic to colonies which sought self-determination through democratic means. "In the 1930s, the future of India was still visualized as being within the British empire and not outside it," wrote Prem Chowdhry in *Colonial India and the Making of Empire Cinema*. Immediate concerns such as economic stagnation and the rise of fascism "rendered the question of Indian self-determination futile."[3]

The Government of India Act in 1835 gave India greater autonomy on the local level, but the legislation reaffirmed Great Britain's overall control over the Asian subcontinent and the Indian Army. That, of course, would change.

Despite its modest economic ties to India, the United States maintained a robust motion picture relationship with the Asian subcontinent; as a matter of fact, India was a major international market for American films. Next to Japan, it was the only Asian nation in the late 1930s with more than 1,000 movie theaters.[4] RKO expected that *Gunga Din* would do well in all world markets, but some early criticisms signaled the possibility of box office trouble in India.

While cinematic villains abound in *Gunga Din*, the film championed the disciplined bravery of the Indian lancers and the sympathetic title character's courageous sacrifice, yet that wasn't enough for audience members in India, who looked at the film through their own prisms of race, history, and culture. Even before its release, the epic motion picture was severely criticized. "Mr. K. A. Abbas, the well-known local journalist, had gone on a world tour [and] while in Hollywood he got the opportunity of visiting some of the foreign studios and watching the shooting of *Gunga Din* which he calls 'a scandalously anti-Indian picture,'" noted the January 1939 issue of *Filmindia*. The "scandalously anti-Indian" claim against *Gunga Din* was also made by Chandular Shah, the Chairman of the Reception Committee of the Indian Motion Picture Congress and President of the Indian Motion Picture Producers Association.[5]

The negative press directed at films made by American and British studios about nineteenth century India was nothing new. Alexander Korda's *The Drum* (1938), which featured its star, Sabu, as a pro-British prince, caused riots in Madras and Bombay, and was subsequently banned.[6] "Such libelous pictures should not be allowed to land on our soil," proclaimed *Filmindia*.[7]

The criticisms continued. "Those who are familiar with the works of that greatest of all Imperialist propaganda poets, Rudyard Kipling, will recall a poem [whose purpose is] to impress the world with the devotion of Indians and to teach the 'natives' that the highest ambition in their lives must be such an opportunity to serve their White masters," stated Abbas in *Filmindia*. He noted that the final "better man than I am" line of the poem "will be exploited to prove that the motive of the story is not anti-Indian."

Abbas' article featured such sub-headlines as "Indians Portrayed as sadistic barbarians," "Indians—no better than dogs!" "Indians cringing before the White masters," "Horrors of the West planted in the East," and "Ridicule of the goddess Kali." For Abbas, there was no diplomatic way to shroud his feelings about the film, and he described the film's plot in blunt terms: "The White 'hero' is kidnapped by fanatic 'native' priests and is kept in a torture chamber with poisonous cobras wriggling uncomfortably near. But, of course, he won't yield to the threats of the

'cursed infidels' and is ultimately rescued, the mutinous pathans routed and the mighty British Empire once again vindicated."

The writer also criticized the film's cultural accuracy and identified several anachronisms: "Kali-worship goes on in the land of Muslim Pathans, people in the frontier are shown wearing loin cloth (instead of the 'Shalwar,' in which every one, Hindu or Muslim, wears over there), elephants tread the camel tracks of the Khyber Pass." Abbas ended his article with a demonstrative call to action: "What are we going to do about it?"[8]

At the conclusion of Abbas' article, the magazine published the film's basic story line that was submitted by Nick Ermolieff of RKO's Foreign Department: "When a revival of Thuggee, ancient murder-religion, threatens Britain's troubled Northwest Indian frontier, the three toughest sergeants in the British Indian Army are sent to the scene, one treasure bound, drags the other two into trouble and the three sergeants and their native water carrier, Gunga Din, are captured by Thugs. A rescue battalion heads directly into a Thug ambush but is warned just in time by Gunga Din at the cost of his life. His heroism averts the ambush, the sergeants are rescued and the uprising is stamped out."[9] Ermolieff's article was an op-ed of sorts, a journalistic attempt to simply describe the film without socio-political commentary. However, it received no sympathy from the Indian press, and the criticism escalated.

Ram Bagai, *Filmindia's* Hollywood correspondent, evaluated *Gunga Din* in the magazine's February issue: "It may be good entertainment for the rest of the world but for India, it resembles the usual Occidental idea of India—seen through the eyes of British imperialism."[10]

George Stevens said the Thugs were not representative of all Indians. "They went their own way and were quite belligerent and self-sufficient," he said. However, he admitted that some who viewed the film may have associated the Thugs with the entire Hindu population. "One thing that isn't clear is that the Thuggees worshiping the goddess Kali were not associated with other tribes and groups in India," said Stevens. "We wanted to create an interest in these people who could ride into town in large numbers, occupy a civilized little village and test the strength of the military platoon system."[11]

Filmindia increased its criticism of the film in its March issue with an editorial titled "This Slander Must Stop," which appeared on its first content page: "[*Gunga Din*] will go all over the world and tell the world that Indians are sadistic barbarians and unfaithful dogs who need the stern rule of their white masters to teach them to behave like faithful dogs, which incidentally is the ideal life prescribed for the treacherous, scheming and unscrupulous 'natives of India.'"[12]

The three-page essay did not view *Gunga Din* as an isolated one-of-a-kind production from RKO. Rather, *Filmindia* viewed the motion picture as merely the latest celluloid assault against the Asian nation. "It will be interesting to recall that far back in 1933 that scandalous picture *India Speaks* was also produced by RKO. A storm of protest swept throughout our country and the tins of *India Speaks* were returned back to America."[13]

Filmindia also noted that Gandhi had been ridiculed in a 1935 RKO two-reel comedy, *Everybody Likes Music*. The publication said that the Gandhi-like character was depicted as an "immoral drunkard dancing with a low woman in a cheap saloon."[14] RKO eventu-

ally removed the sequence from the film for Indian audiences. The magazine's editorial stated that *Gunga Din* should be not only be banned in India but in every other country. Furthermore, *Filmindia* demanded that all prints be withdrawn from world markets and the original negative destroyed "in the presence of Indian officials."[15] Years later, British film historian Jeffrey Richards justified India's rejection of the film. "With its dhoti-clad Indian village villain, the Guru, looking like a sort of demented Gandhi and with Indian customs flouted wholesale, this ban is not perhaps surprising," he stated.[16] "The enemies of the British Empire are invariably mad-eyed fanatics, seeking the extermination of the whites and the establishment of personal power."[17]

Filmindia also criticized such previously released India-based films as *The Charge of the Light Brigade* (1936) and *Lives of a Bengal Lancer* (1935). Chandular Shah and Rai Saheb Chuni Lall, Vice-President of the Motion Picture Society of India, condemned *Gunga Din* and praised *Filmindia* for its efforts to ban the film.[18] Shah warned American and British studios not to make films that insulted "Indian prestige and nationalism."[19]

Filmindia dedicated its April issue to *Gunga Din*. Highlighted on a single page, the issue described Kipling's title character, who "died like a faithful dog for his white masters and in dying left behind an excuse to the white-men to slander his country and countrymen." The issue also criticized various reviews of the film which celebrated the British role in India.[20]

Despite protests from India, Hollywood was optimistic about forthcoming releases that had India-based story lines. In April, 20th Century Fox announced a future production titled *The Khyber Rifles*. "A story of heroic action . . . as British regiments and native hordes clash for the gateway of India . . . historic blood-drenched Khyber Pass," read an announcement in *Variety*.[21] However, it would take another fourteen years for the studio to release *King of the Khyber Rifles*.

A tragic incident occurred on April 9, 1939, at a showing of *Gunga Din* in Shanghai. A gunman shot and killed Cheng Si-Keng, a Chinese controller of customs, and Charles Glauser, a Swiss engineer. The unidentified gunman also wounded Talat Mansurov, a Russian who attempted to capture the shooter. The gunman "chose his moment when there was almost constant gunfire as part of the talkie film, and most people in the theatre knew nothing of the act."[22] On April 11, *The San Luis Obispo Daily Telegram* identified Cheng Si-Keng as "director of the Federal Reserve bank." The shooting became a major diplomatic incident when Japan insisted that British authorities were responsible for apprehending the gunman. However, no information directly associated the shooter with anti-*Gunga Din* sentiments.

As a result of a "protest resolution passed unanimously by the Indian Motion Picture Congress," *Gunga Din* was subsequently "banned by different provincial governments in India" in April, 1939.[23] Ironically, the Bengal Board of Film censors allowed the motion picture to be shown after it was edited—not because of India's criticisms, but because part of the film depicted British soldiers "in a bad light."[24]

Filmindia editor Baburao Patel traveled to the United States during the summer of 1939, and expressed his concerns to the Hays Office, headed by Will H. Hays, which established morality guidelines in films via its Production Code. Prior to his departure, Patel met with Gandhi, who approved his mission. Patel told the American press about "unsympathetic treatment accorded the Indians in several recent pictures." He believed that *Gunga Din* was in violation of the Production Code, since the guidelines included a ban on "willful offense to any nation, race or creed," and recommended "avoiding picturizing in an unfavorable light another country's religion, history, institutions, prominent people and citizenry."

"We don't want to quarrel with the American filmmakers," said Patel in a *New York Times* interview. "But neither do we intend to sit back and see Indians portrayed before the entire world as savage barbarians. The anti-Indian attitude of RKO pictures was manifested in *Gunga Din*." Patel also criticized American filmmakers for utilizing only the services of "ex-servicemen from the British Army as technical advisers."[25] The film's primary advisor, Robert Erskine Holland, was somewhat sympathetic to the Indian point of view, and had written numerous memos to George Stevens about his concerns during and after production.

During his stateside visit, Patel met with Stevens and explained his complaints about the film. "Next time I produce an Indian subject, I hope to please India," said Stevens. "Time alone will provide whether we can rely upon the promises of the West," replied Patel."[26]

David Platt, the film critic of the New York-based *Daily Worker*, the official publication of the Communist Party of America, also criticized *Gunga Din*—but for a different reason. The writer mentioned that the film, along with other motion pictures, was decidedly pro-war and pro-British.[27] Despite Platt's posturing, the Union of Soviet Socialist Republics joined Great Britain in the fight against Nazi

Germany, Imperial Japan, and Fascist Italy during World War II.

Japan banned *Gunga Din* in January 1940, due to the nation's "sympathy with the Indian protest" against the film. *Variety* reported that Japan's action was taken "in order to prevent undesirable reactions in Indo-Japanese relations."[28] Japan's "sympathy" with India was primarily based on its anti-British position as an Axis member during World War II (Germany, Japan, and Italy signed the Tripartite Pact on September 27, 1940, in Berlin). The United States became increasingly concerned about India's role in the world conflict. "By late 1938, American officials in India were expressing doubts about the loyalty of the Indian army to the Raj and the susceptibility of nationalist sentiment to German and Japanese propaganda."[29]

Japan was also an important Asian market for American films. Despite the international saber rattling, Hollywood remained focused on the bottom line. "Of the country's 1,800 theaters, 65 show American pictures exclusively, while about 100 others book [American] films irregularly," noted *The Hollywood Reporter*. "A Chaplin, Tarzan, or a serial can play more than 1,000 of the houses."[30] After December 7, 1941, American film releases in Japan became an irrelevant issue.

The ban on *Gunga Din* extended to Hong Kong, then a British colony, following protests organized by the Hindu Association of Hong Kong. Anti-British sentiment reached a higher level when Gandhi asked for an end to British rule in 1942. On November 10, 1942, British Prime Minister Winston Churchill delivered a speech in London and said, "I have not become the King's First Minister to preside over the liquidation of the British Empire." Events would prove otherwise.

Gunga Din's re-releases in the early 1940s were criticized by Ezra Goodman, the film critic for *Common Sense*, a left-wing political magazine published in the United States between 1931 and 1946. "The fact that Hollywood's presentation of foreign groups and minorities has usually been a distorted one," wrote Goodman in a piece for *Asia Magazine* in 1943. "And yet, at this time, a motion picture company has seen fit to revive *Gunga Din*, a film that depicts the Hindus as deep-dyed villains. The ill-will sowed by *Gunga Din* and pictures like *The Lives of a Bengal Lancer* is reaping its harvest now. India's distrust of the white man's concept of India has been appreciably conditioned by such films."[31]

Writer Jeffrey Richards justified the distrust, suggesting that the big-screen enemies of the British Raj were usually depicted the same way. "More often than not they are devotees of the goddess Kali and members of the strangling brotherhood of Thuggee," said Richards.[32]

The fight over *Gunga Din* included covert operations. The United States Office of War Information (OWI), which was created in 1942 to disseminate propaganda favorable to the allies, and its companion war-time agency in Great Britain, the Ministry of Information (MoI), were concerned about films that championed Great Britain's imperialism over the nation's democratic heritage. An OWI survey found that "some Americans believed that Britain was not a democracy at all." Furthermore, many Americans felt that Britain was fighting for "selfish reasons," including "the defense of her Empire."[33] The OWI, which examined all the studio's scripts (Paramount refused to provide its screenplays), was concerned that films which heralded British imperialism might be criticized as hypocritical, considering the denounced imperialist policies of the enemy Axis Powers.

In 1942, RKO planned another worldwide re-release of *Gunga Din*. Lowell Mellett, a former *Washington Daily News* editor and head of OWI's Bureau of Motion Pictures, was concerned about India's wartime view of the film. "I am told that at the time of its first release there was a great deal of criticism from Indian leaders who resented the manner in which the people of India were presented," noted Mellett. "If that is true, the resentment at this time doubtless would be much greater and the consequences of such resentment might be serious." The OWI recommended that the film not be re-released in European and Asian markets, but RKO appealed. The OWI countered the studio's request by stating: "The assumption of the picture is that it is right for Britain to hold an alien country by force of arms. At a time when we are stressing that the current war is a people's war, this is an obviously inopportune comment."[34] At that particular juncture, RKO was attempting to raise additional box office revenue to pay off the film's initial big-budget costs. Furthermore, the studio had already invested additional dollars to promote the re-release, but RKO managed to generate an additional $705,000 at the box office before it was withdrawn from the British and Indian markets. The film became profitable in 1942 with "a profit of $445,000."[35]

"*Gunga Din* . . . was not re-released [in the British empire] at the behest of the MoI and the OWI. [The] decision taken to shelve the reissue of *Gunga Din* is a testament to the fact that the OWI was trying to reshape ideas about the British and minimize the negative connotations of Empire."[36] Furthermore, the film was also banned because of the "fear of offending Indians whose cooperation was needed in the war effort."[37]

In Great Britain, previously held stereotypical views on the country's colonial peoples were changing. "War has taken multitudes of us abroad to see something of other lands and their peoples," wrote Harold Stewart in the April 1945 issue of *The Kipling Journal*. "As a result, we've learned quite a lot about 'subject races' and 'lesser breeds without the Law.' We've learned that all Indians aren't 'Lazarushian-leather.'"[38]

To some, those changing views were evolving too slowly. When World War II ended, large-scale anti-British protests erupted in India and mutinies broke out by native military personnel. The most tragic event associated with the Indian protests of *Gunga Din* occurred in Greece less than a month after the war ended in Europe.

The April 1946 issue of *Filmindia* later reported: "Joginder Singh, a young Punjabi electrician attached to a unit in the Indian army stationed in Greece . . . was sentenced to transportation for life on a charge of shooting dead a British guard." According to the monthly, Singh and a group of other Indians had been outside a movie theater protesting its showing of *Gunga Din* by the British military authority. They later entered the theater and disrupted the showing. "A British guard fired at him but he escaped. Joginder Singh retaliated by firing at the guard who was instantly killed." Singh was immediately captured and sent to a court martial where he was sentenced to death, but the sentence was later changed to "transportation for life," which equated to life imprisonment at a penal colony. The magazine made no comment on Singh's crime but added: "*Gunga Din* is the same obnoxious anti-Indian film which was banned ... because the film constituted a slander on the fair name of our country and its people."[39]

However, British military authorities found a number of errors in *Filmindia's* report. Captain F. S. Jafri sent a complete description of the events and requested that the magazine publish it in its next [June 1946] issue. Jafri pointed out that on the evening of June 1, 1945, Singh and five other Sepoys of the 7th India Infantry Brigade transport company "took exception to the fact that the Attikon Cinema in [Kavala] ... advertised the film *Gunga Din* which they considered [a] 'bad' film." The group subsequently entered the theater, where *Marie Walewska* (1937), a film (also known as *Conquest*) about Napoleon's Polish mistress, was being shown—not *Gunga Din*. "Armed, some with Tommy guns and other rifles, they entered the hall where approximately 50 people were present and opened fire indiscriminately." A corporal named Curtis, who was on duty, was fatally wounded with two bullets, but he never fired at his attackers nor did he engage in any conversation with them. The six Indian soldiers were convicted of murder and sentenced to "transportation for life." The British report also noted that the cinema booked its films and that the military authorities "had no power to prevent its being shown."[40]

On August 15, 1947, India became an independent nation. Five months later, Gandhi was assassinated. Coincidentally, RKO did not authorize a 1948 re-release of *Gunga Din*.

Chapter Twenty Notes

1. B. R. Crisler, "Poets and the Cinema," *The New York Times*, January 29, 1939, Screen, 5.

2. Raghavan, *India's War*, 212.

3. Prem Chowdry, *Colonial India and the Making of Empire Cinema: Image, Ideology and Identity* (Manchester, UK: Manchester University Press, 2000), 181.

4. T. Ramsaye, ed., *The 1939-1940 Motion Picture Almanac* (New York: Quigley Publications, 1940), 944, cited in *Glancy, When Hollywood Loved Britain*. Japan had 1,749 movie theaters; India had 1,025, which represented 25% of all the theaters in Asia. According to *The Hollywood Reporter* in its January 26, 1939 issue, Japan had 1,800 movie theaters. The *Motion Picture Almanac* noted that the United States had 16,228 motion picture houses; Great Britain had 5,300.

5. *Filmindia*, January 1939, 34; *The Cine Technician*, July-August 1939, 47. Shah is also identified in other publications as Sardar Chandulal Sha.

6. Richards, *The Age of the Dream Palace*, 137.

7. *Filmindia*, January 1939, 34.

8. Ibid., 26-27, 31.

9. Ibid., 31.

10. Ibid., 24.

11. George Stevens, Jr., *Conversations*, 226.

12. *Filmindia*, March 1939, 3.

13. Ibid.

14. Ibid., 4.

15. Ibid., 5.

16. Richards, *The Age of the Dream Palace*, 137.

17. Richards, *Visions of Yesterday* (London: Routledge & Kegan Paul, 1973), 211.

18. *Filmindia*, March 1939, 23, 25.

19. *The Cine-Technician*, July-August, 1939, 47.

20. *Filmindia*, April 1939, 2, 26.

21. *Variety*, April 19, 1939, 14.

22. *Marietta Journal*, June 9, 1939, 1.

23. *Filmindia*, October 1939, 45.

24. Ibid., March 1940, 4.

25. *The New York Times*, September 10, 1939, Amusements, 4.

26. *Filmindia*, December, 4.

27. *Motion Picture Herald*, April 27, 1940, 9.

28. *Variety*, February 21, 1940, 11.

29. Srinath Raghavan, *India's War*, 212.

30. *The Hollywood Reporter*, January 26, 1939, 18.

31. Ezra Goodman, "Hollywood and Minorities," *Asia Magazine*, 1943, 84.

32. Richards, *Visions of Yesterday*, 211.

33. Glancy, *When Hollywood Loved Britain*, 187-188.

34. Ibid., 191.

35. Richard B. Jewell, "RKO Film Grosses, 1929-1951," cited in Glancy, 232.

36. Sara Rose Johnstone, *A Special Relationship: The British Empire in British and American Cinema, 1939-1960*, Ph.D thesis, University of Warwick, Canada, 2013, 21.

37. Richards, *The Age of the Dream Palace*, 143.

38. Harold Stewart, "Goodbye to Gunga Din," *The Kipling Journal*, April 1945, 6.

39. *Filmindia*, April 1946, 53.

40. Ibid., June 1946, 48-49.

CHAPTER TWENTY-ONE
Gunga Din: TV's "First" Film

Gunga Din has a unique place in television history: it was one of the first big-screen films to be broadcast on the small screen.

The New York Times stated that "the first motion picture to be made expressly for television will be *Gunga Din*, according to arrangements completed between RKO-Radio Pictures and the National Broadcasting Company."[1] *Gunga Din* wasn't "made expressly" for the home screen, but an abbreviated version of it was.

On March 11, 1939, *Motion Picture Herald* announced that a ten-minute television version of *Gunga Din*, "with medium and close-up scenes, with special sound effects, and a smooth continuity," has been shipped to NBC studios in New York for tests. The film's selection was also based upon its use of vivid, contrasting outdoor lighting, a tribute of sorts to cinematographer Joseph H. August. "This television version of *Gunga Din* is a groundbreaker," said RKO's Pandro Berman.[2] One month later, *Variety* reported that "RKO has prepared a two-reel version of *Gunga Din* designed strictly for television broadcasting."[3]

A few weeks later, *Motion Picture Daily* noted that RKO had entered into an agreement with NBC-television to show a specially edited version of *Gunga Din*. "NBC is scheduled to start regular daily broadcasts April 30, coincidentally with the opening of the World's Fair," reported the publication. ["*Gunga Din* will be the] first film to be televised in this manner." The special 18½ minute showing, which aired on April 30 and

May 26, seemed to be nothing more than an interesting broadcast idea.[4] However, other studios took notice and followed. On April 27, 1939, *Motion Picture Daily* reported that Columbia Pictures provided a *Mr. Smith Goes to Washington* (1939) trailer to NBC-television.

Radio Today magazine featured an article titled "Television's First Film" in its May 1939 issue. "RKO Radio Pictures' *Gunga Din* is the first film being adapted especially for television. The picture is being condensed to 1,000 feet for use by NBC over its television transmitter on top of the Empire State Building."[5]

Television in 1939 was an embryonic industry, and speculations arose about its future. "There are dozens of guesses about what practical form television may take," wrote syndicated news correspondent Paul Harrison.[6] On August 26, 1939, television made its presence more widely known when WXBS broadcast the first major league baseball game, a contest between the Brooklyn Dodgers and the Cincinnati Reds at Brooklyn's Ebbets Field.

Still, the new medium did not seem to be a threat to the motion picture business. After all, *Motion Picture Daily* estimated the number of television sets in the New York metropolitan area to number "about 500." However, one person saw the special broadcast as a wake-up call. George Gold, the president of the Allied Theatre Owners of New Jersey, sent a letter of concern to George J. Schaefer, the president of

RKO. "It has come to our attention that RKO Radio Pictures, Inc. has been furnishing films for use over television systems," wrote Gold. "We are greatly surprised that any producer should provide a source of competition to its exhibitor customers. We strongly oppose such action by any distributor-producer, and urge that you discontinue this practice."[7]

On June 13, 1939, *Motion Picture Daily* ran a headline that read: "No Television Peril Visioned For Theaters." The accompanying article included portions of a letter written by W. J. Merrill, Schaefer's assistant, to Gold in which the RKO spokesperson stated that months ago a special trailer for *Gunga Din* was broadcast to television owners in San Francisco as "an experiment with a new medium of exploitation for feature product." Merrill added that "the present outlook of a threat to motion picture theatres seems very small, indeed."[8] Statistics at the time supported Merrill's remarks. Approximately 7,000 television sets were sold in the United States between 1939 and 1941, which hardly seemed to present a "threat" to the big screen.

Gunga Din helped promote the Dumont company in 1945, when the manufacturer previewed its television set of the future: a big-screen model that could project an image up to 4½ by 6 feet. At the press demonstration held at Dumont's New York station, WABD, viewers saw the condensed version of *Gunga Din* that NBC had broadcast in 1939. Dumont selected the film "because of its well-lit scenes, excellent close-ups, and the dramatic impact of its story."[9] The Dumont Home Theater Unit carried a $1,800 price tag, which was a higher price than the cost of an average automobile at that time. Large-screen televisions wouldn't become affordable for the average consumer until the twenty-first century.

However, the sales of normal-sized television sets increased dramatically. Over 3,600,000 TV sets were sold in the 1940s, and nearly 10 million were sold in 1950 alone. Conversely, total film box office revenue in the United States peaked in 1947, and began a seventeen-year decline that resulted in a 78% drop in movie ticket sales. George Gold's prediction was correct.

Another new broadcast technology made its official debut in 1951, and *Gunga Din* was part of it. Phonevision was Zenith Radio Company's attempt to create a pay television service in Chicago. It was an innovative financial practice that was designed to provide the television station with additional revenue besides its advertising income. For consumers, the new technology featured the innovative "Lazy Bones" remote control, which was promoted by the company for its convenience. "Simply touch the button," read a Zenith information advertisement that appeared in newspapers. "Touch it again for still another channel. No more walking across the room to change stations." The company also noted that it would broadcast feature films "free of advertising for a small fee."[10]

In 1951, 300 families were "supplied by Zenith with Phonevision-equipped TV receivers [and] were given the opportunity to view ninety Hollywood feature films in their own homes" during a ninety-day period at a price of $1 per picture.

One of the motion pictures offered to participating families was *Gunga Din*. The action-adventure classic generated $89 during the trial period, which translated to a potential $2,967,000 gross (or a producer's share at 50% of $1,483,500) based on 10,000 theoretical television receivers. *Gunga Din* was also one of the more popular films selected by participants in a survey. However, pay television in the 1950s was about three decades premature, despite positive feedback from its selected customers.[11]

Chapter Twenty-One Notes

1. *The New York Times*, January 22, 1939, Art-Radio, 10. Among earlier films shown on television was *The Crooked Circle* (1932), which was broadcast in 1933 in its entirety on TV when experimental Los Angeles station W6XAO-TV beamed it out from the corner of 7th and Bixel Streets in downtown.

2. *Motion Picture Herald*, March 11, 1939, 35.

3. *Variety*, April 12, 1939, 47.

4. *Motion Picture Daily*, February 17, 1939, 1.

5. *Radio Today*, May 1939, 47.

6. *Lexington Herald* (Lexington, Kentucky), June 4, 1939, 5.

7. *The Film Daily*, June 8, 1939, 1, 6; *Motion Picture Daily*, June 8, 1939, 8. See also David Pierce, "'Senile Celluloid:' Independent Exhibitors, the Major Studios and the Fight over Feature Films on Television, 1939-1956," *Film History*, Vol. 10, No. 2, Indiana University Press, 1998.

8. *Motion Picture Daily*, June 13, 1939, 12.

9. *Motion Picture Herald*, May 5, 1945, 30.

10. *Greensboro Daily News* (Greensboro, North Carolina), October 3, 1950, 2.

11. *Film Daily Year Book* 1951, 766-768. *Welcome Stranger* (1947) was the most popular Phonevision selection in 1951 with sales of $179. Other popular films were *Silver River* (1948), *Song of the South* (1946), *The Hunchback of Notre Dame* (1939), *The Hucksters* (1947), and *Lost Horizon* (1937), a Sam Jaffe film.

CHAPTER TWENTY-TWO
Cast and Crew After *Gunga Din*

For those who were identified in the film's opening credits, *Gunga Din* was another stepping stone towards greater success in the entertainment business, but many of the uncredited cast and crew members also went on to have rewarding careers in Hollywood. However, one cast member became caught up in the anti-Communist purge of the post-World War II years.

Gary Grant became one of Hollywood's all-time greats, appearing in such memorable films as *His Girl Friday* (1940), *The Philadelphia Story* (1940), *Penny Serenade* (1941), *Arsenic and Old Lace* (1944), *None But the Lonely Heart* (1945), *An Affair to Remember* (1957), *North by Northwest* (1959), and *Operation Petticoat* (1959), among many others.

Grant recalled a *Gunga Din*-related story about his *Operation Petticoat* co-star, Tony Curtis. "When Tony was living aboard ship in the Navy during World War II, the crew would go out for long periods of time," said Grant. "They only had a limited number of films on board. One of them was *Gunga Din*. They got so tired of listening to it over and over that they turned the sound off and acted out the different roles. Tony played me."[1]

Cary Grant was nominated for two Best Actor Oscars—*Penny Serenade* (1941) and *None But the Lonely Heart* (1945)—and won an honorary Oscar in 1970. A year later, his work in *Gunga Din* was acknowledged by British author Ian Allan in the *Cary Grant Film Album*. In his later years, Grant ac-knowledged that *Gunga Din* was his favorite film.[2] Grant died on November 29, 1986.

Victor McLaglen's acting career included such memorable John Ford-directed films as *Fort Apache* (1948), *She Wore a Yellow Ribbon* (1949), *Rio Grande* (1950), and *The Quiet Man* (1953), for which he received a Best Supporting Actor Oscar nomination. One of his last films, *The Abductors* (1957), was directed by his son, Andrew V. McLaglen. He continued to act into his seventies. On October 9, 1959, Victor McLaglen appeared in the TV Western, *Rawhide,* episode "Incident of the Shambling Man," his last professional appearance. He died on November 7, 1959.

Douglas Fairbanks, Jr. appeared in many films, including such swashbucklers as *The Corsican Brothers* (1941), *Sinbad, the Sailor* (1947), and *The Fighting O'Flynn* (1949). During World War II, he served with distinction in the United States Navy, and helped create the Beach Jumpers, an amphibious diversion-deception unit that operated in the Mediterranean Sea. For his service, Fairbanks received numerous awards and citations, including the United States Navy's Legion of Merit, Great Britain's Distinguished Service Cross, and a Silver Star, the United States' third highest combat decoration.

He hosted his own television series, *Douglas Fairbanks, Jr. Presents,* from January 1953 to February 1957, and appeared in a *Gunga Din*-like comedy sketch, "Lives of a Bungle Lancer," on *The Red Skelton Show* in 1964.

Whenever he and Cary Grant crossed paths, they greeted each other in a memorable way. "Until he died, Grant and I always addressed each other as Cutter and Ballantyne [sic]—from that film of 1938."[3] Douglas Fairbanks, Jr. died on May 7, 2000, and was buried in his famous father's tomb at the Hollywood Forever Cemetery.

Sam Jaffe acted in a wide range of important films, including *Gentleman's Agreement* (1947), *The Asphalt Jungle* (1950), in which he earned a Best Supporting Actor Oscar nomination, and *The Day the Earth Stood Still* (1951).

He also appeared in a number of Broadway plays, including *Cafe Crown* (1942) and *This Time Tomorrow* (1947). Jaffe was also active in supporting actors' rights while a member of Actors' Equity Association, but he came under scrutiny for his union activities by Congressman William P. Lamberston, who stated that the performer and six others on the Equity Council were Communists. "I was never a member of the Communist Party and never entertained any idea of joining it and have no affiliations, whatsoever, in any red organization," stated Jaffe.[4]

Jaffe had been active in a number of actors-related organizations, including The Forum, whose members "were a mix of advocates and Communists."[5] His Forum association was "proof" enough for his critics, and on June 22, 1950, he was listed among 151 performers, writers, and broadcasters in *Red Channels*, an anti-Communist pamphlet. Jaffe also belonged to the End Jim Crow in Baseball Committee, which attempted to break professional baseball's color line. His career suffered after he received a subpoena in 1951 from the House Un-American Activities Committee.

"Sam refused to testify before the House Un-American Activities Committee, but he was never a Communist or a Communist sympathizer because he believed that any philosophy that endorsed the-ends-justify-the-means was unethical," said Bob Ackerman, Jaffe's brother-in-law.[6]

When Nate Spingold, the President of Columbia Pictures, asked about his alleged political affiliations, Jaffe replied on May 22, 1953: "I have never at any time been a Communist. I have never at any time been under Communist Party discipline. I have at all times followed my conscience and independent judgment and have repeatedly been in public opposition to the 'Communist Party line.'"[7]

After several years on Hollywood's "black list," Jaffe returned to the big screen with appearances in such films as *Les espions* (1957), *The Barbarian and the Geisha* (1958), and *Ben Hur* (1959).[8]

One of Jaffe's most memorable roles was that of Dr. David Zorba in the *Ben Casey* television series, which ran from 1961 to 1965. His wife, Bettye, co-starred in the program. "We did a benefit a short while ago and we met a doctor who was the president of the local *Gunga Din* club," said Ackerman in 1964. "He'd seen the picture 86 times. It seems that no one ever sees that picture just once." Despite his many roles on stage, screen, and television, Jaffe was primarily identified with his famous *bhisti* characterization. "In New York, where I go, they call me Gunga," said Jaffe.[9]

Roxanne Ackerman Spencer, Jaffe's niece, remembered an incident in 1975. "I remember when Uncle Sam and my Aunt Bettye were living in Beverly Hills," she said. "There was a zoo near them where you drove through it. I was visiting their home and they took me to the zoo. I rode an elephant and the guides tried to get Uncle Sam to ride. He declared that he had done his time on the back of an elephant in *Gunga Din* and it was very uncomfortable."[10] In 1983, Jaffe and his wife received honorary degrees from Drew University. Sam Jaffe died on March 24, 1984.

Eduardo Ciannelli worked in nearly 150 productions following his riveting role as the Guru in *Gunga Din*. The Italian-born actor returned to his homeland for a number of films, and worked in numerous stateside productions, including scores of appearances on television in the 1950s and 1960s. He died on October 8, 1969.

Joan Fontaine was nominated for a Best Supporting Actress Oscar for *Rebecca* (1940), and followed it with a Best Actress Oscar for her performance in *Suspicion* (1941), which co-starred Cary Grant. She was nominated for a Best Actress Oscar for her work in *The Constant Nymph* (1943), which included such *Gunga Din* cast members as Montagu Love and Eduardo Ciannelli. Fontaine starred in *Jane Eyre* (1943), *Kiss the Blood Off my Hands* (1948), *Ivanhoe* (1952), and other films, before adding numerous television productions to her resume. She died on December 15, 2013, at age ninety-six, making her the oldest and last surviving member of the *Gunga Din* cast.

Montagu Love had appeared in about 150 films, including numerous silent motion pictures, before working in *Gunga Din*. Afterwards, he performed in over two dozen films, including *Northwest Passage* (1940), *The Sea Hawk* (1940), and *The Mark of Zorro* (1940). He died on May 17, 1943, which made him the first major cast member to pass, although George Regas, who played one of the uncredited Thug Chieftains, died on December 13, 1940.

Robert Coote's acting career was later filled with film, stage, and television performances. He portrayed Aramis in *The Three Musketeers* (1948) and appeared in *Soldiers Three* (1951). In the theater, he originated the role of Colonel Pickering in *My Fair Lady*, a performance which earned him a Tony Award nomination for Best Featured Actor in a Musical in 1957. He continued to act into the 1980s, appearing as Theodore Horstmann in the 1981 TV series *Nero Wolfe*. Coote died on November 26, 1982.

Abner Biberman continued to play supporting characters in films. He served as an Army Air Corps flight instructor during World War II, and after the war, continued his acting career while serving as an acting coach at Universal. He directed his first film, *The Golden Mistress* (1954), and later directed hundreds of television episodes on such programs and series as *Tightrope*, *The Fugitive*, *Mr. Novak*, *Hawaii Five-O*, *Ironside*, *The Virginian*, *The Twilight Zone*, and *Ben Casey*, where he teamed up again with Sam Jaffe. Biberman died on June 20, 1977.

George Stevens went on to direct some of the best-remembered films in Hollywood history. He earned a Best Director Academy Award nomination for *The More the Merrier* (1943), and led an important film unit in the United States Army Signal Corps during World War II. Using the same 16mm home-movie camera that was used on the set of *Gunga Din*, Stevens filmed such important historical moments as the D-Day Invasion, the liberation of Paris, and the emancipation of the Dachau concentration camp.

After the war, he directed *I Remember Mama* (1948), and won a Best Director Oscar for *A Place in the Sun* (1951), which included such *Gunga Din* crew veterans as Fred Guiol (associate director) and Charles Gemora (make-up). Stevens earned another Academy Award nomination for *Shane* (1953), which featured a *Gunga Din*-inspired fist fight involving Alan Ladd, Van Heflin, and bunch of Emile Meyer's "thugs."

Stevens won an Academy Award for his grand epic, *Giant* (1956), and earned another Oscar nomination for *The Diary of Anne Frank* (1959). He followed with *The Greatest Story Ever Told* (1965) and concluded his career with *The Only Game in Town* (1970). Stevens died on March 8, 1975.

In 1984, George Stevens, Jr., created a wonderful documentary tribute to his father: *George Stevens: A Filmmaker's Journey*, which featured a superb segment on *Gunga Din*. In his review of the biographical film, critic Roger Ebert said: "Stevens . . . saw his own way through the standard scripts he was handed, freeing his actors so that *Gunga Din*, for example, became a high-spirited comic masterpiece instead of just another swashbuckler."

Alfred Newman's music credits are among the greatest Hollywood soundtracks of all time. During his career he was nominated for an amazing forty-five Academy Awards, and won nine of them: the aforementioned *Alexander's Ragtime Band* (1938), *Tin Pan Alley* (1940), *The Song of Bernadette* (1943), *Mother Wore Tights* (1947), *With a Song in My Heart* (1952), *Call Me Madam* (1953), *Love is a Many-Splendored Thing* (1955), *The King and I* (1956), and *Camelot* (1967). He died on February 17, 1970.

Cinematographer Joseph H. August provided his skills to the likes of *Man of Conquest* (1939), *The Hunchback of Notre Dame* (1939), *The Devil and Daniel Webster* (1941), *They Were Expendable* (1945), and *Portrait of Jennie*

(1948), which earned him his second Academy Award nomination for black-and-white cinematography. He died on September 25, 1947.

The prolific costume designer Edward Stevenson worked with Joan Fontaine and Cary Grant in *Suspicion* (1941). He created the costumes for *It's a Wonderful Life* (1946), provided the gowns for Maureen O'Hara in Douglas Fairbanks' *Sinbad, the Sailor* (1947), and shared a Best Costume Design, Black and White Academy Award with Edith Head for *The Facts of Life* (1960). He also accumulated over 200 costume design credits, working on such Lucille Ball television shows as *I Love Lucy*, *The Lucy Show*, and *Here's Lucy*. Stevenson died on December, 2, 1968.

Among the uncredited cast and crew members who worked on *Gunga Din*, several became important figures in the motion picture industry.

Camera operator William H. Clothier became an accomplished cinematographer who worked in many John Wayne films, including *The Horse Soldiers* (1959), *The Alamo* (1960), *The Man Who Shot Liberty Valance* (1962), *Donovan's Reef* (1963), *McLintock!* (1963), and *The Train Robbers* (1973), among others. He died on January 7, 1996.

Edward B. Powell had composed, arranged, or orchestrated three dozen films prior to *Gunga Din*, but contributed to another 350 motion pictures, including such superb musicals as *Carousel* (1956), *The King and I* (1956), and *South Pacific* (1958). Another uncredited orchestrator, Robert Russell, who arranged Richard Rogers' memorable theme music for TV's *Victory at Sea* series, won a Best Music, Scoring of a Musical Picture Oscar for *Oklahoma!* (1955). He died on February 28, 1984.

Richard Farnsworth continued to display his stunt skills, whether he was riding a horse in *Arrowhead* (1953), handling a covered wagon team on television's *The Adventures of Kit Carson* (1954), or riding a chariot in *The Ten Commandments* (1956). By the 1970s, he devoted himself more to acting, and performed splendidly in such films as *Comes a Horseman* (1978), which earned him a Best Supporting Actor Academy Award nomination; *Resurrection* (1980); *The Grey Fox* (1982); *The Natural* (1984); and *The Straight Story* (1999), which resulted in another Best Actor Oscar nomination. He died on October 6, 2000.

Charles Gemora continued to work as a make-up artist, but the "King of the Gorilla Men" also reprised his ape-playing roles in such films as *The Monster and the Girl* (1941), *Road to Utopia* (1945), and *Phantom of the Rue Morgue* (1954), although he competed for such parts with actors Emil Van Horn and Ray "Crash" Corrigan. Gemora also played a Martian in *The War of the Worlds* (1953) and an alien in *I Married a Monster from Outer Space* (1958). Gemora died on August 19, 1961.

Chapter Twenty-Two Notes

1. Nelson, *Evenings with Cary Grant*, 230.
2. *State Journal Register* (Springfield, Illinois), January 26, 1980, 22.
3. Fairbanks, Jr., *The Salad Days*, 285.
4. Lorrance, *Sam Jaffe*, 243.
5. Ibid., 341.
6. *Les espions* director Henri-Georges Clouzet "had helped Jaffe to break the barriers against him." See Lorrance, *Sam Jaffe*, 392.
7. Lorrance, *Sam Jaffe*, 369.
8. Bob Ackerman to author, January 14, 2016.
9. *Boston Record American*, March 15, 1964, 65.
10. Roxanne Ackerman Spencer to author, December 30, 2015.

CHAPTER TWENTY-THREE
Re-releases and Offshoots

During the 1940s, *Gunga Din* was scheduled in American movie theaters every year except 1948, although it would not be surprising if a random print of the film was shown in at least one American movie house that year. Portions of Alfred Newman's *Gunga Din* score—used when Cutter and Din are riding Annie towards the bridge, and the other when the Guru explains his plan to massacre the approaching British Army—were used in the "News on the March" sequence in RKO's *Citizen Kane* (1941). Bernard Herrmann, the film's composer, also incorporated musical passages from such other previously released RKO films as *Bringing Up Baby* (1938), *A Man to Remember* (1938), *Five Came Back* (1939), and *Curtain Call* (1940), among others, in Orson Welles' classic motion picture.

The 1941 re-release of *Gunga Din* had a significant impact on one audience member: Bettye Ackerman, an aspiring young actress, who had moved from her home in Cottageville, South Carolina, to New York City. The twenty-four-year-old wasn't attracted to Gary Grant or Douglas Fairbanks, Jr., but to Sam Jaffe, who was nearly thirty-seven years older than she. "That's the kind of man I want to marry," recalled Ackerman about the sensitive and humble character Jaffe created on the big screen. "The hair wasn't showing then; he had that turban on. And he was covered up in chocolate. But he was lit up from within." Years later she met him. "The minute I saw Sam in person I knew I was going to marry him," she said. "I knew it was an unlikely match and I didn't know he was looking for anybody."[1] The couple wed in 1956.

The 1942 re-release of *Gunga Din* was particularly successful since it was part of a summertime twin bill that included *King Kong*. "*Gunga Din* Still Rated Top Picture," stated the *Evansville Courier and Press*. "Pictures laid in India have a peculiar charm for this reviewer, and there is nothing she likes better than temples of gold, where prisoners are about to be fed to the snakes, and cavalry charges of the Bengal Lancers with pennants flying and lances at the ready," wrote critic Leah Bodine Drake.[2] The two-film package had it greatest success at the RKO-Albee in Providence, Rhode Island, where it took in an impressive weekly total of $9,800, a sum $3,800 greater than its usual weekly take. The tandem bill also did better than average business at the Twentieth Century in Buffalo, New York; the Lyric in Indianapolis; and the Loew's-Poli Palace in Hartford, Connecticut.[3] The popular two-picture package was reissued in 1943 and 1944, which added to *Gunga Din's* profitability.

Gunga Din remained a favorite film among among military service personnel during World War II; in fact, a United States Navy survey published in *Motion Picture Daily* in 1945 showed the results of "return engagement films" (in addition to new releases) that sailors would like to view at sea or in foreign ports. *Gunga Din* was selected one of the top fifty films in the survey.[4] The film's domestic release in 1945 was also successful at the box office, especially early in the year. For example, the Family Theatre in Cincinnati reported "pleasing" business during the week that included Valentine's Day.[5]

In 1946, *Gunga Din* was double-billed with both RKO films and motion pictures produced from other studios. It was joined with 20th Century Fox's *Rings on Her Fingers* (1942) at Cleveland's Almira theater in May, and *The Dark Corner* (1946) at Springfield, Illinois' Tivoli theater. *Gunga Din* was matched with Laurel and Hardy's *Nothing but Trouble* (1944), an MGM film, at the Orpheum theater in Malden, Massachusetts, in December.

In 1947, *Gunga Din* was usually doubled-billed with other RKO films. For example, in January 1947, *Gunga Din* was teamed with *The Ex-Mrs. Bradford* (1936) in San Diego's North Park theater, and two months later it was supported with *Lady Takes a Chance* (1943) in St. Louis. *Gunga Din* was joined by *The Informer* (1935) as part of a successful four-week summer "revival of oldie box office winners" at New York City's Palace Theatre.[6]

During its reissue, *Gunga Din* appeared as an illustrated story in the March 18, 1947 issue (#50) of *Junior Films*, a Spanish language publication. The entire film was recreated in a two-page storyboard that featured images based upon a mix of production stills and scenes from the movie. The back cover of the publication featured a *Gunga Din* movie ad that proclaimed a cast and crew of 5,000, which was more than twice the actual number, but a total that probably made members of the RKO publicity department blush with pride.

Some 1947 newspaper ads in European countries featured photos of Cary Grant and Joan Fontaine, rather than Fairbanks and the actress. The advertisement's text even billed Grant and Fontaine ahead of the other actors. It was a trend that would continue in subsequent re-release publicity campaigns as Grant's world-wide popularity grew and overshadowed his male costars.

Gunga Din was teamed up with *The Lost Patrol* (1934) in 1949 as a major studio reissue. The double-bill pressbook noted that *Gunga Din* still maintained its original release length of 117 minutes.

Gunga Din's influence on other films began in the 1950s. *Soldiers Three*, a Kipling story that made it to the big screen in 1951, had several *Gunga Din* connections. The film was produced by Pandro Berman and featured Robert Coote as Major Mercer. Cyril McLaglen, one of Victor McLaglen's brothers, appeared as an uncredited background player. Technical advisor Clive Morgan appeared as an uncredited soldier, and one of the contributing writers was Vincent Lawrence, one of *Gunga Din's* first writers. In fact, the first ten minutes of the movie is replete with *Gunga Din* elements: a soldier, who had been involved in a brawl, is interrogated by an officer; three soldiers have a second-floor fight with a group of Scots; and singing soldiers march along a trail with majestic mountains in the background. The film includes references to a place called Chotapur, which recalled the name of Abner Biberman's Chota character.

Like *Gunga Din*, the principals in *Soldiers Three* were not the first actors sought to fulfill the roles. In 1938, MGM announced that the starring roles would go to Clark Gable, Robert Taylor, and Wallace Berry. The completed film focused on the fortunes of three soldiers in the British Army. One of the enlisted men, Archibald Ackroyd (played by Stewart Granger), shared Cary Grant's actual first name. The other two enlisted men leads were played by Robert Newton and Cyril Cusak. Interestingly enough, Victor McLaglen was considered for a role when the film was originally going to be made in the 1930s.

Recalling the severe criticism over *Gunga Din* in India, Berman had some reservations about making the film. "We are making a rough and tumble brawling comedy with three British soldiers out of a Kipling work as major characters and that presents major problems," said Berman in a September 24, 1950 article in *The New York Times*. "The people of India hated Kipling. As to the British, how they will react when we show three roistering, drunken Tommies on the screen is a question. When I produced *Gunga Din* at RKO in 1938, it was banned in India and efforts were made to stop it being shown in the British Isles. But if we were to film *Soldiers Three* to please either Britain or India we would have to make it much too dull for our much bigger audience here at home."

Nevertheless, Berman made changes to the story and the cast of characters, which reduced the aggressiveness in *Soldiers Three*. The film reached theaters just a few months after Kipling's *Kim* (1950) was released. Surprisingly, the *Soldiers Three* movie posters featured the laughing heads of the major characters, a composition which looked very similar to the original *Gunga Din* posters. MGM promoted its film with such publicity statements as "Adventure, escapades, hi-jinx, romance!" and "Rough and tough and riotous!"

A Kipling-inspired character, Gunga Ram, played by young Nino Marcel, was the leading role in *Sabaka* (1954), aka *The Hindu*, a low-budget color film directed by Frank Ferrin, which was part *Gunga Din* and *The Jungle Book,* and included several *Gunga Din* story

lines. The film's opening credits begin with the sound of a gong and the image of a large gong-shaped logo that features the name of writer-director Frank Ferrin's production company. *Sabaka* has torch-carrying cultists, deadly snakes, a whipping and torture scene, elephants (Gunga Ram is an elephant trainer and driver), the British military (commanded by Boris Karloff), a large gold-like idol, and a fanatical cult leader (the High Priestas of Sabaka) who warns that infidels will "grovel" in the dirt. Gunga Ram helps save the day when he convinces the cultists to stop their evil ways. In the film's conclusion, Ram enjoys a ride on the Maharajah of Bakore's elephant, during a spectacular processional.

Marcel later appeared as "Gunga, the East India Boy" in episodes that were written and directed by Ferrin on *Andy's Gang*, a children's television program that aired from 1955 to 1960.

There's a bit of *Gunga Din* in *Cult of the Cobra* (1955), a Universal-International horror film that begins in East Asia, and features a group of American soldiers who are "very close," hooded cult members, poisonous snakes, a temple illuminated by torchlight, and a nearly-bald high priest (John Halloran) who cries, "One by one, you will die!," to a group of ceremony crashers.

Not counting the specially edited version of *Gunga Din* that aired on a handful of television sets in 1939, the theatrical print finally reached a widespread home audience in the 1950s. It's appearance on the small screen came about as a result of actions initially taken by Howard Hughes, who gained control of RKO in 1948. The daring entrepreneur and airplane pilot had *Gunga Din* edited down to ninety-four minutes in 1954 for its theatrical re-release.[7] The shortened version allowed theaters to efficiently combine the film with another motion picture for a more audience-friendly two-feature bill. However, several scenes were missing from the edited version (which was later broadcast on television), including the initial attack on Captain Markham's patrol; the complete punch-bowl sequence; the meeting of MacChesney, Ballantine, Higginbotham, and Emmy on the road to Tantrapur; the appearance of the Kipling character; and some shots of Sam Jaffe climbing the temple, among others.

Like other film re-releases, *Gunga Din's* film stock had changed. "Prior to 1950, films were shot on a dangerously flammable nitrate stock; projection booths in theaters had to be lined with bricks or concrete," explained Joseph Musso, an accomplished Hollywood production artist and storyboard illustrator. "Around 1949, Kodak developed a nonflammable celluloid film stock. All the film studios immediately began transferring their libraries from the nitrate stock to the new, more stable, and archival 'safety film,' as it was referred to. To justify the cost, the studios re-released these older films on the new 'safety film' stock to the theaters, usually on a double bill. Sometimes, they did a formal re-release with new ads on their classics like *Gunga Din*. Other times, and more often than not, they just offered them to theaters on a double bill at a much cheaper flat rate than the new releases."[8]

Later, Hughes sold his film interests to General Teleradio in 1955. The new owner, a subsidiary of General Tire and Rubber, made the RKO film library of 742 titles available to fifty-eight television stations on July 1, 1956, in exchange for commercial ad time. RKO wasn't the only studio that released its titles; in fact, some 3,000 feature films not previously seen on television were made available by the other Hollywood studios in 1956.[9] Fans who had seen the originals in theaters decades earlier were able to watch the classic films at home on the small screen, and Baby Boomers were introduced to such motion pictures as *King Kong* (1933), *Top Hat* (1935), *The Hunchback of Notre Dame* (1939), and *Gunga Din*, which were part of RKO's "Finest 52" film titles package.

Television station managers soon realized that their ratings significantly increased when they aired the so-called "new features" in place of old films that had been broadcast in previous seasons. Philadelphia's WCAU-TV, for example, "increased its average late-evening ratings by 221% within a month by putting one of the newly released Hollywood libraries into the time slots where it used to run older features."[10]

Gunga Din first aired on WOR-TV, an independent network based in New York, the nation's largest television market, on April 1, 1957. It aired twice in the evening and multiple times on the weekend during its weeklong run. Along with *Top Hat* (1935), it was one of the most popular RKO films that aired on American television that year. The station usually ranked fourth after the other three major networks (WRCA-TV, WCBS-TV and WABC-TV), but the broadcasting of the RKO classic films helped elevate WOR-TV to second place on some evenings.

Screen Gems planned to produce a new half-hour TV film series titled *The Adventures of Gunga Din*. Since the character had died bravely in the motion picture, one idea was to create prequels, episodes about the legendary *bhisti's* earlier life. A precedent had been established in 1955, when *Walt Disney's Disneyland* television series broadcast

THE CAST:

Cutter........................CARY GRANT
MacChesney....VICTOR McLAGLEN
Ballantine
........................DOUGLAS FAIRBANKS, JR.
Emmy..................JOAN FONTAINE
Gunga Din.....................SAM JAFFE
Guru............EDUARDO CIANNELLI
Col. Weed..................MONTAGU LOVE
Higginbotham.........ROBERT COOTE
Chota......................ABNER BIBERMAN
Maj. Mitchell..........LUMSDEN HARE

THE MAKERS:

PANDRO S. BERMAN, in Charge of
Production; Produced and Directed
by GEORGE STEVENS; Screen
Play by JOEL SAYRE and FRED
GUIOL; Story by BEN HECHT and
CHARLES MacARTHUR; From RUD-
YARD KIPLING'S Poem, "Gunga
Din"; Music by ALFRED NEWMAN;
Director of Photography, JOSEPH
H. AUGUST, A.S.C.; Art Director,
VAN NEST POLGLASE, Associate,
PERRY FERGUSON; Photographic
Effects by VERNON L. WALKER,
A.S.C.; Set Decorations, DARRELL
SILVERA; Gowns by EDWARD
STEVENSON; Recorded by JOHN
E. TRIBBY and JAMES STEWART;
Edited by HENRY BERMAN and
JOHN LOCKERT.

An RKO RADIO Re-Release
FOOTAGE: 8546
RUNNING TIME: 94 MINUTES

HIGHLIGHTS:

Produced with the sweep
and power befitting Rudyard
Kipling's saga of colorful and
adventurous army life in India
as it existed in the Nineties,
GUNGA DIN is truly one of
the great film classics. Rated
as one of RKO Radio's greatest productions, this magnificent movie loses none of its
impact through the changing
events of world history.

Quite as famous as Dumas'
"Three Musketeers" but portrayed with more down-to-
earth realism are the three
sergeants of GUNGA DIN. As
characterized by Cary Grant,
Victor McLaglen and Douglas
Fairbanks, Jr., they are perhaps the most fascinating
three-some ever brought to
the screen. Vigorous in their
approach to life, lusty in their
humor and brave in their attack on adventure, their loyalty to each other is not les-
sened even when the romance
between Fairbanks and Joan
Fontaine becomes a major
factor in their existence.

Several thousand players
were used by Producer-Di-
rector George Stevens in re-
creating the battle scenes and
some of the biggest location
sets ever constructed were
employed as backgrounds for
other action. Much of the production was filmed at the
base of snow-capped Mount
Whitney in California's High
Sierras, where the terrain
matched the Khyber Pass
country of India's frontier.

GUNGA DIN has been en-
thusiastically recommended
by the Motion Picture Committee of the National Education Association. Exhibitors
can capture an extra audience through tie-ups with
schools, libraries, community
organizations and the film activities of women's clubs.

THREE SHEET

FROM **RKO**

1957 Pressbook. Author's collection.

"Davy Crockett's Keel Boat Race" and "Davy Crockett and the River Pirates," two fictional episodes that depicted the famous Tennessean's earlier life. The three original television episodes were "Davy Crockett, Indian Fighter," "Davy Crockett Goes to Congress," and "Davy Crockett at the Alamo." Although Crockett died at the Battle of the Alamo, Disney successfully resurrected his coonskin cap-wearing frontier hero in the two prequels. If Disney could bring an historical character "back to life" without too much difficulty, Screen Gems believed it would be even easier to bring back a fictional personality. Despite the fanfare, *The Adventures of Gunga Din* was never produced.[11]

Gunga Din also had a major re-release in theaters in 1957, and the studio produced a new trailer, although edited from previous trailers and filmed footage. The 94-minute version of the film was promoted with an attractive large four-page pressbook, which boasted that "this magnificent movie loses none of its impact through the changing events of history." The pressbook also included a convenient review for local newspapers, advance and current press releases, available posters, and advertising mats, which featured updated photos of Cary Grant and Joan Fontaine. Cognizant of the negative reaction to the film in India a decade earlier, the pressbook explained the two terms that composed the title character's name: "Kipling applied them to the heroic native water carrier of his classic and the mixture of Hindu and Mohammedian nomenclature avoided any injured feeling in India and ultimately registered indelibly in the field of literature."

The 1957 re-release was part of numerous double-bills. *Gunga Din* was teamed with such new films as Disney's *Westward Ho, the Wagons!* (1956) in Cleveland, and *The Prince and the Showgirl* (1957) in Boston; film fans in Portland, Oregon, saw *Gunga Din* with a re-release of John Wayne's *Flying Leathernecks* (1951). An interesting ad in the *Oregonian* listed *Gunga Din's* leads as Cary Grant, Joan Fontaine, and Victor McLaglen.[12] Unfortunately, Fairbanks was lost in the publicized reshuffled cast list.

Gunga Din's antagonists, the Thuggees, became the focus of *The Stranglers of Bombay* (1959), a Hammer Films production directed by Terence Fisher, and starring Guy Rolfe as an early nineteenth century officer in the British East India Company. The film has a few *Gunga Din*-like touches: Rolfe's Captain Harry Lewis character is confronted by a deadly cobra; George Pastel's High Priest of Kali looks and sounds (with chants of "kill!") like Eduardo Ciannelli's bald-headed Guru; and the film concludes with a quote by William Henry Sleeman, who battled the Thugs in the 1800s. Hammer, Great Britain's well known horror films studio, advertised the motion picture, which was released by Columbia Pictures, as filmed in a process called "Strangloscope."

In 1961, *Gunga Din* was re-released in Italy. However, the posters featured an image of Cary Grant and Joan Fontaine in a romantic pose instead of Fairbanks and Fontaine. At the time, the two men's big screen careers had been going in opposite directions. Many years later, the film was dubbed in Italian and made available as a two-part video disc package.

A year later, *Sergeants 3* (1962), a Western comedy that was based on the *Gunga Din* story line, debuted in American theaters. Directed by John Sturges, who had worked on *Gunga Din* as an uncredited editor, *Sergeants 3* traces the exploits of three non-commissioned

Italian re-release poster, 1961. Author's collection.

officers stationed in Native American territory. Sturges was well-suited to handle the Western, since he had directed *Escape From Fort Bravo* (1953), *Gunfight at the O. K. Corral* (1957), *Last Train From Gun Hill* (1959), and *The Magnificent Seven* (1960).

The cast was primarily composed of Frank Sinatra's fellow Rat Pack buddies. Sinatra played First Sergeant Mike Merry, Dean Martin portrayed Sergeant Chip Deal, and Peter Lawford played Sergeant Larry Barrett, a soldier who is preparing to leave the service and get married. Sammy Davis Jr. portrayed Jonah Williams, a trumpet-playing former slave, who wants to be a soldier. He eventually comes to the rescue of the soldiers after the group is captured by a band of Indians. However, the horn player survives. Since the *Sergeants 3* story was similar to *Gunga Din,* the production company had to secure permission to release it.

The film received mixed reviews, but performed surprisingly well at the box office; as a matter of fact, *Sergeants 3* was #1 for three consecutive box office weekends in February 1962, bumping the epic *El Cid* (1961) from the top spot. *Sergeants 3* earned over $1.7 million during its first week and nearly a million dollars in its second week. The film took in over $700,000 during its third week and eventually made over $4 million.

In 1963, *Gunga Din,* a 66-page French photo novel composed of 333 film frames and detailed text, was published. It coincided with the release of *Charade* (1963), a comedy-mystery set in Paris that starred Cary Grant. Capitalizing on Grant's international fame, the photo novel's cover featured an updated illustration of the actor dressed in an officer's uniform, and a depiction of Sam Jaffe blowing the bugle. No other actor from the film was featured on the cover.

In *Help!* (1965), the Beatles tangle with a Thuggee-like cult led by a high priest (a near bald Leo McKern), who has an affection for bloody sacrifices. Chanting cult members, a torch-filled temple, and a statue of Kali (with eight arms) add to the *Gunga Din* garnishing of this rock music-comedy.

The Blake Edwards-directed comedy, *The Party* (1968), featured Peter Sellers as the bumbling Hrundi V. Bakshi, an Indian actor, who stars in the faux film *Son of Gunga Din.* The motion picture parodies the 1939 film's famous dramatic sequence in which Sam Jaffe's character blows the bugle atop the temple. Thanks to Sellers' performance, the scene becomes nonsensically funny. His character climbs to the top of a rocky hill and begins to blow the alarm call. After about twenty seconds, the rebellious natives start shooting him and he falls, but he continues to play—and play. The scene recalls Sonny Gianotta's humorous "The Last Blast of the Blasted Bugler" novelty 45-rpm single release. Although hundreds of rifle and Gatling Gun shots are fired at him, Bakshi manages to blow the bugle for over two minutes. After yelling "cut," the film's director shouts, "What is that idiot doing?"

Gunga Din's popularity among film buffs remained strong in the 1970s. On January 10, 1970, the film was screened at the Metropolitan Museum of Art in New York. Dennis Belafonte, the brother of singer Harry Belafonte and the author of *The Films of Tyrone Power,* invited two of his friends, Mike and Phil Boldt, a pair of New Jersey-based musicians, who had only seen the film on television, to the museum. "After the battle of Tantrapur, the three of us were so overcome by seeing

Gunga Din *French photo novel, 1963. Author's collection.*

Concluding page from the French photo novel. Courtesy of Mike Boldt. Author's collection.

this fabulous scene unfold on the big screen, we gave it a standing ovation," said Mike Boldt. "Needless to say, we were the only ones to stand up, and we received a lot of 'New York looks,' but we didn't care. The film was great!"

Gunga Din topped Don Miller's roster of the "Favorite Films of the Year: 1939" in the popular film appreciation magazine *The New Captain George's Whizzbang* in 1973. Miller called it "a walloping robust tale of Her Majesty's Forces in old India" and saluted the efforts of George Stevens, the cast, and cinematographer Joseph H. August. At the time of publication, however, Miller lamented about the film's edited state. "Today, the ravages of time and television have taken toll: the present owners have edited the original length to around 100 minutes, making a hash of many sequences and seriously harming the version presently shown on TV," wrote Miller. In the next issue, reader William A. Thomaier, a well-known New York metro area classic film fan, agreed and identified the missing scenes that he had seen when the movie was reissued in the 1940s. The subsequent removal of the Kipling character writing the poem created a problem in the edited story, explained Thomaier: "The absence of this scene makes it appear as if Montagu Love had written it himself when he suddenly produces it and reads it over Din's body."[13]

On May 23, 1973, George Stevens spoke about his career at the American Film Institute's Center for Advanced Film Studies. James R. Silke, a faculty member at the Center, hosted and conducted the event, which included film clips from some of the director's most celebrated works. "I think *Gunga Din*, which we looked at today, with all of the hazards that existed there, has a tremendous excitement about it to me and to the audience at the time," said Stevens.[14]

Classic film aficionados were encouraged, when it was announced that *Gunga Din* would be shown at Radio City Music Hall's Art Deco festival on January 30, 1974. It was more than a nostalgic event; it was a homecoming for a film that had debuted there thirty-five years earlier. Unfortunately, the version that was screened that night was a poor 16mm copy of the edited print that had been shown on television.[15] During the screening, some audience members laughed at the visible string lines that animated some of the rubber snakes in the snake pit scene.

Despite its editing, original prints of *Gunga Din* existed, and in 1977, the *Seattle Daily Times* reported that a restored 35mm print of *Gunga Din* was going to be shown at the Edgemont Theater in Edmonds, Washington. A few years later, *Gunga Din* was made available as a home video product, although in an edited 94-minute version. However, in 1983, a 117-minute, grainy version of *Gunga Din* was released on VHS by Vid America as part of the New York company's "classic series" collection. The video company also included *Gunga Din* in a handsome "Collector's Limited Edition" box set, which also contained VHS copies of *Citizen Kane* and *King Kong*.

In 1984, George Stevens Jr. created an excellent tribute to his father with the documentary *George Stevens: A Filmmaker's Journey*. Among the numerous films clips in the production were scenes from *Gunga Din* and commentary segments from some of the actors and actresses who worked with him, including Cary Grant and Douglas Fairbanks, Jr.

Gunga Din was issued on laser disc in 1991 by Turner Home Entertainment and distributed by Image Entertainment as part of "The RKO Classic Collection." The disc's box back cover notes incorrectly state that the film's story is set in the "late 1890s."

Gunga Din *monument in Lone Pine, California. Photo by Craig R. Covner.*

On October 11, 1992, Douglas Fairbanks, Jr. attended an event in Lone Pine, California, which celebrated the epic film. The actor dedicated the plaque—titled "Gunga Din" Filmed Here—that was donated by the Lone Pine Sierra Film Festival and the people of Lone Pine. Perhaps in anticipation of Fairbanks' appearance, the plaque elevated his name above Victor McLaglen's in the ranks of the posted cast.

Turner Home Entertainment presented a colorized VHS version of the film in 1993.

Notes on the videotape's box stated: "This is a colorized version of a film originally marketed and distributed to the public in black and white. It has been altered without the participation of the principal director, screenwriter, and other creators of the original film." Many classic film purists were aghast—and they were correct. It was not the motion picture that George Stevens had envisioned or made. The most obvious flaw in the colorized version was the distortion of the brilliant black and white contrasts that cinematographer Joseph H. August had captured in the original film. Cary Grant, though, had other thoughts. "And I've seen a reel of *Gunga Din* in color," said Grant. "It's absolutely marvelous. The uniforms are exactly what they should be."[16]

In 1995, the 1991 *Gunga Din* laser disc was repackaged as a "Special Collectors Edition by Image Entertainment, with an added disc side of supplemental information. The essential contents of the laser disc was included in a 2004 Turner Entertainment Company-Warner Bros. DVD. The DVD featured the complete 117-minute film, a "making of" on location feature, a commentary track provided by film historian Rudy Behlmer, and two re-release trailers—although the DVD case states incorrectly that one is an "original" trailer. The DVD itself features a photo of Cary Grant's Cutter and Jam Jaffe's title character being swayed dangerously on the wooden suspension bridge by Annie.

Chapter Twenty-Three Notes

1. Lorrance, *Sam Jaffe*, 376.

2. *Evansville Courier and Press*, July 21, 1942, 7.

3. *Motion Picture Daily*, July 16, 1942, 7; July 27, 1942, 6; July 29, 4; September 4, 1942, 4.

4. Ibid., February 19, 1945, 6. According to the article, the sailors rejected most war films unless they seemed "authentic." Ironically, one of the top fifty films on the seamen's roster was *Mutiny on the Bounty*.

5. *Variety*, February 14, 1945, 10.

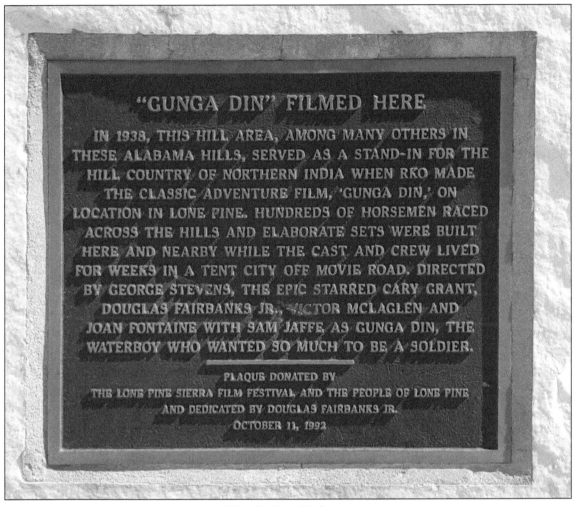

Photo by Craig R. Covner.

6. Ibid., March 5, 1947, 17; September 3, 1947, 11.

7. *Gunga Din's* various theatrical print lengths include 119, 117, 115, 107, and 94-minute versions.

8. Musso to author, July 12, 2016.

9. *Sponsor*, October 15, 1956, 27. In the late 1980s, "Ted Turner acquired the U.S. distribution rights from the new RKO owners for his television stations, like today's Turner Classic Movies," explained Musso. "In 1996, Time Warner, the parent company of Warner Bros., bought out Turner Entertainment and inherited Turner's American distribution deal with RKO. However, the RKO company and the actual rights to its extensive film library, including *Gunga Din*, are now owned by Post Cereals heiress and actress, Dina Merrill, and her husband, Ted Hartley. They, in turn, occasionally produce one or two films a year as a limited liability company."

10. Ibid., October 15, 1956, 27, 29.

11. *Broadcasting Telecasting*, April 29, 1957, 94.

12. *Oregonian*, January 26, 1957, 5.

13. *The New Captain George's Whizzbang*, No. 15, 1973, 6-7; 16, 32.

14. *Dialogue on Film: George Stevens*, 22.

15. *The Hollywood Reporter*, January 26, 1939, 2. The venue had installed a 16mm projector in January 1939 to show color newsreels and some small gauge black and white films.

16. Nelson, *Evenings with Cary Grant*, 105.

CHAPTER TWENTY-FOUR
Gunga Din's Socio-Political Legacy

The post-World War II years featured an increase in nationalism, the erosion of the colonial system, and the birth of new nations. Hollywood films that had celebrated British imperialism before the war were frequently looked upon through a new world socio-political lens as anachronistic tributes to oppressive empires. "Anti-imperialism in Gunga Din, however, remains a subtext because the film simultaneously glorifies the British Raj and operates primarily as an adventure tale, not a political-message movie, even though it has fallen to scholars of political cinema since then, most of whom have viewed empire cinema before World War II as an apologia for the white man's burden."[1]

The intense criticism of both *Gunga Din* and Kipling in India after its release did not subside with the passage of time. Rasipuram Krishnaswami Narayan, a celebrated Indian writer, criticized Kipling during a speaking tour of the United States in 1958, a year after *Gunga Din* was released on American television. At Michigan State University, he called Kipling "the supposed expert writer on India," and cautioned those who embraced the West's distorted opinions of the Asian subcontinent.

That same year, Harold R. Isaacs wrote *Images of India: American Views of India and China*, which was based upon a series of interviews conducted between 1953 and 1957. Isaacs noted that nearly forty percent of those interviewed "mentioned Kipling as a source for early impressions relating to India [but] few mentioned *Gunga Din*." However, the author pointed out that the film "introduced post-Kipling generations to the cringing and rather pathetic creature whose dog-like devotion and ultimate sacrifice for his British masters might have pleased the bearers of the burden but could hardly have made him a folk hero in India."[2]

Isaacs also complained that in the film "tall, brawny British troopers are engaged for a good part of the total footage in brawling free-for-alls with dozens and scores of Indians whom they hurl around like so many dolls." He criticized Kipling as being racist for describing *Gunga Din* as "'white, clear white inside,' when he acted like a brave man, and black all the way through the rest of his time when he was his cringing pathetic self."[3]

In 1964, German poet-playwright Bertolt Brecht described the dichotomy of *Gunga Din's* cultural sensitivity and the film's entertainment value in *Brecht on Theatre: The Development of an Esthetic*. "[Gunga Din] betrayed his compatriots to the British, sacrificed his life so that his fellow countrymen should be defeated, and earned the audience's heartfelt applause," noted Brecht. "My heart was touched, too: I felt like applauding and laughed in all the right places. Despite the fact that I knew all time that there was something wrong, that the Indians are not primitive and uncultured people...and that this *Gunga Din* could also be seen in a very different light, e.g., as a traitor to his people."[4]

However, Brecht assumed that all of the film's Indians were exclusively Thugs, which they were not. The writer also did not explain why he thought it was appropriate that Gunga Din hopelessly remain at the bottom of India's socio-economic order. Hardly "uncultured," the Guru was depicted as one of the most educated members of the cast, a man who spoke English with precision, and displayed knowledge of Chandragtupa Maurya, Hannibal, Julius Caesar, and Napoleon Bonaparte. The Guru's final "India farewell" speech also reflected the sophisticated complexity of the celluloid character.

Prem Chowdhry of the Nehru Memorial Museum and Library in New Delhi, continued the condemnation of the RKO film in *Colonial India and the Making of Empire Cinema: Image, Ideology and Identity*, an empirico-historical inquiry into motion pictures made in Hollywood and Great Britain in the 1930s and 1940s. The book's central focus is on three films: *The Drum* (1938), *The Rains Came* (1939), and *Gunga Din*. Chowdhry suggested that the possibility of an independent India and its potential impact on the British Empire raised concerns in the West, which needed to be appeased, and *Gunga Din* provided that reassurance of stability in the world. "*Gunga Din* epitomises the affection, love, dependence and awesome loyalty of the 'common man'—the teeming multitudes of India—who wanted to maintain the colonial connection rather than sever it." The author contended that *Gunga Din* presented colonialism in a positive way to a white audience, and as a result, "the film rearticulated colonial race relations that subverted rather than promoted the colonists' intent in the context of the non-white audience."[5]

In a broader sense, Jennifer M. Jeffers, in *Britain Colonized: Hollywood's Appropriation of British Literature*, was even more blunt.

"The global hegemony over knowledge and naming that white European males exerted for hundreds of years over the colonial world (from Africa to the Far East to America) is analogous to the postwar capitalist and military dominance the United States had displayed," said Jeffers, an English professor at Cleveland State University. "Hollywood reproduces the American's fantasy—global American hegemony—through historical and literary figures borrowed from this older European tradition."[6]

The film's title character continued to be held in contempt. "For Indian nationalists, loyalists were little more than collaborators with the British Raj; *Gunga Din's* 'heroism,' which led to the death of so many Indians, was a bitter pill for an Indian audience to swallow," wrote Chowdhry.[7] Like the film's other critics, Chowdhry never fully addressed Gunga Din's effort to improve his status within the context of the Indian caste system, which upheld the segregation of people based upon their birth.

To others, the *bhisti's* legacy is depicted more optimistically. In a review of *Gunga Din*, an illustrated book for young readers published in 1987, Jo Enever noted: "The poem illustrates the issues associated with colonization, but also the hope that can arise post-colonization; hope for a better world where all people are treated as they deserve to be regardless of their cultural heritage."[8]

One media source intimated that all of *Gunga Din's* socio-political liabilities might be forgotten if a change in casting was made. "[The] 1939 classic *Gunga Din* might denounced as racist, sexist and colonialist today, but [it] could be remade with a feminist heroine," stated the Maturity News Service, in the Cleveland *Plain Dealer's* TV section, for the week of June 3, 1991.[9]

Film historian Philip Leibfried was critical of those who assessed the film with modern eyes. "There are some who decry the 'political incorrectness' of the British soldiers' treatment of the Indians, but *Gunga Din*, like any historical work, must be taken in context."[10] Leibfried also reminded critics that Kipling held the Gunga Din character in the highest regard: the *bhisti* was more than a good man, he was, in fact, "the finest man I knew."[11]

Not surprisingly, the Victorian Military Society, which was established in Great Britain in 1974, has maintained a favorable opinion of *Gunga Din*. The film "is still as popular as ever with cinema and television audiences who watch the story of the brave water-*bhisti* who eventually got his wish to join the army," wrote George Robinson in *Soldiers of the Queen*, the organization's official publication.[12]

The Kipling Society in Great Britain has also held *Gunga Din* in obvious high regard. The motion picture's emotional finale, in particular, still resonates among the faithful. "The film ends with an emotionally charged scene—the torchlight burial of the dead, accompanied by skirling pipes and the super-imposed image of a smiling *Gunga Din,* now promoted Bugler and wearing the Queen's uniform, while the Colonel's voice-over delivers the poem's finals lines," wrote Alan D. Wolfe in *The Kipling Journal*. "Some may be able to watch that without a lump in their throat. I cannot."[13]

Chapter Twenty-Four Notes

1. Frederic Cople Jaher and Blair B. King, "Hollywood's India: The Meaning of RKO's *Gunga Din, Film & History: An Interdisciplinary Journal of Film and Television Studies*, Vol. 38.2 (Fall 2008), 33.

2. Harold R. Isaacs, *Images of India: American Views of India and China* (New York: Harper & Row, 1958), 241-242. The Harper Torchlight paperback edition was printed in 1972.

3. Ibid., 276-277, 281.

4. John Willett, ed. and trans., *Brecht on Theatre: The Development of an Esthetic* (London: Macmillan, 1964), 151.

5. Chowdhry, *Colonial India*, 131.

6. Jennifer M. Jeffers, *Britain Colonized: Hollywood's Appropriation of British Literature* (New York: Palgrave Macmillan, 2006), 107. Although Jeffers makes no note of Kipling or films based upon his works, she criticizes the "buddy movie" as a creative work "frequently appropriated by stereotypical popular Hollywood genre films."

7. Chowdhry, *Colonial India*, 176.

8. Enever's review was submitted as part of the course work for Post-Colonial Literature for Children at Latrobe University in Melbourne, Australia.

9. The Maturity News Service is a trademark of the American Association of Retired Persons (AARP).

10. Philip Leibfried, *Rudyard Kipling and Sir Henry Rider Haggard on Screen, Stage, Radio and Television* (Jefferson, NC: McFarland & Company, 2000), 29.

11. Some may assert that "the finest man I knew" passage in *Gunga Din* does not refer to all men but only those in "them black-faced crew." However, the soldier in the poem acknowledges Gunga Din as "a better man" which underscores "the finest man" statement.

12. George Robinson, "Gunga Din," *Soldiers of the Queen*, September 1994, #78, 28.

13. Alan D. Wolfe. "Kipling in Hollywood," *The Kipling Journal*, December 1996, 32-33.

CHAPTER TWENTY-FIVE
The Influential *Gunga Din*: Pop Culture and the Planned Remake

Since the release of *Gunga Din* in 1939, Kipling's famous *bhisti* has lived on in various forms of popular culture, including spoken-word and musical recordings, filmed cartoons, illustrations, proposed new motion pictures, and other forms of creative expression.

Kipling's literary creation also manifested itself in unconventional forms. In 1947, the legendary Vincent "Gunga Din" motorcycle made its debut in Great Britain. The record-setting bike made headlines for its speed, but the enterprise that manufactured it went out of business in the mid-1950s. The original "Gunga Din" vehicle was later recovered and restored, and continues to be a topic of interest among motorcycle enthusiasts.

An innocuous cartoon of *Gunga Din* appeared in the comical *Through History with J. Wesley Smith* "text book" in 1950. Author-artist Burr Shafer's caption read: "Oh, that's just our water-boy, Gunga Din—you wouldn't find him interesting, Mr. Kipling."

Kipling's poem continued to be recorded. Among the more memorable recordings was one delivered by opera star Leonard Warren on the *Songs of Rudyard Kipling* album in 1951. Warren, who began his professional career as a member of the Radio City Music Hall chorus in 1935, displayed a vocal performance that recalled the grandiose style of Charles Gilbert Spross' 1925 version. Well-known narrator Alexander Scourby delivered an excellent reading of *Gunga Din* on the 1962 album, *A Golden Treasury of Poetry*.

Race horses with the name "Gunga Din" have been running on tracks around the world since 1896, when an Australian equine was born and named after Kipling's famous character. Over the course of more than a century, none of the horses have achieved major race victories, although a number of European-based Gunga Dins have achieved some level of success in the post-World War II years. As recently as 2016, a four-year-old gelding, owned by France's Corine Barande-Barbe, placed six times in ten outings on European tracks. Alas, none were victories.

In 1959, the Crew Cuts, a pop vocal group known best for their chart-topping cover song "Sh-Boom," released "Legend of Gunga Din." The RCA recording's lyrics were somewhat serious, but the tune featured a periodic, novelty background refrain of "Gunga Din, bring water!" The single was released two years later on the Warwick label.

Bobby Darin's 1960 top ten Atco Records hit, "Beyond the Sea," featured "That's the Way Love Is" on the single's flip side. The B-side's lyrics included the refrain: "And you're a better man sir, than I, Gunga Din."

A jazz version of Alfred Newman's *Gunga Din* theme was performed by trumpeter Tommy Turrentine on his eponymous 1960 Time Records album. After a few familiar bars, Turrentine's melody dissolves into a hard bop sojourn.

A year later, Johnny Duncan and his Blue-grass Boys recorded "The Legend of Gunga

Din" on England's Pye Records. The lyrics were original but were based on Kipling's character. On the recording, Duncan's *bhisti* was a seventeen-year-old, who blew a bugle warning and "saved his regiment."

In 1962, Sonny Gianotta (with Phil Camarta and Tommy Cardinale) recorded "The Last Blast of the Blasted Bugler," a satiric ABC-Paramount production that begins on a serious note ("The legend of Gunga Din," says the narrator. "Let us recreate that moment.") before evolving into a never-ending bugle call that slowly weakens after each blast of gunfire.

Also in 1962, the Gold Coast Singers (George Cromarty and Ed Rush) released "Gunga Din" as a single on World-Pacific Records, but it failed to chart. Two years later, the song was included on the blues-folk *Hootenanny Saturday nite* album (World Pacific Records).

On October 10, 1964, the animated TV series, *The Famous Adventures of Mr. Magoo*, featured an episode titled "Gunga Din." The nearsighted character, voiced by Jim Backus, portrayed the famous water boy in the episode.

No Heaven For Gunga Din, a fictional tale about heaven, purgatory, and hell, written by Ali Mirdrekvandi, was published in 1965. Coincidentally, the book was reviewed by Joel Sayre in the September 25, 1965 issue of *Life* magazine. "[It is] filled with imagination-rich situations and uproarious action," wrote Sayre, who pointed out that the author, an Iranian, had been nicknamed Gunga Din by an American officer whom he had worked for during World War II. In the book, the deceased title character and a group of American and British officers, who perished during a futuristic twenty-first century war, attempt to enter heaven.

In 1966, Frank Sinatra recorded Kipling's poem and released it on his Reprise label. The recording coincided with the thirtieth anniversary of the celebrated poet's death. However, only several hundred copies of "Frank Sinatra Reads From Gunga Din" were pressed as 45-rpm recordings.

Singer-songwriter Jim Croce recorded "Gunga Din" on his 1966 album *Facets* (Croce Records). Croce set the poem to an accessible melody, and later included the song on his 1975 *The Faces I've Been* album (Lifesong Records).

The Contenders, a doo-wop vocal group, released "Gunga Din" (Whitney Sound Records) in 1966. The tune, written by Jack Strong during the height of the Beatles-led British Invasion, featured classic street corner harmonies and a story line about the title character who eventually "got a rock and roll group."

In 1969, the Byrds recorded "Gunga Din," a modern-story tune written by Gene Parsons that had little to do with Kipling except for a lyrical line that said: "You know that it's a sin/Gunga Din." The song appeared on the band's *Ballad of Easy Rider* album (Columbia Records). That same year, a funk band called Gunga Din released "Snake Pit," a single release on Valise Records, which suggested a musical reference to the film's memorable torture chamber, but the tune was nothing more than an upbeat dance tune that featured the repetitive background chant, "snake pit, oh yeah!"

The Vaudeville parodies of Kipling's legendary character were revived in issue #125 of *Mad* magazine in 1969 (and in issue #239), and a dozen years later in issue #81 of *Crazy* magazine. The Gunga Din character was also depicted in cartoons that were included in more conventional periodicals such as *The New Yorker*.

Veteran DJ announcer Ralph Paul recorded a narrated version of "Gunga Din," a promotional 45-rpm record adapted and arranged by songwriter-producer Alex Zanetis, for Nashville's Mega Records in 1971.

In the earlier 1970s, a professional wrestler called Gunga Din battled it out with the likes of "Hippie" Boyette, Cowboy Bob Kelley, and Thundercloud in the Southern United States circuit. He joined forces with Kubla Kahn and won the tag-team championship in 1973.

Gunga Din was set to music in 1976 on *Peter Bellamy Sings the Barrack-Room Ballads of Rudyard Kipling*, a 12-track collection that was released a year later in Great Britain. The track was also included on Bellamy's *Wake the Vaulted Echoes*, a three-CD package, which was issued two decades later.

In 1978, forty years after *Gunga Din* was filmed, Andrew McLaglen, Victor McLaglen's son, announced that he was going to direct a remake of the classic film, a production that would star Richard Burton, Roger Moore, and Richard Harris. The four had been working together on *The Wild Geese*, an adventure film in South Africa, when they "just decided they were all having too much fun for it to stop."[1] It was suggested that Sam Jaffe could reprise his role, although the 87-year-old actor may have thought otherwise. Reginald Rose, who wrote the screenplay for *The Wild Geese*, was scheduled to write the script. However, the fun never got started on the *Gunga Din* remake.

Efforts to remake *Gunga Din* coincided with comments made by screenwriter William Goldman during a 1979 interview with *Hollywood Reporter* columnist George Christy. "[*Gunga Din*] is "the child adventure that's

never been captured again," said Goldman, who earned a 1970 Oscar for Best Writing, Story and Screenplay Based on Material Not Previously Published or Produced for *Butch Cassidy and the Sundance Kid* (1969), and a 1977 Oscar for Best Writing, Screenplay Based on Material from Another Medium for *All the President's Men* (1976). "The scene where *Gunga Din*, played by Sam Jaffe, crawls to the top of the Temple of Gold and blows a warning to the British troops—it's always overpoweringly moving."[2] In another interview, Goldman said that *Gunga Din* was "the greatest movie ever made," and acknowledged that the cliff-jump scene he wrote in *Butch Cassidy and the Sundance Kid* was inspired by the 1939 classic.[3]

Another *Gunga Din* project was on the horizon. On December 1, 1980, the Associated Press announced: "Stuart Whitman, filming *Butterfly*, will produce a remake of *Gunga Din*. Whitman, who plans to play one of the major roles, acquired the right from the National Historical Trust of England."[4] Whitman "would play a missionary and three British actors, as yet unnamed, would take the roles of the soldiers."[5] However, Whitman's project was never made, but he continued his acting career in numerous film and television productions.

Whitman is credited as securing permission to include an excerpt from Kipling's poem in *This Year's Blonde* (1980), a movie made for television about Marilyn Monroe's early career. Near the end of the movie, Lloyd Bridges' character, Johnny Hyde, asks Constance Forslund's character, Marilyn Monroe, if she ever read Kipling's poem in junior high. "No," she replied, "But I saw the movie." Hyde follows by reciting a few make-shift lines from *Gunga Din*: "You may talk of wine and beer, when you're quartered safe out here; but when it comes to slaughter, you will do your work on water." Like the famous water carrier, the Hyde character's demise soon follows.

In Roger Dooley's 1981 book, *From Scarface to Scarlett: American Films in the '30s*, *Gunga Din* is celebrated among other great motion pictures in the epilogue chapter, "1939: The Best of Everything—Almost." The classic film became a staple of revival house screenings, library, and institutional presentations, including showings at Seattle Central Community College in February 1981, and the Lincoln Library in Springfield, Illinois, in July 1981.

Goldman later commented on *Gunga Din* in *Adventures in the Screen Trade: A Personal View of Hollywood and Screenwriting*. In an advance piece about the book, syndicated Hollywood reporter Liz Smith said, "He claims the movie *Gunga Din*, which won not a single Oscar in 1939, is 'infinitely superior to any of the five Lucas-Spielberg winners.'"[6]

Adding to the renewed interest in *Gunga Din* in 1982, Ted Mahar, film critic of Portland, Oregon's *Oregonian*, said, "*Gunga Din*, of course, is one of the great adventures of all time, with vast vistas filmed in the American Southwest, and with great performances, [and a] score by Alfred Newman, one of his best."[7]

On June 23, 1982, Gunga Din producer Pandro Berman hosted a special luncheon in Hollywood to acknowledge the donation of RKO's archives to the University of California at Los Angeles' film archives. Sam Jaffe was among those who attended the event.

The scattered attention given to *Gunga Din* was soon about to manifest itself into something more concrete. The most adventurous project associated with Kipling's famous poem was the Cannon International-Golan-Globus Productions' effort to remake the motion picture. A plane carrying a banner over the Cannes Film Festival in 1981 promoted the film and one of its stars, Roger Moore. However, according to syndicated entertainment columnist Marilyn Beck, the actor "had no intention of doing it." Moore, who had recently finished starring in his fifth title role as James Bond in *For Your Eyes Only* (1981), was displeased at the aerial promotion. "They even had my name on the back of an airplane flying around advertising it," said Moore, who would later add two more Bond films to his resume. "And I don't even believe there is a script."[8]

Moore's comments notwithstanding, Golan-Globus Productions went ahead with its promotional efforts and remained steadfast in retaining Moore's services. "The Remake of the Century! Principal photography commences with an all-star cast in spring of 1982," announced the Hollywood, California-based company in a two-page trade ad.

An all-star cast it was. The film, scheduled to be written by Joseph Goldman and James Silke, had allegedly lined up Sean Connery, Roger Moore, Michael Caine, and Ben Kingsley to star in the motion picture. The cast would feature two of filmdom's James Bonds (Connery and Moore); two actors, who had teamed up on a previous Kipling film, *The Man Who Would Be King* (Connery and Caine); and one (Kingsley), who had just completed the title role in *Gandhi*. Caine was eager to work with Connery again. "He is probably the nearest person to me I've ever played," said Caine in 1982.[9]

In all probability, Kingsley would assume the title role, Connery would play MacChesney, Moore would portray Ballantine, and Caine would take the role of Cutter. "I'd love to do some of the films Cary Grant did," said Caine.[10] It was, indeed, a cast of big names; however, the quartet's services would be costly for any studio, especially for the budget-conscious Cannon, which began in 1967. Its two co-founders, Chris Dewey and Dennis Friedland, had little success at the box office (with the exception of *Joe* in 1970), and sold the company to Menahem Golan and Yoram Globus, who were cousins. The two new owners focused on making inexpensive B-films, but a number of them, including *Lady Chatterley's Lover* (1981) and *Death Wish II* (1982), directed by Michael Winner, resulted in financial success. The company had several big hits later in the 1980s, including *Missing in Action* (1984), *Invasion USA* (1985), *Delta Force* (1986), *Runaway Train* (1985), and *The Assault* (1986), which was distributed by Cannon and won an Academy Award for Best Foreign Language Film.

Golan and Globus began to market their *Gunga Din* project, but they had some problems with the proposed roster of actors, particularly Moore who became angry once again when his name was "used in vain as the projected star" in the remake. Golan and Moore exchanged counter claims. "Golan insists he never said Moore was set for the picture," wrote Marilyn Beck. "He does admit that he asked Roger to star in the production, but says the Cannon Group decided they wanted a younger man, and withdrew the offer before Roger had a chance to say no." Moore, who turned fifty-five in 1982, admitted that he couldn't accept the part. "We're older than any dead field marshal, let alone a live one," quipped Moore. "How can we play corporals in the Indian Army?"[11]

Still, the project remained alive. At the Cannes Film Festival in 1984, a small private plane carried an advertisement banner over the site for Michael Winner's remake of *Gunga Din*. Despite Moore's pessimistic appraisal of the film, it appeared that the Cannon production was still alive, and Winner was on board to direct. Ultimately, though, Cannon's production of *Gunga Din* only went as far as the banner that flew over the French Riviera during the *Festival de Cannes*.

It was a missed opportunity, because the original film story was still embraced by critics and fans. In 1985, John R. Starr, writing in the *Arkansas Democrat*, stated that the best film he saw all year was *Gunga Din*, despite the release of *Back to the Future*, *Out of Africa*, *The Color Purple*, *Pale Rider*, and *Witness*. Starr had viewed the film on Cinemax, the first time he had seen the film since its 1939 release. He noted that *Gunga Din* and other films of the era were made by moviemakers who "concentrated on entertainment instead of messages."[12]

In *Heaven Help Us* (1985), a comedy drama about Catholic high school students in the mid-1960s, two films clips from *Gunga Din* (the body of the deceased water bearer and "The End") appear on a TV screen inside the operator's office of the Carroll Street Bridge in Brooklyn. As an approaching boat threatens four teens trapped in a car on the bridge that extends over the Gowanus Canal, bridge operator Calvert DeForest laughs hysterically at Montagu Love's narration during the film's final moments. It is, arguably, the most off-beat pop culture use of the classic motion picture. Despite its inclusion in the film, *Gunga Din* is not mentioned in the final credits.

Meanwhile, Cinecom Pictures released *The Deceivers* (1988), which starred Pierce Brosnan, a future big-screen James Bond, as British Captain William Savage, who battles the Thugs in India in 1825. The film's opening scene begins like *Gunga Din* with a nighttime massacre of a small British patrol. *The Deceivers* uses a few early *Gunga Din* story lines: Brosnan disguises himself as an Indian, the practice of Suttee is included, and an elephant is featured (as a means of capital punishment). The film ends with a successful cavalry charge and a message: "It took twenty years to wipe out Thuggee. Rather than betray the cult, over 400 Thugs put the hangman's noose around their own necks. Thuggee had claimed almost two million victims." *The Deceivers* was unsuccessful at the box office and may have played a role in Manahem Golan's decision to abandon his *Gunga Din* remake project—at least for a while.

Golan subsequently left Cannon in 1989 and formed the 21st Century Film Corporation. He eventually worked with Moore and Caine in a so-called *Gunga Din*-substitute project, *Bullseye!* (1991), an adventurous comedy film.

Golan's 21st Century Films went bankrupt in 1996, but three years later, a new Los Angeles-based company, FilmWorld, Inc., headed by Chairman Menahem Golan and President John Daly, announced that its first film would be *Gunga Din*. On the Animation World Network's website, David Kilmer stated that the production, written by Joseph Goldman and James Silke, "will be based on Rudyard Kipling's story about a young Indian boy's adventures with the British Army in India." The animated film was scheduled to be completed and released during the "2000 holiday season in theaters throughout the world." However, that holiday season passed without any on-screen references to Kipling's heroic water carrier.

The 1939 film did have an influence on one of Hollywood's biggest releases in 1984:

Steven Spielberg's *Indiana Jones and the Temple of Doom*, which was preceded by the *Gunga Din*-flavored *Raiders of the Lost Ark* (1981). *Temple of Doom* is garnished with a number of *Gunga Din* elements, including its India location, a man hammering a large gong, a search for fortune, the appearance of a Thuggee cult and its blood-thirsty leader, the worship of Kali, a deteriorating rope bridge, and elephants.

"I liked *Raiders of the Lost Ark* all right but it was not in a class with *Gunga Din*," wrote syndicated *New York Times* columnist Russell Baker, who called *Gunga Din* "indisputably the best boys' adventure film ever made." Baker added, "I can watch *Gunga Din* twice a year without yawning. One viewing of *Raiders of the Lost Ark* will hold me for a lifetime."[13]

Syndicated Knight News Service film critic Glenn Lovell was more generous. He placed *Raiders of the Lost Ark* on his list of "Top Ten Adventure Films," and identified *Gunga Din* as one of the others. "They broke the mold when they made this nineteenth century India adventure," stated Lovell. "It has everything—intrigue, bloodthirsty religious fanatics, a forbidden city of gold, knock-about camaraderie, swashbuckling action, and an ambush averted by local coolie Sam Jaffe on bugle. Steven Spielberg's snake-filled room in *Raiders [of the Lost Ark]* is but one of countless debts owed this classic adventure."[14]

One critic even suggested a *Gunga Din-Star Wars* connection. "Eduardo Ciannelli as a Darth Vader prototype, complete with faith in a demon worship akin to The Force. Cary Grant, Victor McLaglen and Douglas Fairbanks Jr. embody many of the virtues of Han Solo, Luke Skywalker and Chewbacca."[15]

Actor Tom Selleck said that *Gunga Din* was his favorite film. He even viewed the film while flying in a private jet on the way to Los Angeles where he was attending the premiere of *High Road to China* (1983). Selleck said that he had seen the epic 1939 movie about twenty times. *High Road to China* was a second cousin of sorts to the *Gunga Din*-influenced *Raider of the Lost Ark*, since it included fast-paced adventure sequences flavored with carefree dialogue.

By the end of the 1980s, interest in remaking *Gunga Din* had disappeared, but Spielberg kept making more *Gunga Din*-inspired Indiana Jones films. *Indiana Jones and the Last Crusade* (1989) and *Indiana Jones and the Kingdom of the Crystal Skull* (2008) combined for over $500 million at the box office.

Standard recitations of the poem continued to be recorded. In 1990, Peter Bellamy, who had originally sung the song in 1976, released a spoken version of Kipling's famous work on *Soldiers Three*, a CD which had a limited private distribution.

Parts of Alfred Newman's score can be heard on *Historical Romances: The Charge of the Light Brigade – Gunga Din – Devotion*, a CD produced by HNH International Ltd. in 1995, which features the music of Newman, Erich Wolfgang Korngold, and Max Steiner. The music, performed by the Brandenburg Philharmonic Orchestra in Germany, under the direction of Richard Kaufman and arranged by William Stromberg, includes the following *Gunga Din* selections: "Main Title," "Alright, I'll sign," "Across the bridge/ Battle at Tantrapur," "Reading the Poem," and "Finale/End Cast."

"They had much of the score at UCLA in the RKO archives," explained John W. Morgan, a film composer, who worked with Stromberg on the project. "Bill did the assembly for our score. I agreed with him about using most of the battle music from the early portion of the film, but if we had done it a bit later, it certainly [would have] deserved an album of its own. There is not a cue in the film that I don't love."[16]

In 1998, a New York-based band called The Gunga Din (not to be confused with Gunga Din, the 1960s funk band) performed its mix of quirky, retro indie rock for the first time. A year later, the band's CD debut, *Introducing the Gunga Din*, an eleven-track collection, was released on the Tractor Beam label. The group followed up with additional releases, but Kipling's poetic inspiration is only found in the band's name.

"Gunga Din" became the title of more songs that were recorded by a host of diversified music acts, including Plainsong in 1993, Dr. Didg in 2002, Dialeto in 2008, Four Day Crawl in 2009 (actually "Gunga Din on the Rock N Roll Hiway"), and Dirty Squad in 2010, although the recordings had nothing to do with Kipling. However, the classic poem was recited by Colonel Mason and the Kids on the wacky *Santa's Movin In* album in 2004.

Kipling's *bhisti* was showcased in *Adventure Classics* #12 (July 1, 2005), an illustrated comic book-style publication.

Sixty years after its release, *Gunga Din* was acknowledged as an important motion picture, when it was added to the United States Film Preservation Board's National Film Registry in 1999. Films added to the roster are recognized as being "culturally, historically, or aesthetically significant." *Gunga Din* is one of eighteen films in the National Film Registry from 1939, a year that has more films in the registry than any other.[17]

Three Kings (1999) recalled *Gunga Din* somewhat with its three roguish Gulf War soldiers (George Clooney, Mark Walhberg, and Ice Cube), its mix of action and light-hearted fun, and the search for gold.

Film critic Roger Ebert said he was intrigued by Indian director Shekhar Kapur's remake of *The Four Feathers* (2002). Ebert anticipated a revisionist retelling of the classic British colonial film; however, it turned out to be "a skilled update of the same imperialist swashbuckler." Ebert noted: "We await the revisionist *Gunga Din*."[18]

Twenty-first century film historians acknowledged the film's status as an outstanding production. In his *2015 Move Guide: The Modern Era*, Leonard Maltin gave *Gunga Din* four stars and called it "*The* Hollywood action-adventure yarn."

One film historian gave the film a mixed review. "*Gunga Din* was a routine film—it was not nominated for anything, nor should it have been," wrote David Thomson in "*Have You Seen...?*," who failed to mention cinematographer Joseph H. August's Academy Award nomination or one of *Photoplay's* "outstanding pictures" of the year awards or Sam Jaffe's "Best Character Performance" award from *Modern Screen*. "But its confidence, its brio, and its fun have hardly faded. If anything, the rest of the world is left with just one objection: not that the film and its follies were uttered, but that America has become so much gloomier and more self-conscious a country, always testing its own motivation.[19]

The film was included in Mark A. Viera's *Majestic Hollywood: The Greatest Films of 1939*. The author concluded his four-page entry with a quote from Douglas Fairbanks, Jr.: "It was not only an enormous hit—it broke every record at Radio City Music Hall—but also an effective goodwill boost toward the British at that uncertain time in international affairs."[20]

Gunga Din is included in *1001 Movies You Must See Before You Die*, an encyclopedic 2015 update of the original 2003 release. The book, which was edited by Steven Jay Schneider, states that the motion picture "is a spectacular visual treat, one of the most impressive action films ever made—the buddy film to end all buddy films."

Two of the modern film world's most creative and accomplished artists, have been sharing their enthusiasm for *Gunga Din* at various film festivals over the years: Craig Barron and Ben Burtt. Barron won an Oscar for Best Effects, Visual Effects for *Batman Returns* (1992), and an Oscar for Best Achievement in Visual Effects for *The Curious Case of Benjamin Button* (2008). Barron also earned an Outstanding Visual Effects Emmy for *By Dawn' Early Light* (1990). Ben Burtt won an Oscar for Special Achievement for *Star Wars* (1978), a Special Achievement Oscar for *Raiders of the Lost Ark* (1982), a Best Sound Editing Oscar for *E.T. The Extra-Terrestrial* (1983), and a Best Sound Editing Oscar for *Indiana Jones and the Last Crusade* (1989). Burtt also gave voice to *WALL-E* (2008) and created the *Star Wars* audio expressions of R2-D2 and the captivating breathing sounds of Darth Vader.

Both Craig Barron and Ben Burtt are also film historians, who presented and hosted panel discussions for *Gunga Din* at the Academy of Motion Picture Arts and Sciences in New York City in 2009, the 2014 Lone Pine Film Festival, and the TCM Classic Film Festival, which was held at Los Angeles' Egyptian Theater in March of 2015. *Gunga Din* remains one of Burtt's favorite movies of all time. "It is in my top five favorites," said Burtt in a *Los Angeles Times* interview. "It's a wonderful adventure movie that still holds up really well. It combines serious action adventure and comedy in the same movie." Burtt credited the music for his initial interest in the motion picture. "Alfred Newman's score is a strong foundation for the film," he said. "His *Gunga Din* theme for that character always caught my attention as a child. I think I was also impressed when my grandfather, watching it with me, recited parts of Kipling's poem."[21]

Burtt also appreciated various audio elements in the film. "The Thuggee yells off screen when our heroes first encounter the Thuggees in Tantrapur is an excellent use of sound which puts you in the point of view of the soldiers about to be ambushed," he said. "The reverberant gunshots recorded at Lone Pine became classic and were used in many later Westerns for Gene Autry's and Roy Rogers' TV guns."[22]

The fight at Tantrapur remains Burtt's favorite scene in the movie. "Terrific editing and stunt work," he noted. "And beautifully choreographed. Of course, the whole suspenseful build-up at the end when Gunga Din is slowly ascending the cupola on the temple to blow the bugle alarm works so well because they make the scene about as quiet as possible. All you hear are the distant bagpipes. Moviemakers today have forgotten about dynamics like that. You can use near silence very effectively; you don't need to have one-hundred-percent music, dialogue, and sound effects going on at the same time. *Gunga Din* shows the real artistry when it comes to dynamics: scenes can seem very loud and impactful when preceded by quietude."

Burtt acknowledged *Gunga Din's* influence on modern motion pictures. "The film might have been the first to successfully combine comedy and realistic action where people die," he explained. "It is common today and was revived by the James Bond and Indiana Jones films, but that style was first invented by *Gunga Din*."[23]

Gunga Din became part of the modern music scene when on July 2, 2015, the Libertines, a British rock band, released "Gunga Din," an advance single from the group's *Anthems for Doomed Youth* album. The song, written by Pete Doherty and Carl Barat, the quartet's chief vocalists and admirers of Rudyard Kipling, is a depressing tale of self-induced anguish, and includes such veiled optimistic lyrical references as "You're a better man than I" and "Dreamt of Gunga Din."

One of the most unconventional items dedicated to Kipling's regimental *bhisti* is Gunga Din Cider, an alcoholic beverage currently produced by the St. Julian Winery in Michigan. The bottle features a color illustration of a mounted nineteenth century British soldier, who looks remarkably like Rudyard Kipling. The winery states: "Crisp acidity and the perfect touch of sweetness make this hard cider perfect until the last drop—Gunga Din!"

Select scenes from *Gunga Din* appear in The Great Movie Ride, a popular attraction at Walt Disney World's Hollywood Studios. The pre-show film sequence, which lasts about 47 minutes and features clips from many classic films on a large movie theater-sized screen, includes 36 seconds of *Gunga Din*. The late Turner Classic Movies host Robert Osborne narrates the pre-show film and says of *Gunga Din*, "It stars the dynamic trio of Cary Grant, Douglas Fairbanks, Jr., and Victor McLaglen as three roguish, wise-cracking British soldiers who romp through colonial India." It's seen every day at the theme park; however, the TCM sponsorship is scheduled to end.

Kipling's famous character and lines from *Gunga Din* are mentioned in *The Man Who Knew Infinity* (2016), a motion picture about the struggles of Srinivasa Ramanujan, a brilliant early twentieth century Indian mathematician, who travels to the University of Cambridge for further studies. In England, Ramanujan, played by Dev Patel, confronts racism and doubts about his intellectual capabilities, but is befriended by Professor G. H. Hardy, who is portrayed by Jeremy Irons. In one scene, Hardy's assistant, Beglan, played by Pádraid Delaney, says, "Don't let it ruin our day with Gunga Din. I'm sure it won't mean war," after the professor reads a newspaper account about the assassination of Archduke Franz Ferdinand of Austria-Hungary. Irons' character responds with, "All this Din Din Din."[24] Later, during a discussion about a mathematical problem, the assistant replies to the professor, "Until now? Din, Din, Din, Gunga Din."

Gunga Din will always be a part of the Museum of Western Film History in Lone Pine, California. Although the museum is primarily dedicated to the many Western motion pictures and television programs that were filmed nearby, the facility properly acknowledges *Gunga Din* as the "largest production ever filmed in the Lone Pine area."

The museum's south exterior wall features a wonderful large mural of colored film frame-like paintings that depict scenes from various productions filmed at Lone Pine. One of the panels, painted by artist Kathy Sexton, shows Cary Grant's Cutter and Sam Jaffe's Gunga Din struggling on the precarious wooden rope bridge as Annie attempts to join them on their crossing.

Inside, the museum features a number of *Gunga Din* items in its collection, including one of Victor McLaglen's helmets, a cartridge belt, plaster chunks from the various buildings, prop firearms and edged weapons, posters, empty blank cartridge casings, lobby cards, and assorted movie stills. One wooden prop sword features the signatures of the film's principals. Many other films and television productions that were filmed in the Lone Pine area are properly documented in the facility. The museum is located at 701 S. Main Street, Lone Pine, California, 93545, USA.

At the Mount Whitney Cemetery in Lone Pine rests the body of Juan M. Perez, who worked for Lone Pine Lumber and Supply, appeared in *Gunga Din* as a background player, and was one of Sam Jaffe's stand-ins. He was "one of the first five boys in Lone Pine to enlist," prior to the December 7, 1941 attack on Pearl Harbor.[25] Perez served with the 24th Infantry Division and was killed at Leyte in the Philippines on January 10, 1945. He was a "better man than I."

Chapter Twenty-Five Notes

1. *Oregonian*, February 2, 1978, 26.

2. *San Diego Union*, September 4, 1979, 11. Goldman's first novel, *The Temple of Gold*, which was published in 1957, was a reference to the temple in *Gunga Din*.

3. William Goldman interview, Writers Guild Foundation, 2000, https://www.youtube.com/watch?v=nCs4gdt-mPY&feature=youtu.be&t=39m

4. *Plain Dealer*, (Cleveland, Ohio), December 1, 1980, 29.

5. Leibfried, *Rudyard Kipling and Sir Henry Rider Haggard*, 29.

6. *Trenton Evening Times*, September 30, 1982.

7. Oregonian, March 14, 1982, 155.

8. Times-Picayune, (New Orleans, Louisiana), July 11, 1981, 46.

9. Lewis Archibald, "An Interview With Michael Caine," *The Aquarian Weekly*, March 31, 1982, 13.

10. Ibid.

11. *Times-Picayune*, (New Orleans, Louisiana), July 14, 1981, 42.

12. *Arkansas Democrat*, Oct. 23, 1985, 73.

13. *Omaha World-Herald*, December 21, 1981, 24.

14. *Arkansas Gazette*, August 14, 1981, 27.

15. *Oregonian*, September 12, 1982, 165.

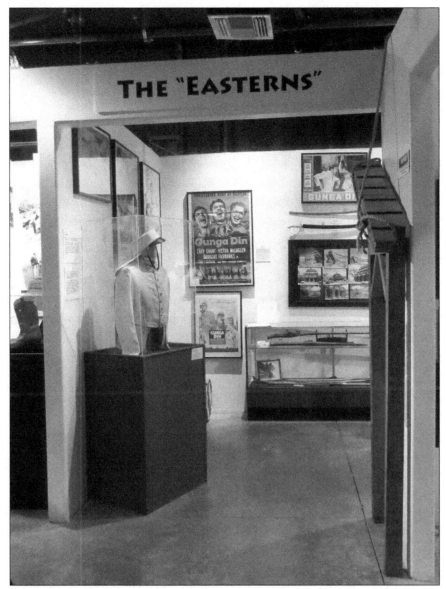

Entrance to Gunga Din displays at the Museum of Western Film History in Lone Pine, California. Photo by Craig R. Covner.

16. John W. Morgan to author, September 30, 2016. "The sad fact is many of our classic American film scores no longer exist in their fully orchestrated, original versions," noted Morgan in the CD's liner notes.

17. Eighteen films from 1928 and 1940 are also in the registry. *Gunga Din*, categorized by the National Film Registry as a "Narrative Feature," was one of twenty-five films added to the roster in 1999. On November 5, 1999, the film was showcased by the New York State Writers Institute at the State University of New York.

18. *Daily Advocate* (Stamford, CT), September 20, 2002, 61.

19. David Thomson, *"Have You Seen...?" – A Personal Introduction to 1,000 Films* (New York: Alfred Knopf, 2008), 353.

20. Mark A. Viera, *Majestic Hollywood: The Greatest Films of 1939* (Philadelphia: Running Press, 2013), 29.

21. Burtt to author, June 7, 2016.

22. Ibid.

23. Burtt to author, June 7, 30, 2016.

24. Although Irons is actually saying "din," as a reference to the loud noises associated with war, the movie's DVD subtitles capitalized the term.

25. "Inyo Serviceman Dies on Leyte," The undated 1945 newspaper clipping reported: "Recently Sgt. Perez has been in numerous South Pacific battles, He has never been home on a furlough in his four years of service."

GUNGA DIN POSTSCRIPT

Unforgettable motion pictures are those that not only entertain but tell memorable stories, usually about characters who confront serious challenges, no matter what the cost may be to overcome them. These special films address fundamental aspects of the human condition, raise questions about the nature of interpersonal relationships, express commonly shared burdens, and contain scenes and characters which excite both heart and soul.

In *Gunga Din*, the title character aspires to be a soldier, a seemingly impossible objective, considering his circumstances. Yet, his determination and extraordinary courage ultimately elevate him to a status beyond that which even he originally sought. Of course, his brave actions result in his death, which raises the question: to what extent does one give up his or her life to save the lives of others? The world was at war less than eight months after *Gunga Din* was released, and the issue of sacrifice would be a topic that would resonate in millions of households.

George Stevens assembled a great staff of writers, crew members, and actors, who contributed to the success of the film, a rousing tale of action, adventure, and joyous escapades, which were strategically punctuated with comedy and playfulness. The film featured excellent cinematography, vivid sets, a glorious mountainous location, and a superb musical score. *Gunga Din* had it all.

Yet *Gunga Din* is much more, because it contains a lesson—one that flows from Sam Jaffe's performance, which is at the emotional core of the film. His inspirational portrayal of the lowly *bhisti* reminds us that achievement is always within our grasp. It is only a question of our resolve.

Appendix A

Gunga Din
By Rudyard Kipling
1890

You may talk o' gin and beer
When you're quartered safe out 'ere,
An' you're sent to penny-fights an' Aldershot it;
But when it comes to slaughter
You will do your work on water,
An' you'll lick the bloomin' boots of 'im that's
    got it.
Now in Injia's sunny clime,
Where I used to spend my time
A-servin' of 'Er Majesty the Queen,
Of all them black-faced crew
The finest man I knew
Was our regimental bhisti, Gunga Din.
He was "Din! Din! Din!
"You limpin' lump o' brick-dust, Gunga Din!
"Hi! *Slippery hitherao*!
"Water, get it! *Panee lao*!
"You squidgy-nosed old idol, Gunga Din!"

The uniform 'e wore
Was nothin' much before,
An' rather less than 'arf o' that be'ind,
For a piece o' twisty rag
An' a goatskin water-bag
Was all the field-equipment 'e could find.
When the sweatin' troop-train lay
In a sidin' through the day,
Where the 'eat would make your bloomin'
    eyebrows crawl,
We shouted "Harry By!"
Till our throats were bricky-dry,
Then we wopped 'im 'cause 'e couldn't serve
    us all.
It was "Din! Din! Din!
"You 'eathen, where the mischief 'ave you
    been?

"Or I'll *marrow* you this minute
"If you don't fill up my helmet, Gunga Din!"

'E would dot an' carry one
Till the longest day was done;
An' e didn't seem to know the use o' fear.
If we charged or broke or cut,
You could bet your bloomin' nut,
'E'd be waitin' fifty paces right flank rear.
With 'is mussick on 'is back,
'E would skip with our attack,
An' watch us till the bugles made "Retire,"
An' for all 'is dirty 'ide
'E was white, clear white, inside
When 'e went to tend the wounded under
    fire!
It was "Din! Din! Din!"
With the bullets kickin' dust-spots on the
    green.
When the cartridges ran out,
You could 'ear the front ranks shout,
"Hi! ammunition-mules an' Gunga Din!"

I sha'n't forgit the night
When I dropped be'ind the fight
With a bullet where my belt-plate should 'a'
    been.
I was chokin' mad with thirst,
An' the man that spied me first
Was our good old grinnin,' gruntin' Gunga
    Din.
'E lifted up my 'ead,
An' 'e plugged me where I bled,
An' 'e guv me 'arf-a-pint o' water green.
It was crawlin' and it stunk,
But of all the drinks I've drunk,
I'm gratefullest to one from Gunga Din.
It was "Din! Din! Din!
" 'Ere's a beggar with a bullet through 'is
    spleen;

" 'E's chawin' up the ground,
"An 'e's kickin' all around:
"For Gawd's sake, git the water, Gunga Din!"

'E carried me away
To where a dooli lay,
An' a bullet come an' drilled the beggar clean.
'E put me safe inside,
An ' just before 'e died,
"I 'ope you liked you drink," sez Gunga Din.
So I'll met 'im later on
In the place where 'e is gone –
Where it's always double drill and no canteen.
'E'll be squattin' on the coals
Givin' drink to poor damned souls,
An' I'll get a swig in hell from Gunga Din!
Yes, Din! Din! Din!
You Lazarushian-leather Gunga Din!
Though I've belted you an' flayed you,
By the livin' God that made you,
You're a better man than I am, Gunga Din!

Explanation of Terms in *Gunga Din*

Out 'ere – in England

Aldershot it – Aldershot, a military camp in Hampshire, England known as the "Home of the British Army"

The Queen – Victoria (ruled from 1837 to 1901)

Bhisti – water carrier (literally, *heavenly one*)

Slippery hitherao – a mock dialect for "slip here"

Panee lao – (a command) "bring the water quickly"

sidin' – a railroad side track

Harry By – O Brother

wopped – hit; beat

juldee – speed; "be quick"

marrow – hit; whip

nut – head

mussick – goatskin water bag

dooli – stretcher

canteen – regimental beer shop

Lazarushian-leather – British military slang for "dark skinned"

Appendix B

Cast and Crew Rosters

Compiled primarily from RKO call sheets and other studio documents. Other sources: IMDB, TCM, AFI Catalog of Feature Films, *American Cinematographer*, and assorted 1939 trade publications. The cast roster includes credited and uncredited cast members. Uncredited cast members who were identified in RKO Studio Records portraying a particular background player are noted. A supplemental roster of background players follows.

Directed by:
George Stevens

Writing Credits:
Fred Guiol (screenplay)
Joel Sayre (screenplay)
Ben Hecht (story)
Charles MacArthur (story)
Lester Cohen (contributing writer)
John Colton (contributing writer)
Vincent Lawrence (contributing writer)
Dudley Nichols (contributing writer)
Anthony Veiller (contributing writer)
Rudyard Kipling (*Gunga Din* poem)

Cast
Cary Grant (Archibald Cutter)
Victor McLaglen (MacChesney)
Douglas Fairbanks, Jr. (Thomas Ballantine)
Sam Jaffe (Gunga Din)
Eduardo Ciannelli (Guru)
Joan Fontaine(Emmy Stebbins)
Montagu Love (Colonel Weed)
Robert Coote (Sgt. Higginbotham)
Abner Biberman (Chota)
Lumsden Hare (Major Mitchell)
Cecil Kellaway (Mr. Stebbins)

Charles Bennett (Telegraph Operator)
George Du Count (Pandu Lal)
Lalo Encinas (Thuggee Executioner)
Ann Evers (Cutter's Dance Partner at Party)
Olin Francis (Fulad)
Bryant Fryer (Scottish Sergeant)
Jamiel Hasson (Thuggee Chief)
Will Jefferies (Orderly)
Audrey Manners (Girl at Party)
Fay McKenzie (Girl at Party)
Lal Chand Mehra (Jadoo)
Clive Morgan (Lancer Captain [also credited as a technical advisor])
George Regas (Thuggee Chieftain)
Olin Francis (Thuggee Chieftain)
Richard Robles (Thuggee)
Reginald Sheffield (Rudyard Kipling)
Leslie Sketchley (Corporal)
Roland Varno (Lt. Markham)

Supplemental Background Roster
Jasin Ali
Arthur Allen
John Alban (Officer)
Buzz Barton
James Bell
Joe De La Cruz
Carl Deloro
Tom Forman
Bryant Fryer
Saret Singh Gill
Sam Harris (Officer)
Abdul Hasson
Jamil Hasson
Frank Levya (Bazaar merchant)
Margarita Luna
Joe McGuinn (Officer)
Toofic Mickey
Art Mix
Juan M. Perez

Satini Pualoa
Rod Redwing
Bob Reeves
Chas Rivero
Bob Sherwood
Allen Schute (Officer)
Dalip Singh
Gurdial Singh(Thuggee)
Paul Singh
Tom Tamarez (Officer)
Charlie Taylor (Officer)
Bruce Wyndham (Officer)

Production Management
Pandro S. Berman

Location Management
Louis Shapiro

Second Unit Director /Assistant Director
Edward Killy (Assistant Director)
Syd Fogel (Assistant Director)
Dewey Starkey (Assistant Director)
Robert Parrish (Assistant Director)

Music
Alfred Newman

Cinematography
Joseph H. August

Film Editing
Henry Berman
John Lockert
John Sturges

Art Direction
Van Nest Polglase

Set Direction
Darrell Silvera

Costume Design
Edward Stevenson

Makeup Department
Mel Berns (makeup department head)
James R. Barker (makeup artist)
Dan Berns (makeup artist)
Irving Berns (makeup artist)
Layne Britton (makeup artist)
Russell Drake (makeup artist)
Charles Gemora (makeup artist)
Abe Haberman (makeup artist)
Joe Hadley (makeup artist)
Walter Hermann (makeup artist)
Dick Johnson (makeup artist)
Ben Libizer (makeup artist)
Harry Pringle (makeup artist)
Louis Sainty (makeup artist [as Louis
    Saintly])
Al Senator (makeup artist)
Howard Smit (makeup artist)
Armand Triller (makeup artist)
William Woods (makeup artist)

Art Department/Property
Perry Ferguson (Associate Art Director)
William Atkinson (swing gang)
Nathan Barragar (props)
Lloyd Bradley (swing gang)
Claude E. Carpenter (set dresser)
Fenton Coe (swing gang)
Thomas Grady (props)
Maxwell O. Henry (props)
James Lane (props)
O. Leffingwell (swing gang)
Tony Lombardo (swing gang)
Kenneth J. Marstella (props)
Glenn Miller (swing gang)
Benafield Millington (drapery)
Carl Riley (greens)
Gene Rossi (props)

Cliff Shair (greens)
Chet Smith (swing gang)
Ralph Warrington (swing gang)

Sound Department
George C. Emick (sound)
John C. Grubb (sound)
Stanford Houghton (sound)
Aubrey C. Lind (sound)
Jack Mark (sound)
Gordon McLean (sound)
Eric Meisel (sound)
Arthur C. Robbins (sound)
Fred Rodgers (sound)
Cecil Shephard sound)
Jean L. Speak (sound)
James G. Stewart (sound recorder [as James
    Stewart])
John E. Tribby (sound recorder)
Kenneth C. Wesson (sound)

Special Effects
Vernon C. Walker (special effects)
Russell A. Cully (special effects)

Visual Effects
P. Brock (photography effects)
William Collins (assistant camera, camera
    effects)
Linwood G. Dunn (photography effects)
Horace L. Hulburd (photography effects)
Mario Larrinaga (camera effects-matte
    artist)
Roger Shearman (photography effects)
Clifford Stine (second camera, camera
    effects)
G. Swartz (photography effects)
M. Zamora (photography effects)

Camera and Electrical Department
Frank Redman (second unit camera lead)

Joseph A. August, Jr. (second camera operator)
H. Barrett (grip)
Pete Bernard (grip)
H. J. Brandon (grip)
Charles Burke (second camera operator)
Tom Clement (grip)
William H. Clothier (camera operator)
T. Connelly (grip [also as Connolly])
Charles Davis (camera operator)
George Diskant (second camera operator)
Thomas East (best boy)
Earl Gilpin (grip)
Ledge Haddow (assistant camera)
Joe Jaslove (camera operator)
Alexander Kahle (still photographer)
George Marquenie (gaffer)
Ross Mesecher (gas generator operator)
C. Noren (grip)
W. Norton (grip)
Edwin Pyle (second camera operator)
William Record (grip)
William Reinhold (assistant camera)
F. Reed (grip)
William Robey (gas generator operator)
Cliff Shirpsir (assistant camera)
Charles Straumer (assistant camera opera-
    tor)
Leon Turon (camera operator)
William Whitaker (camera operator)
Joe Zaslove (camera operator)

Costume and Wardrobe Department
Morris Berger (tailor)
Ray Camp (wardrobe)
Harold Clandening (wardrobe)
Bill Durant (wardrobe)
Eugene Joseff (costume jeweller)
Harry Lawrence (wardrobe)
Bill Rabb (wardrobe)
[…] Singh (wardrobe)
Fred Starnes (wardrobe)

Edward Stevenson (gowns)
Wesley Trist (wardrobe)
Pat Williams (wardrobe)

Music Department
Robert Russell Bennett (orchestrator)
Edward B. Powell (orchestrator)
Conrad Salinger (orchestrator)

Unit Manager
Gordon Jones

Stunts
Red Blair
Alva Baudelio
Gordon Carveth
Tom Coleman
Pat Deasy
Jimmy Dundee
Calvin Emory
Richard Farnsworth
Jack Fitzpatrick
George Flynn
Clem Fuller
Duke Green
Bryan "Slim" Hightower
William Kahale
Ahmed Kalane
Bernard Kikume
Mike Lally
Jack Lindell
John McCafferty
Buddy Mason
Otto Metzetti
Thom Metzetti
Victor Metzetti
Art Mix
Al Munia
Barney O'Toole
Walt Robbins
Max Rose

Rube Schaeffer
David Sharpe
Barlow Simpson
Tom Steele
Otto Victor
Shorty Woods
Louis Young

Carpenters
W. Allendorf
B. Alison
D. Christy
C. Doble
D. Donaldson
R. Donaldson
M. Snyder

Laborers
E. Belane
R. Brown
R. Orkin
J. Struch, Jr.

Other Crew
Charles Anders (painter)
Harold Barry (construction superintendant)
William Briers (technical advisor [as Sergeant Major William Briers])
Barney T. Cole (first aid)
Abdulla Abbas (masseur)
Robert Erskine Holland (technical advisor [as Sir Robert Erskine Holland])
Art Bruggerman (stand-in [for Victor McLaglen])
Phoebe Campbell (stand-in [for Joan Fontaine])
Gordon B. Clarke (stand-in [for Douglas Fairbanks, Jr.])
Hilda Grenier (technical advisor)
Sam Harris (technical advisor)

Malcolm Merrihugh (stand-in [for Cary Grant])
Ralph E. Peckham (painter)
Barlow Simpson (elephant trainer)
Lester G. Schuler (first aid)

Transportation/Drivers
Robert Alexander
Arnold Ballard
Bernie Breakstone
Booth Bowers
Al Caya
F. Coon
Al Fredrickson
Leon Gracy
Smiley Grams
Irving Hedeen
Orville Hilton
Ben Keables
Tom King
Wilkie Kleinpell
John McLaughlin
John P. O'Conner
Fletcher Pierce
Winston Platt
Vernon Sperry
George Sullivan
Archie Towne
Charles Ware
Jarrett Watson
William White
William Whittaker
Ray Yates

Appendix C

Negative Cost "Gunga Din"
At March 23, 1940

Classification	Total Charges	Budget	Classification	Total Charges	Budget
Story	34,234.96	34,235.00	Departmental		
Continuity	113,354.52	107,833.00	Supervision	12,198.00	6,200.00
Directors	105,050.92	73,507.00	Photo Effects		
Cast	465,374.53	329,685.00	(Production)	3,873.81	3,663.00
Extra Talent	97,256.91	53,201.00	Cutting & Editing	11,525.88	5,426.00
Tests	2,083.19	2,000.00	Projection	3,780.21	1,880.00
Production Staff	22,651.24	14,563.00	Music	37,856.99	10,697.00
Cameramen	26,383.76	18,646.00	Music Scoring –		
Sound Recordings	16,779.45	9,431.00	Sound & Lab.	3,690.53	1,184.00
Laboratory			Rerecording	17,600.07	8,552.00
Shooting	29,206.70	17,763.00	Checkup &		
Stills	4,770.12	4,026.00	Master Prints	1,232.30	1,000.00
Art Direction	12,558.92	10,000.00	Main &		
Set Construction	105,968.23	102,400.00	End Titles	2,363.25	500.00
Set Maintenance	8,539.42	3,000.00	Inserts	1,364.28	1,550.00
Standby			Miscellaneous	30,492.58	18,075.00
Laboratory	18,255.89	8,071.00	Photographic		
Set Striking	4,590.73	3,500.00	Effects	5,724.06	6,121.00
Properties &			Total Direct		
Drapery	79,466.75	49,218.00	Cost	1,549,005.67	1,065,620.00
Lighting	22,082.03	11,925.00	Overhead	360,663.61	239,817.19
Wardrobe	35,175.64	29,155.00	**Total Picture**		
Make-up	16,128.45	6,799.00	**Cost**	1,909,669.28	1,305,437.19
Transportation	65,902.17	40,295.00			
Location	115,586.96	62,888.00			
Mechanical					
Effects	1,124.79	4,881.00			
Unclassified					
Expense	4,877.43	3,750.00			

Source: *Gunga Din: Special Collector's Edition* [laser disc], directed by George Stevens, Image Entertainment, 1995.

Appendix D

Eulogy for Sam Jaffe
Written and presented by Robert Ackerman

I am viewing this occasion as a celebration of the life of Sam Jaffe. I keep thinking of Tennyson's Ulysses:

"I am a part of all that I have met;
Yet, all experience is an arch where through
Gleams that untraveled world."

All of us here, and countless others, have been enriched by our association with Sam. He is part of us, and we are richer for it. We, therefore, have a genuine reason to celebrate.

I am here, of course, as Bettye's brother, as a member of that Southern family into which Sam courageously married twenty-eight years ago. I can assure you that that South Carolina Methodist family of rural origins was enriched by Sam. We were enthralled by his kindness, by his inordinate generosity. Without exception, we loved him, and he loved us.

Significantly, the children loved him instantly and enormously. He gave them attention and care; he listened to them, even when my three-year-old daughter, on first seeing him with a beard, demanded that he take it off. Sam came South for a number of family occasions, and he was part of us.

We were awed by Sam's brilliance, by his learning, and by the obvious fact that his learning was unending. Our awe was made all right by Sam's unassuming nature. Last year my school, Drew University, awarded honorary degrees to Sam and Bettye. After listening to a rather lengthy citation filed with those achievements which led to an honorary degree, Sam got the microphone for a moment to say, "What about my modesty?"

We were impressed and entertained by Sam's wit. I am convinced that life for us is more enjoyable because Sam is part of us. I not only remember some of those stories that he told, but more important I recall the joy with which he told them.

We were impressed by Sam's marvelous stubbornness. One night at dinner Sam and I were arguing about where Vassar is located. One of the children got an encyclopedia and found that it located the college not where Sam thought. Sam retorted that it must be an old encyclopedia.

Bottom line, I agree with Kipling:

"By the loving God that made you,
You're a better man than I am, Gunga Din."

John Tobias once said that Sam was one of those saintly people for whom there ought to be a special dispensation to live forever. But it was not to be. For Sam, like Job, died "full of days." What a full life—for which we can all celebrate.

I close with two lines from D. H. Lawrence, for Sam and us:

"And it is time to go, to bid farewell
To one's own self, and find an exit."

Additional Comments About Sam Jaffe
By Bob Ackerman

The line in my eulogy for Sam which got the loudest audience response was "You're a better man than I am, Gunga Din." Sam was aware of the Indian cult which was portrayed in the movie. I have wondered whether Sam was bothered by the element of racism implicit in the movie. That thought notwithstanding, many always thought of Sam as *Gunga Din*. I have always thought that his role as the High Lama in *Lost Horizon* best reflected the essence of Sam, but my favorite role for him was in *Asphalt Jungle*.

He was one of the most ethical people I ever met. Karl Malden once said that he had never known an actor who turned down so more scripts because they were unethical or flimsy. And he didn't believe in life insurance because he thought it was unethical that others would benefit from someone else's death.

Sam had great sympathy for animals, which also came about when he was a very young age. At one time, he lived with relatives who had cattle. A calf was slain and he told me that its mother actually moaned and she walked back and forth in mourning. Sam became a vegetarian but he ate fish.

Bibliography

Archives and Manuscripts

William Faulkner: Notes and Screen Treatments for RKO
film *Gunga Din*
The New York Public Library
Berg Collection
New York, NY

Howard Hawks Papers
L. Tom Perry Special Collection
Harold B. Lee Library
Brigham Young University
Provo, UT

Joel Sayre Papers
The New York Public Library
Humanities and Social Sciences Library
Manuscripts and Archives Division
New York, NY

RKO Radio Pictures, Inc. Studio Records, ca.1928-1958
Library Special Collections, Performing Arts
Gunga Din
UCLA Film & Television Archive
Los Angeles, CA

Audio-Visual Resources

Gunga Din [DVD], directed by George Stevens
Warner Brothers Entertainment, Inc., 2004

George Stevens: A Filmaker's Journey [DVD], directed by
George Stevens, Jr.
Warner Brothers Entertainment, Inc., 1984

Gunga Din [laser disc], directed by George Stevens, 1991,
Turner Home Entertainment and distributed by Image
Entertainment

Gunga Din [Super 8 film], directed by George Stevens
Ken Films, Inc. c. 1970

Books

Alan, Ian. *Cary Grant Film Album.* London: Ian Allan Ltd.,
1971.

Anderson, George K. and William E. Buckler, eds,. *The
Literature of England: An Anthology and a History From
the Dawn of the Romantic Movement to the Present Day.*
Glenview, IL: Scott, Foresman and Company, 1966.

Behlmer, Rudy. *Behind The Scenes: The Making of...The Mal-
tese Falcon, Singin' in the Rain, Snow White and the Seven
Dwarfs, Stagecoach, A Streetcar Named Desire, Tarzan and
his Mate, The Adventures of Robin Hood, The African Queen,
All About Eve, Casablanca, Frankenstein, The Grapes of
Wrath, Gunga Din, High Noon, Laura, Lost Horizon.* Hollywood: Samuel French, 1990.

Breivold, Scott, ed. *Howard Hawks: Interviews.* Jackson,
Mississippi: University Press of Mississippi, 2006.

*Census of the British Empire: Compiled From Official Returns of
the Year 1861.* London: Harrison, 1864.

Chowdhry, Prem. *Colonial India and the Making of Empire
Cinema: Image, Ideology and Identity.* Manchester, UK:
Manchester University Press, 2000.

Dodson, George A., ed. *Twelve Years of a Soldier's Life In
India: Being Extracts from the Letters of Major W. S. R.
Hodson, B. A.* Boston: Ticknor and Fields, 1860.

Durand, Ralph. *A Handbook to the Poetry of Rudyard Kipling.*
London: Hodder & Stoughton, 1914.

Eliot, Marc. *Cary Grant: A Biography.* New York: Random
House, 2004.

Fairbanks, Jr., Douglas. *The Salad Days.* London: William
Collins Sons and Company, Ltd., 1988.

Featherstone, Donald. *Weapons & Equipment of the Victorian
Soldier.* Poole, Dorset: Blandford Press, Ltd., 1978.

Fontaine, Joan. *No Bed of Roses.* New York: William Morrow
and Company, 1978.

Glancy, H. Mark. *When Hollywood Loved Britain: The Hollywood "British" Film 1939-1945.* Manchester, UK: Manchester University Press, 1999.

Groves, Percy. *History of the 42nd Highlanders—"The Black
Watch."* Edinburgh & London: W. and A. K. Johnston,
1893.

Harris, Warren G. *Cary Grant: A Touch of Elegance.* New
York: Doubleday, 1987.

Higham, Charles and Roy Moseley. *Cary Grant: The Lonely
Heart.* New York: Harcourt Brace Jovanovich, 1989.

Hitchman, Francis. *The Public Life of the Right Honourable
the Earl of Beaconsfield.* London: Samson Low, Marston,
Searle & Rivington, 1881.

Holland, Dave. *On Location in Lone Pine: A Pictoral Guide
to one of Hollywood's Favorite Movie Locations for 85 Years.*
Santa Clarita, CA: Holland House, 2005.

Isaacs, Harold R. *Images of India: American Views of India and
China.* New York: Harper & Row, 1958.

Jeffers, Jennifer M. *Britain Colonized: Hollywood's Appropriation of British Literature*. New York: Palgrave Macmillan, 2006.

Leibfried, Philip. *Rudyard Kipling and Sir Henry Rider Haggard on Screen, Stage, Radio and Television*. Jefferson, NC: McFarland & Company, 2000.

Lorrance, Arleen. *Sam Jaffe: An Actor of Character*. Scottsdale, AZ: LP Publications, 2012.

McCann, Graham. *Cary Grant: A Class Apart*. New York: Columbia University Press, 1996.

Nelson, Nancy. *Evenings with Cary Grant: Recollections in His Own Words and by Those Who Knew Him Best*. New York: William Morrow and Company, 1991.

Raghavan, Srinath. *India's War: World War II and the Making of Modern South Asia*. New York: Basic Books, 2016.

Richards, Alfred Bates ("An Old Oxnian"). *A Short Sketch of the Career of Captain Richard F. Burton*. London: William Mullan and Son, 1880.

Richards, Jeffrey. *Visions of Yesterday*. London: Routledge & Kegan Paul Books, 1973.

_____, *The Age of the Dream Palace: Cinema and Society in Britain 1930-1939*. London: Routledge & Kegan Paul Books, 1989.

Said, Edward S. *Orientalism*. New York: Vintage Books, 1979.

Stevens, George, Jr. *Conversations with the Great Moviemakers of Hollywood's Golden Age at the American Film Institute*. New York: Vintage, 2006.

Taylor, Captain Philip Meadows Taylor. *Confessions of a Thug*. London: Richard Bentley, 1839.

Thomson, David. *"Have You Seen...?"—A Personal Introduction to 1,000 Films*. New York: Alfred Knopf, 2008.

This Fabulous Century: 1930-1940. New York: Time-Life Books, 1969.

Turner, George, ed. *The Cinema of Adventure, Romance & Terror*. Hollywood: The ASC Press, 1989.

Turner, Pierre. *Soldiers' Accoutrements of the British Army 1750-1900*. Ramsbury, UK: Crowood Press, 2007.

Viera, Mark A. *Majestic Hollywood: The Greatest Films of 1939*. Philadelphia: Running Press, 2013.

Wansell, Geoffrey. *Haunted Idol: The Story of the Real Cary Grant*. New York: William Morrow and Company, 1984.

Wilkinson-Latham, Robert. *North-West Frontier 1837-1947*. Oxford, UK: Osprey Publishing, 1977.

Wilson, Robert, ed. *The Film Criticism of Otis Ferguson*. Philadelphia: Temple University Press, 1971.

Younghusband, Major-General Sir George. *Forty Years a Soldier: A Volume of Recollections*. London: Herbert Jenkins Ltd., 1923.

Newspapers

Age, The [Melbourne, Australia]
Arkansas Democrat
Arkansas Gazette
Augusta Chronicle [GA]
Boston Record American
Boston Herald
Charleston News and Courier
Columbus Daily Enquirer [Columbus, GA]
Daily Advocate [Stamford, CT]
Daily Illinois State Journal
Daily Inter Ocean [Chicago, IL]
Daily Nonpareil [Council Bluffs, IA]
Dallas Morning News
Evansville Courier and Press [IN]
Evening Star [DC]
Gadsden Times [Gadsden, AL]
Greensboro Daily News [Greensboro, NC]
Heraldo de Brownsville [Brownsville, TX]
Lexington Herald [Lexington, KY]
Marietta Journal [Marietta, GA]
Milwaukee Journal Sentinel
Morning Star [Rockford, IL]
Morning Telegraph [New York]
New York Clipper
New York Daily Mirror, The
New York Herald Tribune, The
New York Journal-American, The
New York Times, The
New York World Telegram, The
Omaha World-Herald
Oregonian [Portland, OR]
Pittsburgh Press
Plain Dealer [Cleveland, OH]
Richmond Times-Dispatch
San Diego Union
San Francisco Chronicle
Seattle Daily Time
Spokesman-Review [Spokane, WA]
Springfield Republican [Springfield, MA]
State Journal Register [Springfield, IL]
Times Picayune [New Orleans, LA]
Trenton Evening News [Trenton, NJ]

Periodicals

American Cinematographer
Aquarian Weekly, The
Asia Magazine
Boys Cinema

Broadcasting Television
Canadian Journal of Regional Science
Cine-Technician, The
Civil and Military Gazette
Colliers
Dialogue on Film
Educational Screen, The
Exhibitor's Trade Review
Film Daily, The
Film Daily Yearbook
Filmindia
Hollywood
Hollywood Filmgraph
Hollywood Reporter
International Photographer
Kinematographic Year Book 1940
Kipling Journal, The
Liberty
Life
Look
Military Collector & Historian
Modern Screen
Morning Telegraph
Motion Picture Daily
Motion Picture Herald
Motion Picture Magazine
Motion Picture News
Motography
National Board of Review
New Captain George's Whizzbang, The
New Movie Magazine, The
Photoplay
Photoplay Studies
Radio Today
Saturday Evening Post, The
Showman's Trade Review
Showplace
Soldiers of the Queen
Sponsor
Variety

Index

A Chump at Oxford 157
A Damsel in Distress 40
A Doll's House 48
A Farewell to Arms 59
A Frozen Ape 8
A Girl in Every Port 43
A Man to Remember 49, 173
A Place in the Sun 170
Abbas, Khwaja Ahmad 60, 158, 159
ABC-Paramount Records 190
Abductors, The 168
Abe Lincoln in Illinois 76
Abel, Walter 26
Academy Award 12, 22, 32, 38, 43,
    50, 65, 103, 104, 149, 168-172, 191,
    192, 193, 196
Academy of Motion Picture Arts &
    Sciences 32, 196
Ackerman, Bettye 169, 173
Ackerman, Bob 91, 169
Ackroyd, Archibald 174
Acooli and Sons 52
Actors' Equity Association 169
Adams Mk II revolver 63
Adams Mk III revolver 63
Adams, Maude 11
Adventure Classics 195
Adventures in the Screen Trade: A
    Personal View of Hollywood and
    Screenwriting 192
Adventures of Gunga Din 176, 178
Adventures of Kathlyn 52
Adventures of Kit Carson 172
Adventures of Robin Hood, The 50, 104
Afghanistan 55
Africa 11, 50
Age, The 145
Alabama Hills 55, 66, 81, 83, 100, 128
Alamo, The 63, 76, 101
Alba Theatre 143
Alexander's Ragtime Band 104, 171
Ali, Jason 54
Ali, Yusef 32
Alice Adams 40, 45
All American Publications 148
All the President's Men 191
Allen, Ian 168
Allied Theatre Owners of New Jersey
    165
Almira Theater 174
Alturas (CA) 55
Amalgamated Clothing Workers of
    America 148

Amazons 52
Ambassador Hotel 149
Ambler (PA) 148
American Cinematographer 60, 98, 143
American Film Institute 183
American Humane Association 91
Ames and Winthrop 7
Amityville (NY) 36
An Affair to Remember 168
Anamosa (IA) 148
Anchor Ranch 103
Anderson, George K. 5
Anderson Boarding and Supply 72
Andy's Gang 175
Angels With Dirty Faces 42
Animation World Network 194
Annie (Anna May) 52, 81, 91, 96, 97,
    115, 116, 118, 148, 173, 184, 198
Annie Oakley 40, 56
Another Dawn 104
Anthems For Doomed Youth 197
Aramis 170
Argentina 145
Arkansas Democrat 193
Arrowhead 172
Arrowhead Springs 56
Arrowsmith 59
Arsenic and Old Lace 168
Asia Magazine 162
Asphalt Jungle, The 169
Assault, The 193
Astaire, Fred 40, 46, 65, 84, 112, 134
Atco Records 189
Attikon Cinema 164
August, Joseph A. 76
August, Joseph H. 75, 76, 84, 91, 108,
    111, 142, 143, 149, 165, 171, 183,
    184, 186
Augusta Chronicle 62
"Auld Lang Syne" 128, 129
Austin, Al 157
Australia 50, 59, 145, 189
Austria-Hungary 198
Autry, Gene 197
Avalon Theater 144
Awful Truth, The 37, 83
Axis Powers 145, 162, 163

Babes in Arms 139
Back to the Future 193
Backus, Jim 190
Bagai, Ram 159
Baghdad 43

Bagley, G. O. 20
Baker, Russell 194
Bakshi, Hrundi V. 180
Balestier, Caroline Starr 2
Ball, Lucille 171
Ballad of Easy Rider 190
Ballantine 24-29, 31-34, 42, 79-81,
    85, 96, 98, 108, 109, 111-120, 125,
    126, 131, 132, 142, 169, 176, 192
Baltimore (MD) 141
Bamberger, Leon J. 152
Banty Tim 4
Barande-Barbe, Corine 189
Barat, Carl 197
Barbarian and the Geisha, The 169
Barnes, Howard 140
Barrack-Rooms Ballads and Other
    Verses 2, 8, 63
Barrett, Larry 180
Barron, Craig 196
Barry, Harold 55
Basich Brothers 72
Batman Returns 196
Battle, The 8
Battle of the Alamo 178
Battle of Loos 6
Battle of Mons 76
Battle of Plassey 1
Baverian Cross 76
Beach Jumpers 168
Beal, John 26
Beatles 180, 190
Beau Geste 60, 63, 139
Beck, Marilyn 193
Beglan 198
Behlmer, Rudy 5, 40, 104, 184
Beirutzoff, Ivy 19, 20
Belafonte, Dennis 180
Belafonte, Harry 180
Belasco Theatre 148
Bellamy, Peter *195*
Beloved Brute, The 43
Ben Casey 169, 170
Ben Hur 169
Bengal Board of Film Censors 161
Bennett, Charles 154
Bennett, Joan 38, 49
Bennett, Robert Russell 105
Benson, John T. 36
Benson's Wild Animal Farm 36
Bentinck, William 114
Benton, Curtis 9
Bergstrom, Wray 52

Berman, Henry 104, 108
Berman, Pandro S. 27, 41, 42, 46, 52, 55, 95, 96, 107, 134, 155, 165, 174, 175, 192; photo 41
Berry, Noah 157
Berry, Wallace 174
Better Times 37
Bevans, Billy 157
Beverly Hills (CA) 169
"Beyond the Sea" 189
Biberman, Abner 50, 54, 58, 96, 107, 132, 170, 174
Bickerton, J. B. 11
Biddeford (ME) 151
Big Parade, The 22, 60
Bishop (CA) 72
Bishop of the Black Canons 50
"Black Hole of Calcutta" 1
Black Arrow, The 8
Black Watch (42nd Highlanders) 50, 143
Black Watch, The 43, 50, 57
Blaisdell, George 143
Blake, Bernie 11
Blockade 12
Blomberg, Ralph 59
Blond Cheat 52
Blondell, Joan 157
Boer War 43
Boehnel, William 140
Bohara 26-28, 32-34
Bohara Street 66
Boldt, Mike 180, 183
Boldt, Phil 180
Bombay (India) 1
Bond, James 192, 193, 197
"Bonnie Dundee" 114
Boston (MA) 178
Box Office Digest 149
Boy Meets Girl 52
Boy Scouts 144
Boy Trouble 140
Boys Cinema 147
Boys Will be Boys 56
Brabin, Charles 25
Brandon, Linda 18-20
Brackettville (TX) 76
Brandenburg Philharmonic Orchestra 195
Brattleboro (VT) 2
Brazee, Marcel 144
Breakstone, Bernard 60
Brecht, Bertolt 186
Brecht on Theatre 186
Bride of Torosko, The 49
Bridgeport (CT) 144

Bridges, Lloyd 191
Briers, William 59, 108
Bringing Up Baby 37, 38, 83, 173
Briskin, Samuel 23, 38
Britain Colonized 187
British Agent 59
British Board of Film Censors 12
British Colombia 48
British East India Company 1, 18, 19, 44, 114, 178
British National Anthem 107
British Raj 1, 162, 186, 187
Brittingham Commissary 72
Broadway 22, 23, 37, 48-50, 169
Bronson Canyon 105
Brooklyn (NY) 92, 143, 193
Brooklyn Dodgers 165
Brooks, Phyllis 92
Brosnan, Pierce 193, 194
Brown, B. C. 148
Brown, Horace 105
Bruggerman, Art 84
Brushwood Boy, The 5
Buck, Frank 36
Buckler, William E. 5
Buffalo (NY) 173
Bulgaria 76
Bullseye! 194
Burglar and the Baby, The 8
Burns, Walter 22
Burton, Richard (actor) 191
Burton, Sir Richard 23
Burtt, Ben 196, 197
Butch Cassidy and the Sundance Kid 191
Butterfly 191
By Dawn's Early Light 196
Byrds 190

Caesar 120, 187
Cafe Crown 169
Cagney, James 42, 157
Cahusac, General 18-20
Caine, Michael 192-194
Calcutta (India) 1, 15, 19, 24, 32, 52, 156
California Department of Fish and Wildlife 83
Call Me Madam 171
Call of the Road 43
Camelot 171
Cameron, Kate 140
Campbell 15
Campbell, Phoebe 84
Canada 43, 136, 147

Cannes Film Festival 192, 193
Canning 15
Cannon Films 192-194
Captain Blood 104
Captains Courageous 6
Carefree 65, 95
Carmody, Jay 140
Carousel 171
Carroll, Madeleine 49
Carroll Street Bridge 193
Caruso, Enrico 9
Cary Grant Film Album 168
Cassidy, Hopalong 55
Castle, Irene 105
Catholic Church 151, 152
Central Theatre 151
Census of the British Empire 1, 3
Chalk Hills (CA) 98
Chandragtupa Maurya 120, 132, 187
Charade 180
Charge of the Light Brigade, The 24, 44, 55, 59, 91, 160
Charlie Chan at the Circus 63
Charleston (SC) 105
Chatsworth (CA) 26
Chewbacca 194
Chicago (IL) 5, 7, 144, 166
China 1
Chota 50, 54, 57, 78, 108, 111, 112, 118-120, 126, 132, 174
Chowdrhy, Prem 158, 187
Christy, George 191
Churchill, Winston 162
Ciannelli, Eduardo 50, 58, 62, 66, 96, 107, 118, 120, 132, 134, 135, 170, 178, 194; photos 123, 124, 146
Cinecom Pictures 193
Cinemax 193
Cincinnati (OH) 174
Cincinatti Reds 165
Citadel, The 22
Citizen Kane 173, 183
City College of New York 49
Civil and Military Gazette 41
Civil War 4, 8
Clark, Sgt. 50
Clarke, Gordon C. 84
Clarke, Mae 22
Cleveland (OH) 135, 147, 174, 178
Cleveland Cinema 147
Cleveland State University 187
Clive, Robert 1
Clive of India 24, 50, 104
Clooney, George 195
Clothier, William H. 76, 171

Coconut Grove 149
Cohen, Lester 17, 19, 23, 24, 105
Colliers 136
Colman, Ronald 42
Colonel Mason and the Kids 195
Colonial India and the Making of Empire Cinema 158, 187
Color Purple, The 193
Colt Army Revolver 63
Colt Model Gatling Gun 64
Colton, John 17-19, 24, 105
Columbia Pictures 8, 38, 165, 169, 178
Columbia Records 9, 190
Columbia University 152
Colonel of the Black Watch 150
Come and Get It 22
Comes a Horseman 171
Common Sense 162
Communist Party of America 169
Comont, Matilde 157
Congress of Industrial Organization 148
Connery, Sean 192
Constant Nymph, The 170
Consumer Price Index 149
Contenders, The 190
Convict Lake 55
Cook, Clyde 157
Coote, Robert 50, 52, 58, 78, 81, 105, 107, 108, 132, 170, 174; photo 47
Corelli, Ed 7
Cormack, Bartlett 22
Corrigon, Ray "Crash" 172
Corsican Brothers 168
Cottageville (SC) 173
Count of Monte Christo 12, 104
Cowboy Bob Kelley 191
Crawford, Clifton 7, 8
Crazy 190
Crew Cuts 189
Crimean War 8
Croce, Jim 190
Croce Records 190
Crone, J. R. 27, 48, 80
Crosby, Bing 52
Cross, Wellington 7
Crisler, B. R. 141, 147, 158
Cromarty, George 190
Crusades, The 50
Cuba 145
Cusak, Cyril 175
Cult of the Cobra 175
Culver City (CA) *65*
Curious Case of Benjamin Button, The 196

Curtain Call 173
Curtis, Tony 168
Cusak, Cyril 175
Cutter 24-29, 31, 32, 34, 37, 57, 80, 85, 91, 92, 96, 103, 108, 109, 111-120, 125, 126, 128, 131, 132, 142, 169, 173, 184, 192, 198
Czechoslovak Republic 145
Czechoslovakia 145

D-Day 170
Dachau 170
Daily Inter Ocean 5
Daily Worker, The 161
Daisy 27-29, 33, 34
Daks, Nicholas 140
Dakuno Kalatare 73
Dallas (TX) 105
Daly, John 194
Damsel in Distress 40, 50, 134
Danny Deever 5
Darin, Bobby 189
Dark Corner, The 174
Dark Victory 139
D'Artagnan 26
Darth Vader 194, 196
Das 15
Dastiger, Sabu 46, 48, 159
Davies, Marion 62
Davis Jr., Sammy 180
Davy Crockett and the River Pirates 178
Davy Crockett at the Alamo 178
Davy Crockett Goes to Congress 178
Davy Crockett, Indian Fighter 178
Davy Crockett's Keel Boat Race 178
Dawn, Hazel 11
Dawn Patrol, The 22, 38
Day the Earth Stood Still, The 169
Deal, Chip 180
Death Wish II 193
Deceivers, The 193, 194
Declaration of Independence 9
Defence of Sevastopol 8
Defense of Lucknow 152
DeForest, Calvert 193
DeHavilland, Olivia 49
Delaney, Pádraic 198
Delhi (India) 3, 14, 132
Delta Force 193
DeMille, C. B. 102
Deming, Bill 58
Denmark 145
Denville (NJ) 142
Denville Theatre 142

Denver (CO) 144
Destry Rides Again 139
Detchard 50
Detroit (MI) 151
Devil and Daniel Webster, The 171
Dewey, Chris 193
Dialeto 195
Diary of Anne Frank, The 171
Dickens, Charles 6
Dirty Squad 195
Disney, Walt 8, 148, 176, 178
Disneyland 176
Disraeli, Benjamin 14, 15
Distinguished Service Cross 168
Dixie Ice Cream 148
Dodge City 64, 139
Doherty, Pete 197
Donat (character) 44, 45
Donat, Robert 42, 44
Donovan's Reef 171
Dooley, Roger 192
Douglas Fairbanks, Jr. Presents 168
Down the Stretch 9
Dow, G. W. 72
Drake, Leah Bodine 173
Dr. Didg 195
Drew University 170
Drum, The 46, 159, 187
Drums 46
Drums Along the Mohawk 139
Duane, Lydia 11
Dueker, Dr. Howard 91
Duffield Theatre 144
Dumas, Alexander 42, 152
Dumont 166
Dunbar, Dixie 62
Dunn, Bobby 157
Dunn, Lin 167
Durand, Ralph 3
Durfee Theatre 143

Earl of Beaconsfield 15
Ebbets Field 165
Ebert, Roger 171, 196
Ecuador 144
Eddy, Nelson 41
Edgemont Theater 183
Edington-Vincent, Inc. 42
Edison, Thomas 52
Edison Diamond Disc 9
Edmonds (WA) 83
Educational Screen, The 152
Edwards, Blake 180
Egyptian Theatre 196
El Cid 180

El Paso (TX) *72*
Elephant Boy 12, 46, 56
Ellensburg Daily Record 141
Ellman, Murray 58
Emerson, George 52
Emmy Award 196
Empire State Building 165
Empire Theatre 11
Encino (CA) 75
End Jim Crow in Baseball Committee 169
Enever, Jo 187
Enfield Mk I revolver 63
Enfield Mk II revolver 63
Enfield Rifle 17, 44
England 1-4, 6, 11, 12, 18, 20, 23, 37, 40, 43, 44, 63, 92, 118, 120, 143, 145, 190, 191, 198
Englewood (CA) 165
Ermolieff, Nick 159
Escape from Fort Bravo 180
E.T. the Extra-Terrestrial 196
Evans, Sgt. 27, 28
Evansville Courier and Press 173
Eve 12, 18
Evening Star 140
Evening Tribune 22
Everybody Likes Music 62
Evers, Ann 52, 115
Ex-Mrs. Bradford, The 174
Express to Hollywood 43

F. P. Tivoli Theatre 144
Faces I've Been, The 190
Facets 190
Facts of Life, The 171
Fairbanks, Douglas 81
Fairbanks Jr., Douglas 38, 42-47, 49-51, 58, 59, 63, 72, 76, 78, 81, 83, 84, 87, 91, 92, 96, 102, 107, 119, 122-124, 131, 134, 139, 142, 145, 148, 168, 169, 171, 173, 174, 178, 183, 184, 194, 196, 197; photos 47, 51, 82, 86, 87, 89, 110, 122-124, 146
Fall River (MA) 143
Family Theatre 174
Famous Adventures of Mr. Magoo 190
Famous Players Film Company 9, 85
Farnsworth, Richard 172
Fat Jones Stables 72, 92
Faulkner, William 14-17, 23, 24, 102, 105, 134
Faust 49
Feature Play Company 9
Ferber, Edna 22

Ferdinand, Archduke Franz 198
Ferguson, Otis 142
Ferguson, Perry 65, 66, 108, 134
Ferrin, Frank 175
Fiddler, Jimmie 72
Fielding, Henry 118
Fields, W. C. 52
Fighting 69th, The 60
Fighting O'Flynn, The 168
Film Journalists Association of India 60
Film Booking Offices of America 14
Film Daily, The 11, 12, 17, 18, 22, 106, 144, 147
Filmindia 6, 159-161, 163, 164
FilmWorld Inc. 194
Films of Tyrone Power, The 180
Finland 145
First National 9
Fisher, Terrance 178
Five Came Back 173
Flanders Cross 76
Flomoton (AL) 156
Flossie 156
Floyd Bennet Field 92
Flying Leathernecks 178
Flynn, Errol 104
Fogle, Syd 103
Fonda, Henry 52
Fontaine, Joan 40, 49-51, 58, 78, 81, 83, 84, 96, 100, 107, 109, 132, 143, 145, 147, 148, 170, 171, 174, 178; photos 51, 146
For Your Eyes Only 192
Forbstein, Leo 104
Ford 7
Ford, John 32, 43, 75, 168
Forslund, Constance 191
Fort Apache 168
Fort William 1
Forty Years a Soldier 3, 132
42nd Street 62
42nd Royal Highlanders 57
Forum, The 169
Foster, Preston 26
Four Day Crawl 195
Four Feathers, The (1939) 139
Four Feathers, The (2002) 196
Fowler, Miss 115
Foyer, Eddie 11
Francis, Olin 96
Franco, Francisco 17
France 6, 14, 145, 189
"Frank Sinatra Reads from Gunga Din" 190
Franke, Gordon 62

Frankenstein 8
Fraser, Sir William 14
French 75mm gun 64
Friedland, Dennis 193
From Hell to Texas 104
From Scarface to Scarlett 192
Front Page, The 22, 23, 25, 31, 40, 79, 96, 114
Froude, James Anthony 14
Fugitive, The 170

Gab 19, 20
Gable, Clark 40, 46, 174
Gaines, Max 148
Galloping Cowboy, The 8
Gandhi 192
Gandhi, Mahatma 62, 63, 152, 158, 160-162, 164
Ganges River 134
Gardner-Gatling gun 64
Gatling gun 60, 64, 126, 135, 180
Gaumont-Haymarket 145
Gay Divorcee, The 65
Gemora, Charles 63, 171, 172
General Teleradio 176
General Tire and Rubber 176
Gentle People, The 148
George II 1
George Stevens: A Filmmaker's Journey 171, 183
George Washington 63
George White's Scandals 62
Georgia Hotel 48
Gerber, H. M. 147
Germany 6, 145, 162, 195
Gettysburg Address 9
Ghunga Din 156, 157
Ghurkas 60
Gianotta, Sonny 180, 190
Giant 171
Gillette, Charles 7
Ginsburg, Walter 152
Give Us This Night 37
Glasgow (Scotland) 136
Glauser, Charles 161
Globus, Yoram 193
Gloria Theater 105
Gloversville (NY) 144
Goebel's Lion Farm 52
Goetz, Harry M. 12
Golan, Menaham 193, 194
Golan-Globus Productions 192, 193
Gold Coast Singers, The 190
Gold, George 165, 166
Golden Treasury of Poetry, A 189

Golden Dawn 37
Golden Gate Theater 140
Golden Mistress, The 170
Goldman, Joseph 192, 193
Goldman, William 191, 192
Goldwyn, Samuel 22, 104
Gone with the Wind 139, 149-151
Goodbye, Mr. Chips 139
Goodman, Ezra 162
Goose Flesh 63
Gorst, Harold Edward 14
Gould, Harry 155, 157
Goulding, Alfred 155-157
Government of India Act 158
Gowanus Canal 173
Graham, Sheila 83, 92
Grainger, Gloria 17
Gran, Albert 157
Grand Duke Peter 38
Granger, Stewart 174
Grant, Cary 37-39, 42-47, 51, 52, 58,
 63, 78, 80, 81, 83-85, 91-94, 96, 99,
 100, 107, 109, 111, 115, 116, 120,
 121, 131, 134, 140, 145, 147, 148 168,
 169, 171, 173, 174, 178, 180, 183,
 184, 192, 194, 197, 198; photos 47,
 51, 82, 86, 89, 93, 110, 121, 124, 146
Great Britain 1, 2, 6, 44, 132, 143, 158,
 161, 163, 168, 178, 187-189, 191
Great Depression 14, 144
Great Movie Ride 197
Great Mutiny (see Sepoy Rebellion)
Greatest Story Ever Told, The 171
Greece 163
Grenier, Hilda 54
Grey Fox, The 172
Griffith, D. W. 8
Griswold (IA) 147
Gruen Curvex 148
Guayaquil (Ecuador) 144
Gubbins, Jeremy 24
Gubbins, Mildred 24
Guiol, Fred 56-58, 78-81, 85, 92, 95,
 96, 98, 105, 107, 155, 170
Gulliver's Travels 139
Gunfight at the O. K. Corral 180
"Gunga Deen" 5
Gunga Din (band) 190
Gunga Din, The (band) 195
Gunga Din (bull) 52
Gunga Din (children's book) 187
Gunga Din (1911 film) 8, 9
Gunga Din (motorcycle) 189
Gunga Din (poem) 2-4, 7-9, 11, 107,
 151, 189, 191

Gunga Din (photo novel) 180
Gunga Din (wrestler) 191
"Gunga Din"(songs) 10, 11, 190, 191,
 195, 197
Gunga Din Bugle, The 52, 75
Gunga Din Cider 197
Gunga Ram 175
Gungha Din 15, 16, 31
Guru 50, 54, 66, 80, 98, 118-120, 126,
 131, 132, 173

Hagney, Frank 157
Hal Roach Studios 40, 56
Haller, Ernest 149
Halloran, John 175
Hamilton, James Shelley 141
Hamilton, Major 27
Hammer Films 178
Handbook to the Poetry of Rudyard
 Kipling 3
Hanna, Colonel J. C. 12
Hannibal 120, 187
Harding, Hugh 12
Hardy, G. H. 198
Hardy, Thomas 6
Hare, Lumsden 50, 58, 78, 108, 132, 134
Harper's Weekly 4
Harris, Richard 191
Harris, Sam 59
Harrison, Paul 63, 165
Harrison's Reports 63, 136
Hart, William S. 75
Hartford (CT) 173
Hasson, Abdul 54, 79
Hastings, Ross 24
"Have You Seen...?" 196
Having a Wonderful Time 134
Hawaii Five-O 170
Hawks, Howard 14, 22, 24, 32, 36-38,
 43, 45
Hay, John 4
Hays, Richard E. 141
Hays, Will H. 161
Hays Office 161
Hazleton (ND) 147
Head, Edith 171
Healy, Ted 62
Heaven Help Us 193
Hecht, Ben 22-26, 27, 31, 32, 40, 50,
 56-58, 79, 81, 105, 107, 111, 114,
 134, 149, 155
Heflin, Van 171
Held, P. G. 147
Help! 180
Hendee, Harold 54

Henry Miller's Theatre 49
Henry VIII 50
Hepburn, Katherine 26, 37, 38, 40
Here's Lucy 171
Hermann, Bernard 173
Hirshfeld, Abe 142
Hirschman, Herbert 14
High Lama 48
High Road to China 195
Hightower, Bryan "Slim" 102
Higginbotham 27, 28, 32-34, 50, 58,
 102, 105, 108, 109, 114-116, 118,
 128, 131-133, 176
Hill Street theater 139, 144
Hillman, Sydney 148
Hindu, The 175
Hindu Association of Hong Kong
 162
"Hippie" Boyette 191
His Girl Friday 168
Historical Romances 195
Hitchcock, Alfred 94
Hitchman, Francis 14
Hitler, Adolph 145
Hodson, George A. 56
Holiday 37, 83
Holm, Paul 15, 16
Holm, Robert 15, 16
Holmes, Capt. 14, 15
Holland, Sir Robert Erskine 59, 60,
 79-81, 85, 108, 131-133, 161
Hollywood (CA) 14, 22, 32, 36, 37,
 40, 42, 43, 46, 48, 50, 53, 56-60,
 63, 64, 72, 75, 76, 84, 85, 103, 129,
 135, 136, 139, 141, 155, 158-160,
 162, 166, 168-171, 176, 186, 187,
 192, 194
Hollywood 48, 81, 136, 141
Hollywood Filmgraph 11
Hollywood Forever Cemetery 169
Hollywood Reporter 72, 105, 139, 149,
 162, 191
Homophone Company 11
Hong Kong 162
Hootenanny Saturday nite 190
Hopalong Rides Again 55
Hopper, Hedda 42
Horse Soldiers, The 171
Horstmann, Theodore 170
House on Un-American Activities
 Committee 169
Howard, Shemp 62
Howe, Milt 149
Hudson River 8
Hughes, Howard 92, 175

Humphrey, Harry E. 9
Hunchback of Notre Dame, The 139, 149, 171, 176
Huntington Park (CA) 105
Hurricane, The 104
Hyde, Johnny 191, 192

I Am a Fugitive from a Chain Gang 26
I Love a Parade 62
I Love Lucy 171
I Married a Monster from Outer Space 172
I Remember Mama 170
Ibsen, Henrik 48
Ice Cube 196
I'd Give a Million 52
If 6
Illustrated Film-Stage 145
Image Entertainment 184
Images of India 186
Immortal Alamo, The 8
Independent Exhibitor's Film Bulletin 46, 103, 105, 136
India 1-5, 11, 12, 14, 18, 23-25, 37, 43, 44, 46, 48-50, 53-60, 62, 64, 67, 81, 98, 92, 102, 104, 107, 111, 114, 120, 131-133, 139, 142, 151, 152, 156, 158, 160-164, 173, 175, 178, 183, 186, 187, 193, 194, 197
India Speaks 160
Indian Army Medical Corps 59
Indian Motion Picture Congress 159, 161
Indian Motion Picture Producers Association 159
Indiana Jones and the Last Crusade 195, 196
Indiana Jones and the Kingdom of the Crystal Skull 195
Indiana Jones and the Temple of Doom 194
Indianapolis (IN) 173
Informer, The 26, 32, 43, 65, 75, 104, 174
International Photographer 76
International Sales 72
Internet Move Data Base 149
Intolerance 65
Introducing the Gunga Din 195
Invasion USA 193
Invisible Ray, The 18
Inyo County (CA) 55
Ireland 145
Iron Cross 76
Ironside 170

Irons, Jeremy 198
Irwin, L. A. 147
Isaacs, Harold R. 186
Island in the Sky 104
Island of Lost Souls 63
Italy 162, 178
It's a Wonderful Life 171
Ivanhoe 170
Iwerks, Ub 8
Iwerks Studio 8

J. Arthur Rank Productions 107
J. S. Otey 72
Jackson, Sammy 147
Jackson Theatre 147
Jaffe, Sam 38, 48, 49, 58, 60, 62, 67, 79, 80, 83, 84, 91, 92, 96, 100, 102, 107, 118, 131, 134, 135, 140, 142, 145, 148, 149, 169, 170, 173, 176, 180, 184, 191, 192, 194, 196, 198; photos 70, 86, 88, 124
Jafri, F. S. 164
Jalna 18
Jane Eyre 170
Japan 158, 162
Jeffers, Jennifer 187
Jenkins, Colonel 4
Jesse James 139, 149
Jessell, George 7
Jezail musket 63
Joe 193
Johaneson, Bland 140
John Church Company 9
Johnny Duncan and the Bluegrass Boys 189
Johnson, Bill 134
Johnson, Hildy 22
Johnson, Jack 43
Jones, Kathleen 14
Joseph, Ellis 36
Joy, Tilmon 4
J. S. Stembridge Company 63
Juarez 139
Jumma (Juma) 3-5, 98, 132
Jungle Book, The 5, 12, 175
Junior Films 174

Kabul 4
Kahle, Alex 76
Kalatare, Dakuno 79
Kali 18, 19, 45, 52, 65, 66, 80, 108, 112, 114, 118, 159, 160, 162, 178, 180, 194
Kanin, Garson 49
Kansas City (MO) 143

Kapur, Shekhar 196
Karloff, Boris 25, 175
Karnatka (India) 52
Kaufman, Richard 195
Kay Katya and Kay 140
Keane, Robert Emmett 7
Keasbey & Mattison Co. 148
Kebbel, Thomas Edward 14
Keep Cool Revue 11
Keith-Albee-Orpheum 14
Keith Memorial Theater 144
Keith Washington Theater 144
Kellaway, Cecil 50, 109, 132, 154
Kennedy, Joseph P. 14
Khan Sufi 24-27, 29, 32-34, 45
Khan, Surat 44
Khyber Hills 14
Khyber Pass 55, 147, 151, 159, 161
Khyber Rifles, The 160
Kildoyle, Geoffrey 18-20
Killy, Edward 45, 48, 80, 91, 102, 108, 134
Kilmer, David 194
Kim 6, 11
King and I, The 171
King of the Khyber Rifles (1929) 12
King of the Khyber Rifles (1953) 161
King Kong 104, 173, 176, 183
Kingsley, Ben 192
Kipling, HMS 136
Kipling, Alice 1
Kipling, Caroline 2, 12
Kipling, Elsie 2, 6, 136
Kipling, John 2, 6
Kipling, John Lockwood 1
Kipling, Josephine 6
Kipling, Rudyard 1-12, 16, 20, 23, 25, 29, 37, 38, 41, 43, 45, 46, 48, 49, 52, 56, 63, 88, 128, 107, 131, 132, 134, 136, 139, 140, 143, 144, 151, 152, 157-160, 174-176, 183, 186, 188-190, 192, 194, 197, 198
Kipling Journal 4, 11, 163, 168
Kipling Society 11, 98, 188
Kiss the Blood Off my Hands 170
Knapp, Evelyn 157
Knight News Service 194
Koenig, William 102
Korda, Alexander 46, 159
Korngold, Erich Wolfgang 104, 195
Korngold, George 164
Krag-Jorgensen rifle 63
Krogstad, Nils 48
Kubla Khan 191

La Cava, Gregory 38
La Fave, J. J. 144
Ladd, Alan 171
Lady Chatterley's Lover 193
Lady Takes a Chance 174
Lake Arrowhead (CA) 55
Lake Sherwood (CA) 65, 75, 103
Lake Singali 32
Lall, Rai Saheb Chuni 160
Lally, Mike 85
Lamberston, William 169
Lang, Fritz 102
Langdon, Harry 11
Lasky, Jesse L. 9
"Last Blast of the Blasted Bugler, The" 180, 190
Last of the Mohicans 63
"Last Post" 128
Last Train from Gun Hill 180
Laurel and Hardy 40, 56, 118, 157, 174
Law, Frederick J. 152, 153
Law of the Underworld 50
Lawford, Peter 180
Lawrence, Colonel 44, 45
Lawrence, Sir Henry 44
Lawrence, Vincent 32, 105
Lawrence of Arabia 63
Lawson, John Howard 12
"Lazy Bones" 166
Le Paris theater 145
Leach, Archibald (see Cary Grant)
Learoyd 42
Lederer, Charles 22
Legally Dead 8
"Legend of Gunga Din, The" 189
Legion of Merit 168
Lee-Metford rifle 63
Leibert, Richard 140
Leibfried, Philip 188
Leonidoff, Leon 140
Les espions 169
Les Miserables 26
Leon Schlesinger Productions 8
Levy, Charles 85, 105
Lewis, Capt. Harry 178
Leyte (Philippines) 198
Libertines 197
Liberty 136
Liberty League 6
Lichtig, Henry H. 59
Lichtig and Englander 59
Lieber, Perry 149
Lieberdorff, Ivan 157
Life 136, 190
Lifesong Records 190

Light That Failed, The 12
Lincoln, Abraham 9
Lincoln Heights (CA) 52
Lincoln Library 192
Lindeman, Edith 103
Little Blue Book 11
Little Charlie 156, 157
Little Minister, The 26
Little Women 12
Lives of a Bengal Lancer 24, 50, 52, 55, 59, 103, 160, 162
"Lives of a Bungle Lancer" 168
Livesey, Roger 43
Lloyd, Clinton E. 7
Lloyds of London 79
Lockert, John 108
Loew's-Poli theater 173
London 6, 9, 11, 107, 156
London Films Productions 46
Lone Pine (CA) 55, 60, 62, 65, 72, 75, 79, 80, 83, 84, 91, 92, 94-96, 98, 100, 102, 103, 184, 196-198
Lone Pine Lumber and Supply Co. 60, 72, 198
Lone Pine Sierra Film Festival 184, 196
Look 136
Looney Tunes 62
Loos-en-Gohelle (France) 6
"Lord Lovat's Lament" 128
Lorrance, Arleen 49
Los Angeles (CA) 11, 23, 49, 52, 55, 60, 75, 79, 103, 104, 139-141, 144, 149, 155, 192, 194-196
Los Angeles Times 140, 142, 196
Lost Horizon 43, 55, 174
Lost Patrol, The 43, 65, 104,
Love, Montagu 50, 58, 78, 107, 108, 131, 132, 134, 170, 183, 193; photo 122
Lovell, Glenn 194
Love Affair 139, 149
Love is a Many-Splendored Thing 171
Love Kiss, The 8
Lucas, George 192
Lucas Ranch 103
Lucknow (India) 43, 45
Lucy Show, The 171
Lynch, S. A. 139
Lyric theater 173

MacArthur, Charles 22-27, 31, 32, 40, 50, 56, 57, 78, 79, 81, 96, 105, 107, 111, 114, 134 149, 155
Mac's Auto Tours 76

MacChesney 24-29, 31-34, 80, 81, 85, 91, 92, 98, 103, 108, 109, 111-120, 125, 126, 128, 129, 142, 147, 176, 192
MacDonald, Jeanette 41, 139
MacDuff, Sgt. 24, 43
MacLaughlin, Thomas 59
MacMunn, Sir George 4
MacMurray, Fred 40
Mad 190
Mad Miss Manton, The 52
Madras (India) 159
Maher, Ted 192
Magazin 145
Magnificent Seven, The 180
Majestic Hollywood 196
Malden (MA) 174
Malibu Beach (CA) 63
Maltin, Leonard 196
Man of Conquest 139, 171
Man Who Knew Infinity, The 198
Man Who Shot Liberty Valance, The 171
Man Who Would be King, The 2
Man Who Would be King, The (film) 63, 192
Mandalay 11
Manhasset theater 154
Mansurov, Talat 161
Marcel, Nino 175
Marianne 52
Marie Walewska 174
Margo 49
Marguerite 49
Mark of Zorro, The 170
Markham, Lt. 108, 176
Marsh, W. Ward 91
Martha 52
Martin, Dean 180
Martini-Henry rifle 63
Mary of Scotland 75, 76
Mary Baldwin College 151
Mask of Fu Manchu, The 25
Mason, Sarah Y. 12
Maturity News Service 187
Max Factor 148
Mayer, Louis B. 40
Mayo, Katherine 152
McCann, Graham 81
McCann, Thomas 11
McClintock (character) 15
McClintock! (film) 171
McCormick, Paul J. 155
McCormick, S. Barret 83, 100, 134-136
McElroy, D. D. 76
McGregor, Angus 19, 20

McLaglen, Andrew 168, 191
McLaglen, Cyril 43, 174
McLaglen, Victor 24, 32, 42-45, 50, 51, 58, 63, 65, 78, 81, 83, 84, 91, 92, 96, 100, 107, 109, 119, 121, 131, 134, 147, 168, 174, 178, 184, 191, 194, 197, 198; photos 47, 51, 82, 86, 88, 110, 121, 123, 124
McKern, Leo 180
Meador, J. E. D. 9, 11
Meador-Robertson Productions 9, 11
Mecca 23
Mega Records 191
Melbourne (Australia) 145
Mellet, Lowell 163
Melrose Theater 105
Menjou, Adolph 22
Mercer, Ruby 140
Mercer, Major 174
Merchant of Venice 48
Merry, Mike 180
Merivale, Philip 37
Merrihugh, Malcolm 83, 84
Merrill, W. J. 166
Metro-Goldwyn-Mayer (MGM) 11, 12, 22, 25, 40, 41, 46, 104, 106, 174, 175
Metropolitan Museum of Art 180
Mexico 145
Meyer, Emile 171
Michigan 197
Michigan State University 186
Mickey Mouse 8, 148
Might Lak' a Rose 9
Mike 157
Milllinocket (ME) 134
Military and Civilian Gazette 2
Miller, Don 183
Milwaukee (WI) 50, 144
Milwaukee Journal Sentinel 62
Ministry of Information 162, 163
Minneapolis (MN) 141
Minney, Rubeigh, J. 12, 155
Mirdrekvandi, Ali 190
Missing in Action 193
Mitchell, Major 50, 108, 114-116, 128, 136
Mix, Art 85
Mix, Tom 148
Moapa (NV) 55
Modern Screen 147, 149, 196
Mong, William V. 157
Monkley, Jimmy 38
Mono County (CA) 55
Monroe, Marilyn 191

Monster and the Girl, The 172
Montgomery, Robert 40
Moore, Gary 144
Moore, Roger 191-194
Mount Whitney 55, 198
More the Merrier, The 170
Moreno, Antonio 105
Morgan, Clive 59, 108, 174
Morgan, John W. 195
Morgan Litho Corporation 135
Morning Star 49
Morning Telegraph 7
Morse Code 107
Mother India 152
Mother Wore Tights 171
Motion Picture Daily 32, 37, 155, 157, 165, 173
Motion Picture Herald 65, 80, 134, 135, 141, 143, 145, 152, 165
Motion Picture Magazine 9
Motion Picture News 8
Motion Picture Society of India 160
Motography 8
Mount Whitney 55, 65
Mount Whitney Cemetery 198
Mountcastle, Gloria 17
Movie Comics 148
Moving Picture News 11
Moving Picture World 9
Mourbhanj, Maharaja 12
Mr. Novak 170
Mr. Smith Goes to Washington 139, 165
Mucky 157
Mulligan, Sgt. 157
Murders in the Rue Morgue 63
Museum of Western Film History 198
Muslims 17, 159
Mulvaney 42
Muri 32, 65, 66, 69, 70, 78, 103, 108, 111, 113
Musso, Joseph P. 64, 176
My Fair Lady 170
Mysore (India) 52

Naidanpore 18
Nana 44, 45
Napier 15
Napoleon 120, 164, 187
Narayan, Rasipuram Krishnaswami 186
Nashville (TN) 144
Nashua (NH) *36*
National Board of Review 147
National Book Award 14
National Broadcasting Company 165

National Education Association 152
National Film Registry 195
National Historical Trust of England 191
National Legion of Decency 151
National Observer, The 2
Natural, The 172
Nazi Party 17, 145
Nehru Memorial Museum and Library 187
Nero Wolfe 170
Netherlands 145
Nevada 55
Neville, Jack 11
New Captain George's Whizzbang, The 183
New Delhi (India) 187
New Jersey 8, 37, 180
New Movie Magazine 63
New Orleans (LA) 5, 144
New Republic 142
New York City 6-9, 11, 12, 16, 22, 37, 49, 92, 139, 141, 148, 165, 169, 173, 180, 183, 195, 196
New York Daily News 140
New York Daily Mirror 140
New York Daily Worker 161
New York Herald Tribune 5, 140
New York Journal-American 140
New York Times, The 37, 38, 42, 43, 46, 49, 104, 140, 141, 147, 158, 161, 165, 175, 194
New York World-Telegram 140
New York's Schools Motion Picture Committee 154
New Yorker 56, 190
Newman, Alfred 38, 104, 105, 107-109, 111-114, 116, 118, 120, 125, 126, 128, 149, 171, 173, 189, 192, 195, 197
Newton, Robert 175
Nichols, Dudley 32, 37, 43, 45, 56, 105
Nikki 37
Niles, C. L. 148
Niles Theatre 148
Ninotchka 139
Nitwits, The 40, 56
No Heaven For Gunga Din 190
Nobel Prize 6, 13, 151
Nolan, Gypo 43
None But the Lonely Heart 168
North by Northwest 170
North Park theater 174
North West Frontier 25, 59
Northwest Passage 60, 170

Norton, Capt. 59
Norway 148
Notes On Sir Richard Burton 23
Nothing But Trouble 174
Nottingham (England) 11
Nutt, William 23, 24, 136, 155

Oakie, Jack 46
O'Brien, Kenneth 12
O'Brien, Pat 22
Of Human Bondage 17
Of Mice and Men 139
Ogle, Charles 8
O'Hara, Maureen 171
Oklahoma 171
Oklahoma Univ. School of Medicine 147
Oland, Warner 157
One Man's Journey 17
1001 Movies You Must See Before You Die 196
O'Neill, Buck 156, 157
Only Angels Have Wings 139
Only Game in Town, The 171
Operation Petticoat 168
Order of the British Empire 59
Oregon 48
Oregonian 178, 192
Orientalism 2
Orpheum Theater 144, 174
Osborne, Robert 197
Oscar (see Academy Award)
Ortheris 42
Out of Africa 193
Owens Valley (CA) 55

Packard 7
Pagano, Ernest S. 59, 134
Palace Theatre 174
Pale Rider 193
Palestine (TX) 151, 153
Palisades (NJ) 8
Pan, Hermes 112
Panama 144
Panama Theatre 144
Pantages theater 139, 144
Paramount Pictures 9, 162
Paris (France) 170
Parsons, Louella O. 22, 23, 36
Parry, Harvey 113
Parsons, Gene 190
Party, The 180
Pastel, George 178
Patel, Baburao 60, 161
Patel, Dev 198

Patton 32
Paul, Ralph 191
Pawnee Wallah 156
Pearl, Buhla 7
Pearl Harbor (HI) 198
Pearson, Pvt. 43
Pearson, Major 58
Penacook (NH) 147
Penny Serenade 168
Pelswick, Rose 140
Peoria (IL) 144
Perez, Juan 60, 61, 84, 97; photos 61, 97
Persia 55
Peshawar (Pakistan) 54
Peter Bellamy Sings the Barrack-Room Ballads of Rudyard Kipling 191
Phantom of the Rue Morgue 172
Philadelphia (PA) 50, 141, 176
Philadelphia Story, The 168
Philippines 198
Phonevision 166
Photoplay 52, 141, 147, 196
Photoplay Studies 152, 153
Pickering, Colonel 170
Pigot, Gov. 50
Pilgrimage Play Theatre 49
"Pibroch of Donald Dhu" 128
Pittsburgh Press 83
Plain Dealer 136,138
Plain Tales from the Hills 41
Plainsman, The 102
Plainsong 195
Platt, David 161
Poland 145
Polglase, Van Nest 65, 66, 108, 134, 149
Portel, Vic 157
Portland (OR) 178
Portrait of Jenny 171
Portugal 145
Powell, Edward B. 105, 171
Powers, Patrick A. 8
Powers Motion Picture Co. 8
Powers Picture Plays 8
Prague (Czechoslovakia) 145
Primrose Path 143
Prince and the Pauper, The 50, 104
Prince and the Showgirl, The 178
Prisoner of Zenda, The 38, 50, 104
Private Lives of Elizabeth and Essex, The 139
Providence (RI) 173
The Public Life of the Right Honourable the Earl of Beaconsfield, The 14
Pukka Sahib 14

Pulitzer Prize 14
Pye Records 189
Quality Street 40
Quebec 142
Queen of Oudh 20
Queen Victoria 1, 2, 14, 15
Queenie 53
Queenie (character) 157
Queens Own Corps of Guides 3, 4
Queen's Own Sappers and Miners 57
Quiet Man, The 168

R2-D2 196
Radio City Music Hall 139, 141, 148, 183, 189, 196
Radio-Keith-Orpheum 14
Radio Mirror 148
Radio Today 165
Raiders of the Lost Ark 194-196
Rains Came, The 24, 139, 187
Raj Batgahl 157
Rajah Joudmapour 156, 157
Ram, Gunga 175
Ramanujan, Srinivasa 198
Rangoon (Burma) 28
Ransom, Sir 20
Rapee, Erno 140
Rawhide 168
Raymond, Gene 139
RCA Records 189
Rebecca 170
Recessional 2
Red Blood of Courage 11
Red Channels 169
Red Skelton Show, The 168
Redman, Frank 100
Reefer Madness 152
Regas, George 125, 170
Regents Examination 154
Reinhardt, Max 49
Reliance Pictures 12, 106, 155
Remos, Paul 140
Rennahan, Ray 149
Rennel, Gloria 17
Reprise Records 190
Republic Pictures 102
Resurrection 172
Rewards and Fairies 6
Rex 40
Rhineland 17
Rhythm on the Range 52
Richards, Jeffrey 160, 162
Richmond Times-Dispatch 103, 141
Rings on Her Fingers 174
Rio Grande 168

Rio Rita 41
Rise of Catherine the Great, The 38
RKO 1, 14, 16, 18, 20, 22, 23-27, 36-46, 48-50, 52, 53-60, 63-66, 72, 75, 78-80, 83-85, 90-92, 95, 96, 98, 100, 102-105, 106, 107, 112, 113, 134-136, 139, 140, 143, 145, 148, 149, 151, 152, 155, 157-160, 163-166, 173-176, 184, 187, 192, 195
RKO Albee theater 173
RKO Hill Street theater 139
RKO Orpheum 143
RKO Ranch 66, 75
Roach, Hal 40, 155, 157
Road to Glory, The 14, 22
Road to Utopia, The 172
Roaring Twenties, The 139
Roast Beef of England, The 118
Roberston, John S. 9
Robertson, Marian 37
Robinson, Christopher 98
Robinson, George 188
Rochfort-John, E. 59
Rockettes 140
Rockford (IL) 49
Rogers, Ginger 40, 46, 65, 84, 134, 139
Rogers, Richard 171
Rogers, Roy 197
Rolfe, Guy 178
Roma Theatre 144
Room Mates 56
Roosevelt, Franklin D. 136
Rose, Reginald 191
Roxy Theatre 147
Royal Air Force 103
Royal Artillery 63
Royal Engineers 34, 57, 59, 109
Royal Navy 136
Royal Small Arms Factory 63
Royal Society of Saint George 6
Rupert of Henzau 38
Runaway Train 193
Russell, Robert 171
"Running W" 91
Rush, Ed 190
Russia 44
Rusty 60, 61

S. A. Lynch's Sheridan theater 139
Sabaka 175
Sabrina Lake (CA) 55
Said, Edward S. 2
Salad Days, The 42
Salinger, Conrad 105

Salkow, Sidney 102
Sally 53
San Antonio (TX) 72
San Bernardino County (CA) 55, 56
San Diego (CA) 174
San Diego Union 140
San Francisco (CA) 140, 166
San Francisco Chronicle 140
San Luis Obispo Daily Telegram 161
Sanders, George 49
Sanders, Matt 144
Santa's Movin In 195
Sappers 5, 45
Sarnoff, David 14
Saturday Evening Post 136
Savage, Maurice 140
Savage, Captain William 193
Sayre, Joel 14, 40, 56, 57, 72, 78-81, 83, 85, 91, 92, 95, 96, 100, 105, 107, 139, 155, 190
Scarface 22
Scarlett Empress, The 38
Schaefer, George J. 136, 165, 166
Schanfield Brothers 72
Schenectady (NY) 48
Schine's Hippodrome 144
Schlesinger, Leon 8
Schmus, W. G. Van 139
Schneider, Steven Jay 196
Scott, Ainsley 7
Scott, Colonel 19
Scott, George C. 32
Scott, Walter 114
Scourby, Alexander 189
Scotstoun (Scotland) 136
Screen Actors Guild 32, 72
Screen Gems 176, 178
Sea Hawk, The 170
Seattle (WA) 140, 141
Seattle Central Community College 192
Seattle Daily Times 141, 183
See India With Me 54
Selig Zoo 52
Selleck, Tom 194, 195
Sellers, Peter 180
Selznick, David O. 94
Sennett, Mack 155
Sepoy Mutiny 14, 17
Sergeants 3 178, 180
Seven Seas 45
Seven Years War 1
7th India Infantry Brigade 164
17th Highlanders 18
Sexton, Kathy 198

"Sh-Boom" 189
Shah, Chandular 159, 160
Shafer, Burr 189
Shaffer, Frank 151
Shakespeare, William 48
Shall We Dance 134
Shane 171
Shanghai (China) 161
Shapiro, Lou 25, 36, 55
Sharpe, Dave *85*
She Done Him Wrong 37
She Wore a Yellow Ribbon 168
Sheffield, John 52
Sheffield, Reginald 52, 128
Sheridan Theater 139
Showman's Hall of Fame 149
Showplace 140
Skywalker, Luke 194
Sierra Mountains 55
Si-Keng, Cheng 161
Sikhs 48, 60, 144
Silke, James 183, 192, 193
Silver Screen 141, 142
Silver Star 168
Silvera, Darrell 66, 75, 108
Simba 157
Simla (India) 2
Simpson, Barlow 52, 118
Sinatra, Frank 180, 190
Sinbad, the Sailor 168, 171
Singapore 36
Singh, Dalip 54
Singh, Joginder 163
Singh, Nama 48
Singh, Paul 54
Singh, Sucha 48, 49
Siraj ud-Daulah 1
Siva 34
Skolsky, Sidney 24
Slade Wallace Equipment 64
Sleeman, William Henry 114, 178
Slipping Wives 56
Small, Edward 12, 14, 16, 17, 134, 155
Smith, Liz 192
"Snake Pit" 19
Soak the Rich 50
Society For the Prevention of Cruelty to Animals 91
Soldiers of the Queen 188
Soldiers Three 2, 38, 41, 42
Soldiers Three (CD) 195
Soldiers Three (film) 170, 174, 175
Solo, Han 194
Son of Frankenstein 139
Song of Bernadette, The 171

Song of the White Men 2
Songs of Rudyard Kipling 189
South Africa 50
South Pacific 171
Souvenirs of France 6
Spainhower, Russ 103, 104
Spanish Civil War 17, 76
Spencer, Roxanne Ackerman 91, 169
Spielberg, Steven 192, 194, 195
Spingold, Nate 169
Spitz, Leo 16, 36
Splinter 157
Spokane Daily Chronicle 142
Spokesman-Review 26
Sporting Life 9
Springfield (IL) 174, 192
Springfield "Trapdoor" rifle 63
Spross, Charles Gilbert 9, 10, 189
Squaw Man, The 9
St. Julian Winery 197
St. Louis (MO) 174
St. Maurice Valley Chronicle 142
Stagecoach 64, 139
Stanwyck, Barbara 40, 52
Stanley and Livingston 139
Star, Charles "Nat" 11
Star of the Indian Order of Merit 98
Star of Midnight 18
Star Wars 196
Starkey, Dewey 108
Starr, John 193
State Theater 11
Staunton (VA) 151
Staunton Military Academy 151
Stebbins, Emmy 27, 33, 34, 49, 109, 118, 119, 131, 132, 176
Stebbins, Mr. 27, 44, 50, 109, 115
Stebbins, Mrs. 45
Steele, Vernon 143
Steiner, Max 104, 195
Stevens, George 40, 41, 45, 48, 54-57, 59, 60, 65, 66, 72, 75, 76, 78-81, 83-85, 91, 92, 95, 96, 98, 100, 102, 105, 107-109, 112-114, 118, 125, 126, 128, 132-134, 139-141, 145 147, 155, 160, 161, 170, 183, 184
Stevens Jr, George 171
Stevenson, Edward 58, 108, 171
Stevenson, Robert Louis 8
Stewart, Harold 163
Stewart, James H. 76, 108
Stewart, Jimmy 40
Stimson, E. 81
Stockton (CA) 48
Stone, Colonel 24, 33

Stone, George E. 23, 157
Storm Over Bengal 102
Story of Vernon and Irene Castle 84
Straight Story, The 172
Strand Theatre 147
Stranglers of Bombay, The 178
"Strangloscope" 178
Strathmore Paper Co. 148
Strauss, Johann 140
Stromberg, William 195
Strong, Jack 190
Sturges, John 178, 180
Stuyvesant High School 152
Suma (see also Jumma)
Sunset Derby, The 9
Suspicion 170, 171
Sullivan, C. Gardner 12
Suttee 17, 20, 194
Sweden *145*
Swing Time 40
Sydney (Australia) 36, 81
Sydney Morning Herald 81
Sylvia Scarlett 38

Taj Mahal 116
Tantrapur 63, 65, 66, 68, 69, 75, 78 79, 81, 84-90, 97, 103, 104, 108, 109, 111, 113, 115, 116, 118, 148, 176, 180, 197
Tarzan 52, 162
Tarzan and the Amazons 52
Tarzan Finds a Son 52
Taylor, Robert 174
TCM Classic Film Festival 196
Ted Healy and his Stooges 62
Temple, Shirley 148
Temple Theatre 148
Ten Commandments, The 171
Tennyson, Alfred Lloyd 152
Texans, The 102
Texas Theatre 151
"That's the Way Love Is" 189
The New Yorker 56, 191
They 5
They Shall Have Music 149
They Were Expendable 171
Thief of Bagdad, The 46
This is the Night 37
This Time Tomorrow 169
This Year's Blonde 191
Thomaier, William 183
Thomas, Tony 105
Thompson, David 196
Thousand Oaks (CA) 52
Three Kings 195

Three Musketeers, The (Dumas) 42, 152
Three Musketeers, The (Kipling) 41
Three Musketeers, The (1935) 26
Three Musketeers, The (1948) 170
Through History with J. Wesley Smith 189
Thuggee 50, 56, 57, 62, 114, 118, 132, 159, 162, 178, 194, 197
Thunderclap 11
Thundercloud 191
Thunder Trail 102
Tightrope 170
Time 6, 62
Time Records 189
Times Picayune 5
Times Square Theatre 22
Tin Pan Alley 171
Toast of New York, The 46, 56
Toland, Gregg 149
Tommy 5
Toomai of the Elephants 46
Tone, Franchot 40, 41
Tony Award 170
Top Hat 65
Torrence (CA) 72
Tractor Beam Records 195
Trader Horn 11
Tracy, Jane 54
Tracy, Spencer 40
Train Robbers, The 171
Tramp Bicyclist, The 8
Translux theater 154
Tribby, John E. 108
Tripartite Pact 162
Troopin' 5
Tully, Ralph 151
Turner Classic Movies 197
Turner Home Entertainment 183, 184
Turrentine, Tommy 189
21st Century Film Corp. 194
Twelve Years a Soldier's Life in India 56
Twentieth Century 22, 23
20th Century Fox 49, 104, 149, 160, 174
24th Infantry Division 198
2015 Movie Guide 196
Twentieth Century Theater *173*
Twilight Zone 170

UCLA 192, 195
Uninvited Guest 9
Union College 48
Union of Soviet Socialist Republics 161
Union Pacific 139

Union Pacific Railroad 55
United Artists 12, 104, 106, 155, 157
United Services College 1
United States Army 60, 170, 198
United States Army Signal Corps 170
United States Navy 168
United States Office of War
    Information 162, 163
Universal 9, 16, 175
University of Cambridge 198
Uprising in Sidi Hakim 145

Valise Equipment 64
Valise Records 190
Valley Forge 37
Van Dyke, W. S. 11
Van Horn, Emil 172
Vancouver (Canada) 48
Variety 7, 9, 11, 14, 16, 63, 64, 95, 104,
    140-142, 145, 147, 155, 161, 162,
    165
Varno, Roland 108
Veiller, Anthony 17, 45, 105
Vernon Theatre 148
Vickburg, Siege of 4
Victor Records 8
Victoria Cross 8, 142
Victoria Memorial 107
Victorian Military Society 188
Victory at Sea 171
Victrola 8
Vid America 183
Vidor, King 22, 25
Vierra, Mark 196
Virginian, The 170
Viroqua (WI) 148
Vivacious Lady 40, 134
Voss, Carl 60, 100

WABC-TV 176
WABD-TV 166
WCAU-TV 176
WCBS-TV 63, 176
WNBC-TV 165, 166
WRCA-TV 176
WOR-TV 176
WXBS-TV 165
Walhberg, Mark 195
Wake the Vaulted Echoes 191
WALL-E 196
Wall Street Journal, The 140
Walker, Vernon L. 66, 108
Walkerville (Canada) 144
Walt Disney World 197
Walton, Douglas 43

"Waltz King, The" 139
Wansell, Geoffrey 42
War of 1812 158
War of the Worlds, The 172
Warner Bros. 40, 42, 104, 184
Warner Dixie 151
Warren, Leonard 189
Warriner, Jerry 37
Warsaw (Poland) 144
Warwick, Captain 17, 28, 32
Warwick Records 189
Washington 43, 48, 141
Washington Daily News 163
Washington D.C. 140
Washington, George 37
Washington Post 140
Watkins, Gen. 156, 157
Waverly theater 154
Wayne, John 76, 171, 178
Weather Source 83
Wedding March, The 8
Wee Willie Winkie (film) 12, 14, 24, 43,
    57, 104
*Wee Willie Winkie and Other Child
    Stories* 2
Weed, Colonel 50, 108, 109, 114-116,
    120, 126, 128, 131
Weeks, Colonel 57, 58
Welles, Orson 173
Weisberg, Frank 7
Weissmuller, Johnny 52
Werewolf of London, The 18
West, Mae 37
West Springfield (MA) 148
Western Costume 57, 64
Western Union 48
Westminster Abbey 6
Westphal, Frank 7
Westward Ho, The Wagons! 178
Wetkins, Corporal 27
What Happened to Mary 52
What Price Glory? 36, 43
Wheeler, Bert 40
Whitbeck, Frank 52
White, George 62
White Wing's Bride, The 11
Whitman, Stuart 191
Wilson, Jack 9
Winner, Michael 193
Witness 193
Whitney Sound Records 190
Whitten-Grey 15
Whittier (CA) 105
Who Wins the Widow 8
Wilkinson, James *75*

Wild Geese, The 191
"Will Ye No Come Back Again" 125
Williams, Earl 22, 23
Williams, Jonah 180
Willard, Jess 43
Wilson, Doc 7
Wilson, Lee 52
Winterset 50, 65
With a Song in My Heart 171
Wilson, Doc 7
Wizard of Oz, The 139
Wolfe, Alan D. 188
Woman's Power, A 8
Women, The 139
Woodley, Sir Thomas 50
Woolsey, Robert 40
World Theater 144
World War I 6, 9, 43, 52, 76
World War II 145, 162, 163, 168, 170,
    173, 186, 190
World's Fair 92, 144, 165
World-Pacific Records 190
Wuthering Heights 139, 149
Wyler, William 22

Yarrow and Company 136
You Can't Cheat an Honest Man 52
Young America 152
Young British Soldier, The 5, 63
Younghusband, Sir George 2-4, 132
Young Mr. Lincoln 139
"You're a Better Man Than I Gunga
    Din" 9
Yugoslavia 145
Yuma (AZ) 25, 26, 36, 55
Yuma Chamber of Commerce 25
Yvonne 156, 157

Zanetis, Alex 191
Zenith Radio Company 166
Zizanla 19, 20
Zora 17
Zorba, Dr. David 69
Zukor, Adolph 9

Note: The term "theater" has been
    used in the Index to identify those
    venues which did not use the term
    "Theatre" or the capitalized term
    "Theater" in their official name.

CPSIA information can be obtained
at www.ICGtesting.com
Printed in the USA
LVHW100354050119
602753LV00022B/443/P